Safe to be Smart:

Building A Culture for Standards-Based Reform in the Middle Grades

TRITON REGIONAL MIDDLE SCHOOL
112 ELM STREET
BYFIELD, MASSACHUSETTS 01922

Safe to be Smart

Building A Culture

for

Standards-Based Reform
in the Middle Grades

by
Anne Wheelock

National Middle School Association

Columbus, Ohio

NMSA

National Middle School Association
4151 Executive Parkway, Suite 300
Westerville, Ohio 43081
Telephone (800) 528-NMSA
Second Printing, July 1999

Sue Swaim, Executive Director

Jeff Ward, Associate Executive Director

John Lounsbury, Senior Editor, Professional Publications

Edward Brazee, Associate Editor, Professional Publications

Mary Mitchell, Copy Editor/Designer

Marcia Meade, Senior Publications Representative

Library of Congress Cataloging-in-Publication Data
Wheelock, Anne
    Safe to be smart: building a culture for standards-based reform
in the middle grades/by Anne Wheelock.
       p. cm.
    Includes bibliographical references.
    "NMSA stock number 1256"--T.p. verso.
    ISBN 1-56090-126-8 (pbk.)
    1. Middle schools--Standards--United States. 2. Middle school
education--United States--Philosophy. 3. Education and state-
-United States. 4. Educational change--United States. I. Title.
LB1623.5.W54   1998
373.236'0973--dc21   98-46633
                                       CIP

Contents

Acknowledgments

A grant from the Edna McConnell Clark Foundation partially funded the writing of this report. I am grateful for the support of the Foundation and especially for the encouragement of Hayes Mizell, Program Officer for the Foundation's Program for Student Achievement.

In addition, special thanks goes to John Lounsbury and Mary Mitchell of the National Middle School Association for their patience and professionalism in the preparation of this manuscript for publication. John Lounsbury, along with Carl Zon and Walt Haney, read an early draft of the report, and I benefitted from their comments and encouragement. Katie Ryan filled a particular hole in the manuscript when it needed filling.

I owe an enormous debt to the many excellent educators around the country, and in Massachusetts in particular, who have deepened my understanding of how good schools work for all students. In writing this report, I have drawn on their generosity, thoughtful reflection, and willingness to discuss and explain their work. Barbara Brauner Berns has provided more support and encouragement than anyone could ever hope for from a friend and colleague. Finally, I am deeply grateful to Michael Kennedy whose steadfast assistance in negotiating the world of drives, disks, commands, and conversions has been indispensible.

— Anne Wheelock

To middle schoolers, present, and future:

Juliana Isabel, John, David, and Matthew, Juliana and Elena, Ilana, Jenna, and Dan.

Foreword

Standards are all the rage. But why the excitement?

After all, "standards" have always been part of schooling. In the days of the one-room schoolhouse "content and performance standards" were whatever the teacher said they were, though those terms were not then in use. Basic literacy was the goal, and the standards for that were relatively straightforward.

Well into the second half of this century, little had changed. While teachers increasingly looked to textbooks, curriculum directors, and state tests for guidance about what to teach, in the final analysis teachers' "standards" were shaped by their professional and personal priorities, preferences, and, occasionally, vision. This approach became more problematic as demands increased for students to develop more than basic skills and as evidence mounted that students' academic performance was lagging. Not all students had access to teachers with "high standards," and the students most dependent on the public schools for learning were the most likely to have teachers who adjusted their "standards" to what they thought were the students' abilities.

The modern standards movement seeks to:

1. delineate what nearly all students should learn, not just what they should be taught,

2. establish more challenging norms for acceptable levels of student performance,

3. ensure that in all classrooms across all schools in a local school system, teachers consistently apply common expectations for what students should learn and how well they should learn it, and

4. hold school systems, schools, administrators, and teachers accountable for students performing at standard.

As a concept, standards are compelling to policy makers at national, state, and local levels who are searching for ways to focus educators and students on increasing their performance. It seems so easy: specify what students should learn, test them to see if they learned it, and hold both students and educators accountable if students do not satisfactorily demonstrate what they know and can do.

In practice, bringing standards to fruition in the classroom is much more complicated. The problem begins with the language of standards; it is often so jargon-laden, complex, and abstract that teachers, students, and parents cannot understand what the standards mean. And persons responsible for developing standards often go overboard; they create such a long list of what students should ideally know that it is overwhelming to teachers who have neither the knowledge nor the time to teach all the content the standards address. Even worse, these comprehensive standards aggravate a long-standing problem in American education; teachers give priority to "covering" content, compromising students' potential to develop deep knowledge and mastery of skills. When policy makers promulgate these standards, they often repeat the mistakes that have sabotaged previous education reforms. They add standards to teachers' existing burdens, and fail to provide the lead time or the money for teachers to learn how to apply standards effectively.

One might reasonably ask whether in light of these difficulties standards are really worth it. Can the reality of their implementation live up to their promise? In this book, Anne Wheelock approaches her examination of standards with the same skepticism. She acknowledges the importance of standards, assessment, and accountability, but critically analyzes the assumptions and wishful thinking of politicians and bureaucrats who use these ingredients to concoct a witches' brew. The result, she warns, is likely to be more rather than less student failure, less rather than more authentic achievement, and mounting cynicism on the part of educators.

The value of this book, however, is not in its critique of the standards movement but in Wheelock's description of educators who value standards but are driven by their vision of better quality student work and "are putting new routines, beliefs about student learning, and relationships into practice to develop a culture of high standards." Wheelock is concerned not with the mechanics of standards implementation but how educators can change their practice and their schools to make it possible for students to perform at standard.

Readers should not begin this book with the hope that Anne Wheelock favors either education-as-we-now-know-it or schooling that demands little of students, particularly those from low-income families and from language and racial/ethnic minorities. To the contrary, she charts an even more demanding course than implementing standards. Much of the book centers on the importance of making student work, not performance on standardized tests, "the standard of accomplishment." This requires teachers to develop "assignments that help students develop thinking skills for deeper understanding: posing questions, gathering information, reasoning, synthesizing different perspectives, communicating conclusions, and applying new learning. Further, routine opportunities for teachers, students, and parents to talk about the quality of student performances, portfolios, and projects are essential to building a school culture of high standards." Anne Wheelock not only explicates this vision but describes the schools, educators, practices, and resources that are bringing it to life.

The first allegiance of educators Wheelock describes is to help their students become self-directed learners who understand and ultimately embrace standards for quality work, and who learn to value the quality of personal relationships within their school community. This is the result of these educators' "rigorous caring" that is manifest both in their constant examination and revision of their practice, and the repeated opportunities they extend to students to learn and demonstrate what they know and can do. In other words, for students to learn more they need to be in the company of adults who care enough to learn, and to apply what they learn, even if it means changing their instruction and their school.

This book, then, is not for the faint-hearted. It lets no one – students, teachers, administrators – off the hook. If readers take it seriously, as they should, it will lead to more hard work. But both the work and results will be infinitely more gratifying than is currently the case in most schools.

—M. Hayes Mizell
Director, Program for Student Achievement
The Edna McConnell Clark Foundation

I. Introduction

With the passage of Goals 2000 and new Title I legislation, and with many elected officials beating the drum for "higher standards," educators around the country are beginning to grapple with the implications of the "standards movement" for their schools. New policies push states to use standards, however defined, to drive curriculum, teaching, professional development, and assessments, bundling all these elements of reform into a neat package. But in districts and schools, educators voice numerous concerns about the application of standards-based reforms in real classrooms. There matters are not so simple. As educators watch the states produce voluminous curriculum frameworks and listen to calls for increased testing, some raise questions that reveal the myriad challenges of turning policy into practices that improve student learning. For example, educators ask:

■ *Our students learn in many different ways. Won't standards force all classrooms into a single mold that will fail to connect with many students?*

■ *Who should decide on what all students will learn? Won't standards dictate what teachers teach and reduce teachers' freedom to respond flexibly to students?*

■ *Our textbooks really determine how we cover the curriculum year after year. How can standards help us respond to students' own questions about their learning, especially when they depart from required curriculum?*

■ *Motivating students to learn is already a challenge. How will standards help us get students to work harder with greater efficacy? What will we do about students who don't meet standards?*

■ *Our state's testing requirements are now at odds with standards the professional associations have developed. How do we keep state standardized testing requirements from getting in the way of good teaching?*

■ *Some in our community already pay scant attention to students' learning needs. How can standards mobilize more citizens on behalf of student learning?*

These questions underscore the complexity of "implementing standards" in all classes for all students. They signal that standards-based reform involves changing the standard operating procedures of schools along with the content of curriculum. Most of all, they force attention away from the policy level to the school site. While discussions of standards become increasingly politicized in the state capitals, the practical meaning of standards-based reform is beginning to emerge most clearly in schools themselves as educators work to create school cultures that can support the weight of standards-based reforms.

Educators build school cultures for standards-based reforms from the mortar of belief and the bricks of action. Indeed, the standards movement is founded on the belief that "all children can learn." But how schools act on that belief depends to a great extent on the ways they perceive what it means to "be smart." When teachers, students, and parents understand "being smart" in terms of developing students' skills in posing questions, gathering evidence, solving problems, communicating, and linking school knowledge to the larger world, they shape school practices to focus on work that demonstrates those skills. When teachers, students, and parents understand that it is smart to take risks, seek help from adults and peers, exert effort to complete challenging tasks, learn from mistakes, and view problems from multiple perspectives, they orient their practices to create schools where students feel it is safe to be smart.

A deep belief that every student can develop thinking skills, learn for understanding, apply knowledge, become smart, and meet standards is fundamental to school cultures that support standards-based reforms. A second belief – that schools themselves have responsibility for developing the conditions that foster learning for understanding – closely follows. Building school cultures to support standards-based reforms also means establishing new routines and practices to match the beliefs that all students can learn well and that teachers are key to helping them do so. The flurry of activity surrounding much standards-setting work at the policy level has obscured this critical reality: Regardless of the standards

Building school cultures to support standards-based reforms means establishing new routines and practices to match the beliefs that all students can learn well...

adopted at the state or even district level, if the school culture does not nurture these beliefs and foster conditions in which students are motivated to work both harder and smarter, students will not succeed.

New beliefs and action are both essential to a culture that supports standards-based reforms, but the process of building this culture does not have a clear beginning or end. In some circumstances, the effort begins with people who cherish a vision of every student producing good work and act to realize that vision by introducing new practices into their classrooms and throughout the school. In other situations, new practices themselves and the visible results in student learning that follow can work to challenge traditional beliefs and lay the groundwork for making bolder interventions possible. In sometimes unpredictable ways, new beliefs and practice reinforce each other in a dynamic, positive, and mutually supportive tension. In schools that are building a culture for standards-based reforms, attention shifts back and forth from belief to practice as old assumptions are dislodged to create room for new "ways of doing things" that can boost student achievement.

The following pages describe some of the strategies middle grades educators across the country are using to reshape schools so that more students meet standards more of the time. Working from a commitment to develop teaching, learning, and school routines that will help students realize higher expectations, these educators follow no formula in their work. Some begin by introducing new organizational structures as a way of mobilizing everyone in the school to focus on student achievement. Some are putting renewed emphasis on instructional approaches and content to create classrooms compelling enough to compete with "real life" for students' attention. All are working to establish school cultures that balance a press for achievement with connectedness and community. Their goal is to help students produce better work that meets standards while avoiding cookie-cutter approaches that leave little leeway for embracing the special strengths of students and teachers and the resources of local communities. They aspire to create a school ethos where young adolescents feel safe to be themselves, each with a particular individual and social identity, and where students will work hard to become smart, accomplished, and confident learners.

Whatever the beginning point of change, the process of moving from the simple statement "All children can learn" to results that match that expectation involves hard work. Such work is executed by real people, all teaching, learning, and growing in such different ways in such diverse schools and communities that the prospect of their conforming to any standardized model of change seems ludicrous on the face of it. Those who work with students day to day, including those who already expect every one of their students to succeed, know that having high expectations for all students is just the beginning. Between those expectations and student performance lies the challenging work of knowing, reaching, and teaching individual students while creating school communities that will support meaningful learning for children and adults alike. The dimensions of this work make it clear that standards-based school reform is an intensely human endeavor.

... the process of moving from the simple statement 'All children can learn' to results that match that expectation involves hard work.

This report focuses on the efforts of middle grades educators who are working to make schools and classrooms places where more students are working harder and smarter to do work of higher quality more of the time. In many cases, these efforts are groundbreaking in the way they reframe notions about how students learn and achieve. They also reflect innovations in school and classroom organization, and they highlight teaching that pushes students to develop not only the knowledge but also the dispositions that will prepare them to meet future learning challenges.

Many of these efforts are all the more intriguing because educators undertake them in an era when the public often seems ambiguous at best about granting real support for public schools. In this climate, some middle grades educators are negotiating the political tangle of curriculum frameworks, testing, and accountability policies and, at the same time, working within the constraints of these policies to harvest real benefits for their students. The strategies they are adopting for doing this constitute a rich legacy of practice wisdom. Through their daily practice, they bequeath this legacy to their professional colleagues, students, and communities. To build on their lead is to spread the wealth. ◼

II. If "Standards" Are the Solution,
What Are the Problems?

For years, educators and parents, policy makers, and the public have documented the myriad problems of American schools. Some of these problems begin with inadequate resources of all kinds, especially in districts where large numbers of children live in poverty. Other concerns touch on schools in suburban, rural, and urban school districts alike: textbook-based curriculum that emphasizes breadth rather than depth, teaching driven by high-stakes standardized testing, and the unequal distribution of opportunities and resources for learning within schools. Additional problems stem from misguided beliefs that only "deserving" students can benefit from challenging classrooms, school climates that discourage caring relationships, practices, and attitudes that marginalize African American, Latino, and poor students, and routines and norms that emphasize compliant behavior over learning (Darling-Hammond, 1997; Fine, 1991; Goodlad, 1984; Hopfenberg, Levin, & Chase, 1993; Kozol, 1991; Kreitzer & Madaus, 1995; Lipman, 1998; McNeil, 1988; Noddings, 1992; Oakes, 1985; Powell, Farrar, & Cohen, 1985; Sizer, 1984; Smith & Rotenberg, 1991).

Taken together, these conditions shape the day-to-day school life of young adolescents in profound and troubling ways. Many students describe school work as "boring" or "too easy;" and although individual classrooms may generate some excitement, students' overall school experience is often mediocre (Farkus & Johnson, 1996; Lounsbury & Clark, 1990). Although engagement, persistence, confidence, risk taking, and pride in work are key to academic and personal success, many students, especially in urban districts, attend schools that define satisfactory work largely in terms of "showing up" (Haberman, 1997). In one urban district, when researchers Dickson Corbett and Bruce Wilson (1997a) asked seventh graders to describe the report card grades they considered "good," many viewed "C" grades as acceptable, and students frequently believed that completing the work in compliance with simple requirements was more important than the quality of the work itself. Further, although students believed that they and their classmates were capable of doing challenging work, many reported that their peers frequently gave up when confronted with requirements of more difficult assignments. Yet, "harder work" alone does not increase engagement. In fact, as students proceed through the grades and encounter more difficult assignments, students disengage even further from their learning (Corbett & Wilson, 1997a, 1997b).

Disengagement from learning in the middle grades becomes epidemic at the high school level.

Disengagement from learning in the middle grades becomes epidemic at the high school level. For example, Laurence Steinberg and his colleagues (1997) found that 40 percent of the students surveyed from a mix of Wisconsin and California high schools felt they were "just going through the motions" in school. These findings validate observations of others (Farrar, Powell, & Cohen, 1985; Goodlad, 1984; McQuillen, 1998; Sizer, 1984) who, observing few classrooms where students developed real passion for learning or believed that learning actually "mattered," described school climates as flat at best, chaotic at worst. In schools organized into "high," "average," or "low" groups, students caught between the push to learn in the "top" classrooms and the social "pull of the peer group" often find it especially difficult to develop a commitment to academic success, a dynamic that may take a particular toll on African American and Latino students (Fordham & Ogbu, 1986; Hammond & Howard, 1986; Nieto, 1992; Yonazawa, Wells, & Serna, 1996).

Now, in the 1990s, layered over these day-to-day dynamics of schooling, comes the "standards movement" with its aspirations for improved learning for all students. But how do the reams of "standards" for what students will know and do offer solutions to the well-documented problems facing students and teachers? Equally important, can educators reframe the "standards movement" in ways that address some of the most intransigent problems of schools, especially those aspects of school culture that feed widespread student detachment from learning?

Student disinvestment from learning is one facet of a larger school context characterized by beliefs about learning and teaching that put students in a passive role in classrooms, school routines that label students and isolate teachers and students from one another, and norms that distribute opportunities to learn unequally within and across schools. Low expectations for students often feed these conditions, justifying decisions as simple as allowing only certain students to use lab equipment, check out library books, or take textbooks home. Despite a variety of new organizational arrangements and technical interventions, these "regularities" of school cultures resist easy change (Fine, 1994; Lipman, 1998; Oakes & Wells, 1996; Sarason, 1982, 1996). Yet, it is exactly these features of school cultures that must change if the current movement for "higher standards" is to have any meaning, particularly for those students most disadvantaged by their enrollment in the country's most impoverished schools. New curriculum frameworks and large-scale assessments, policy-makers' tools-of-choice, on their own do not have the power to address the persistent problems of schooling that are rooted in school cultures.

The promise of the "standards movement" for better learning and teaching lies in embracing new norms and routines that can turn schools into places that celebrate all kinds of accomplishments, where it is both desirable and safe for every student to become smart, work hard, and learn through risk taking and effort.

The promise of the 'standards movement' for better learning and teaching lies in embracing new norms and routines that can turn schools into places that celebrate all kinds of accomplishments, where it is both desirable and safe for every student to become smart, work hard, and learn through risk taking and effort.

Students need schools characterized by what Ted Sizer (1994) calls "rigorous caring" between teachers and students and where they can engage in meaningful tasks to create high quality work. Students need schools where teachers meet standards of practice in a professional community. Everything in the culture of the school must attend to these purposes. However, because current "standards-based policies" offer little guidance or recognition for developing such cultures, schools must feel their way toward such changes on their own.

The political context of the standards movement

What can middle schools learn from the standards movement? As developed by professional teacher associations that represent different subject areas, standards can be tools to enrich teaching and learning for all students. By promoting idea-rich content and complex problem solving, they anticipate the kinds of teaching and learning for understanding that can enliven classrooms and counteract student disengagement. As descriptions of the endpoints of learning, they can prompt teachers to direct students toward generating products that demonstrate their mastery of basic skills within content areas. Viewed in their most promising light, standards for what students should understand and be able to do to demonstrate their understanding have the potential to guide schools toward better practice for all students. Standards developed by national professional associations can elevate expectations for student learning. They can offer a gauge against which teachers can assess the degree to which all students experience opportunities to learn challenging academic content. They can provide encouragement for teachers to infuse practices that produce high-level learning into all classrooms and a focal point around which whole faculties can center their restructuring work. As the linchpin for a comprehensive school reform strategy, standards can become tools for judging the value of decisions regarding every aspect of schooling from textbook selection to professional development (Wheelock, 1995).

...standards can become tools for judging the value of decisions regarding every aspect of schooling from textbook selection to professional development.

However, as decision makers at policy levels in the states have developed long lists of topics for study, called them "standards," and adopted assessments to match, they have often ignored, diluted, or circumvented the standards of teachers' own professional associations. Drawing steam from Congressional passage of Goals 2000 and the Improving America's Schools Act of 1994, standards-based reform efforts have intensified in both policy and practice circles. Thus, in the 1990s, state departments of education and local school districts have compiled volumes of written "content standards," "curriculum frameworks," and "standards of learning," all meant to guide teaching and ensure that all students have access to similar material. Some "new" standards look like old wine in new bottles, amounting to little more than lists of topics or authors to be covered in prescribed courses. A few provide more guidance for teachers by including descriptions of classrooms where teachers are putting standards into practice, providing samples of work students might be expected to produce, connecting specific teaching and learning processes with high-quality work.

Standards and the economy. Despite the flurry of activity in education policy circles, the words of political officials and corporate officers suggest that they mean to use standards primarily as tools for bullying schools into showing proof of better performance. Gathered at the National Education Summit in March 1996 in Palisades, New Jersey, elected officials including governors from 40 states pledged to support standards-based reforms developed at the state and local levels. At that time, chief executive officers from such corporations as IBM and Proctor and Gamble proclaimed that they would base future hiring decisions on the quality of applicants' school records. Further, they emphasized, standards and student achievement would be a "high priority" in decisions regarding the location of their business operations. Assumptions about the correlation between educational attainment and economic growth, standards, and student achievement have been at the core of claims that achievement would improve by a process of standard setting, assessing student performance, aligning curriculum and teaching to match standards, and "holding schools and students accountable for demonstrating real improvement."

...the words of political officials and corporate officers suggest that they mean to use standards primarily as tools for bullying schools into showing proof of better performance.

But however logical they may seem, assertions that standards, achievement, and economic strength are inevitably connected fall short of the mark. For example, while some policy leaders hold that national standards will improve achievement, results of a cross-country comparison of the performance of 13-year olds in math and science placed the achievement of American students at above or about the same level as students in countries like Germany and France where national standards already shape schooling. Moreover, although private corporations may claim that higher student achievement will influence location of their industries, the migration of corporate jobs from the Northeast or Midwest to the Southeast, Texas, or Mexico suggests that other factors – a state's tax incentives, location in relation to resources, or cheap energy and labor – work more powerfully to affect such decisions. For those who weigh decision-makers' words against these realities, exhortations for "higher standards" have a hollow ring.

For individual students, test scores, whether on conventional norm-referenced tests or more complex assessments, have little connection with employment success in the real world. Reviewing available research, Henry Levin (1998) found no evidence that the use of standards and new assessments could boost worker productivity. Warning that linking standards to anticipated job performance could both undermine overall economic efficiency and narrow students' future opportunities for employment, he noted:

> There is danger in reinforcing the belief that existing and emerging educational performance standards have high predictive powers regarding worker productivity. Such beliefs can lead to

the establishment of a system at the local, state, or federal level that certifies job candidates for employment who meet some arbitrarily adopted "new standards," and employers will likely believe that such standards have been validated on worker productivity. (p. 8)

Levin further reminds us that the earning potential of individual students is ultimately tied more powerfully to graduation from high school and years of education completed than on higher test scores. The challenge of the standards movement, then, is to boost students' achievement while strengthening their commitment to learning and their sense of membership and belonging in school. One without the other leaves little cause for celebration.

Standards and competing visions of learning. Schools should pursue standards-based reforms, then, for educational, not economic, purposes. However, varying definitions of what is meant by "standards" still leave schools struggling to create a common vision for lasting and meaningful learning. For example, in some states, controversy over content standards for social studies and mathematics reveals distinct differences between those educators who define learning in terms of higher-order skills and deeper content and others who support a familiar "just-the-facts" approach (Manzo, 1997; Steinberg, 1997). Some teachers who focus on conceptual learning even find themselves at odds with their own unions' endorsements of standards that threaten to overwhelm classrooms with minutia (Diegmueller, 1996). These tensions play out in other arenas as well. For example, in California, corporate interests have lobbied successfully for approval of math textbooks that emphasize traditional drill and practice despite educators' concerns that the publisher's materials fell short of professional standards (Pham, 1994).

Some reformers originally hoped that grade-level learning goals included in state standards would help weed trivial content from curriculum. In practice, however, some state curriculum frameworks and the assessments that accompany them may instead crowd out strategies that emphasize teaching and learning for understanding. For example, in Virginia, some middle school science teachers report that the state's fact-heavy content standards have meant that they must abandon in-depth learning about science

...some state curriculum frameworks and the assessments that accompany them may crowd out strategies that emphasize teaching and learning for understanding.

concepts involving hands-on work with laboratory equipment so that they can teach about punnett squares, a measurement of genetic variability (Mathews, 1997). Likewise, in Massachusetts, a new social studies curriculum framework puts teachers in the position of having to trade in in-depth projects for "covering" multiple topics, however superficially, because they may appear on the state test (McNamara, 1998). As Brockton, Massachusetts, social studies department chairperson Susan Szachowicz explains:

> If you put the time available in a school year against the scope of what is required by the standards, it's immediately clear that there is simply too much; it's too dense. So how do you carve out a month or two for our award-winning curriculum – a unit called "Election 96: Once Every Four Years" – without neglecting the required content outlined in the framework? Since students are going to face high-stakes assessment, a teacher would be irresponsible in omitting any of the core knowledge requirements. Yet shouldn't students have the benefit of experiencing a focused, comprehensive study of a Presidential election as it is unfolding? How can you resolve this type of dilemma?[1]

Competing visions of what constitutes standards-based teaching further cloud discussions of standards-based reform. Appeals of conservative policy advocates for more drill and practice in "the basics" often appeal to those who harbor mistrust of schools and fear talk of critical thinking. In some states, those who oppose standards developed by the professional associations portray standards-based reform as "experimental," a description that taps into parents' fears that any change in the status quo will put their children at a disadvantage (Jackson, 1997). Attacks on the standards of professional organizations like the National Council of Teachers of Mathematics are grounded in such arguments; advanced through nationally syndicated opinion columns and nation media, they have reached millions, providing ammunition for those wary of professionally developed curriculum that promotes conceptual learning (Cheney, 1997a, 1997b).

Appeals of conservative policy advocates for more drill and practice in 'the basics' often appeal to those who harbor mistrust of schools and fear talk of critical thinking.

---

[1] Quotations not otherwise cited are derived from interviews or other personal communications.

In this highly politicized context, those who support teaching for understanding through problem solving, reasoning, communicating, and making connections across subject areas often encounter difficulties in conveying new knowledge about learning to the general public. Thus, although frameworks for learning adopted in some states and districts may be little more than old curriculum objectives, the familiar factual content and specificity of such "standards," especially compared to the more complex ideas of standards of the professional associations, are reassuring to many parents and teachers. Likewise, in states where organized right-wing interest groups have used the standards-development process to attack multicultural content or eliminate the study of evolution from the curriculum, standards may serve to ensure that little of a nontraditional nature will touch students' recommended course of study.

Against the backdrop of these political debates, many educators are struggling to make sense of what the "standards movement" might mean for their own students, classrooms, and schools. Within this context of unresolved tensions, fundamental questions emerge:

Will educators use standards to tackle the problems identified by respected reformers over the past two decades, including unequal access to knowledge, lockstep curriculum, tedious assignments tied to standardized testing, and impersonal instruction?	Or will standards-based "reforms" simply reinforce the status quo?
Will the teaching practices that educators anticipate will develop in tandem with standards take hold to transform all classrooms into vibrant centers for learning?	Or will only some students in some classes benefit from teaching for understanding?
Will schools and communities use "standards" to expand opportunities to learn to all students?	Or will "standards" reinforce existing labeling and sorting practices?

Illusions of standards: Standardized testing, grade retention, and bureaucratic accountability.

As policy makers on both national and local levels attempt to spell out what standards mean to a public seeking concrete evidence that students and schools are "performing," many increasingly turn to standardized tests to measure progress. In the process, policy makers and the public alike come to view test scores as if they were "standards." Then, as the public applauds policies designed to convey "zero-tolerance" for lackadaisical performance, these scores become the means for sorting those students who have "met standards" from those who have not, a process that often translates into decisions regarding grade retention and ability grouping. At the same time, decision makers designing policies meant to motivate students to work harder through "tough consequences" also seek to motivate educators through monetary awards and sanctions allocated according to degrees of progress also measured by test scores. Despite the widespread popularity of these practices, both fall short of effecting lasting improvement in either student or school performance, least of all for the most vulnerable students in the most vulnerable schools.

Standards and grade retention. Couched in terms of "holding students accountable," retaining students in grade aims to provide additional learning time for students who have not mastered the learning requirements in a given grade. As proponents of non-promotion see it, repeating a grade may be painful for students in the short term, but, they claim, over time students will learn that they must work harder to meet standards. Moreover, say supporters of non-promotion, retained students will be fully prepared for the more difficult work of subsequent grades. Indeed, President Clinton in his 1998 State of the Union Address linked the movement for higher standards to a national test for fourth and eighth graders and called for an end to what he called "social promotion."

Equating standards with test scores and grade retention, however, is likely to backfire. Fueled by the notion that "standards" should sort students into categories, separating the "ready" from the "unprepared," grade retention actually depresses student achievement and motivation, making many students vulnerable to behavior that risks both school engagement and social well-being. And when large numbers of a school's students are overage for their grade, the entire school takes on the characteristics of low-track classrooms, with the overall school climate reflecting depressed expectations for learning.

13

Grade retention actually depresses student achievement and motivation, making many students vulnerable to behavior that risks both school engagement and social well-being.

Actual numbers on grade retention are difficult to come by. The U.S. Department of Education does not routinely gather data on the practice, and data collection in the states is idiosyncratic. For example, states like Illinois, Iowa, Missouri, New York, and Pennsylvania collect no data on non-promotion. California last collected these data for the 1991-92 school year. Others routinely compile data statewide, but may not disaggregate them by race or ethnicity, as in Tennessee and North Carolina, or by grade, as in Indiana. Still others gather data for particular grade spans only. For example, Michigan collects grade retention data only for grades 9-12. Moreover, counting methodology varies from state to state.

Data available suggest that far from an occasionally used practice, grade retention is a familiar experience for many students. In the middle grades, the National Educational Longitudinal Survey of 1988 (NELS:88) found that one fifth of all eighth graders had repeated at least one grade, with the proportion climbing to one out of three eighth graders from low-income and minority families. A more recent report from the National Longitudinal Study of Adolescent Health put the prevalence of adolescents who were retained in grade at least one year at 21.3% (Resnick, Bearman, Blue, Bauman, Harris, Jones, Tabor, Beuhring, Sieving, Shew, Ireland, Bearinger, & Udry, 1997). Moreover, data compiled by some of the states suggest that the numbers of students retained in grade every year may be legion. For example, in the 1994-95 school year, the last year for which data are available in some states, Michigan retained 10,312 students in the high school grades alone, Kentucky retained 15,289 in fourth through twelfth grades, and Texas retained 128,369 for all grades. In 1995-96, Florida retained 96,753 students; Georgia retained 51,044; Tennessee retained 45,498; Wisconsin retained 19,391; Massachusetts retained 18,298; and Arizona retained 17,817.

Over all the states, four million students were retained in grade in 1994, according to Columbia University's Linda Darling-Hammond (1997). Moreover, in many urban districts, more than half of all students repeat at least one grade before they leave school, often without a diploma (Feldman, 1997). Not surprisingly given these numbers, grade retention proves to be an expensive "reform" that reaps few benefits. For example, with an average per-pupil cost of $4,504, Texas spends an estimated $578 million for each extra year of schooling required from retained students (Texas Education Agency, 1996).

Increasingly, some districts and states mandate non-promotion for students who fail to meet certain standardized test score levels. For example, in June 1997, Chicago schools notified about one quarter of their eighth-graders and 48 percent of their ninth graders that promotion would be contingent on achieving a specified grade-equivalent cutoff score on the Iowa Test of Basic Skills after summer school remedial help. The superintendent predicted that some 2,000 to 2,500 eighth graders would not achieve the required score of 7.0 and would be repeating the grade the following year. Commenting on Chicago's policy, Kathy Christie, a spokeswoman for the Education Commission of the States said, "[Chicago's] a little ahead of the game. We're going to be seeing a lot of this around the country in the next year or two" (Johnson, 1997). News reports confirm this prediction as growing numbers of students in states such as North Carolina and Florida are retained in grade (Kurtz, 1997; Swirko, 1997).

If a second year in grade resulted in higher achievement and a stronger commitment to school, educators might be justified in retaining so many students. However, research on grade retention reveals that no such thing occurs. Students who repeat a grade typically do worse academically than those in carefully matched control groups who are promoted(Darling-Hammond & Falk, 1997; Smith & Shepard, 1989). In districts with high percentages of students retained in the elementary grades, many students reach middle school already overage for their grade; when they experience a second grade retention in the middle grades, they begin to disengage from schooling altogether. For example, a multi-year study of Boston middle school students found that truancy in the middle grades correlated most strongly with the school students attended, placement in low-track classes, and overage-for-grade status (Weitzman, 1985). Far from stimulating students to perform "at standard," being overage for grade gnaws away at students' sense of efficacy, with the impact especially severe for African American students (Spurlock, Munford, & Madhere, 1995). Moreover, students retained in grade do not go on to higher achievement levels in subsequent grades. Compared to on-grade students, overage students are twice as likely to be retained in grade (Texas Education Agency, 1996). In addition, they often end up in the lowest ability groups or special education in later grades, or, in middle schools, may repeat the grade at a lower track level (Alexander & Entwisle, 1996; Smith & Shepard, 1989; Dentzer & Wheelock, 1990). As a result, these vulnerable students are

Students who repeat a grade typically do worse academically than those in carefully matched control groups who are promoted.

often those who also experience the most diluted curriculum and diminished opportunities to learn (Oakes, 1985, 1990; Raudenbush, Rowan, & Cheong, 1993).

In the middle grades and beyond, as schools fill up with overage and under-motivated students, the school culture itself becomes vulnerable to depressed expectations. In schools enrolling large numbers of students who are both poor and overage for their grade, "regular" classrooms succumb to practices typical of the low track. For example, in one such school, a seventh grade class profiled in the *Washington Post* included students ages 12 to 16, with one half already overage for grade (Wilgoren, 1998). Working with inadequate numbers of books, and assigned the task of copying word definitions for study at home, these students faced another grade retention if their reading scores did not improve on spring tests.

As schools fill up with overage and under-motivated students, the school culture itself becomes vulnerable to depressed expectations.

Likewise, although schools may offer students extended-year remediation as a way of avoiding grade retention, summer school may offer little more than the same conditions that left students floundering the first time around, and at some cost to out-of-school learning. Thus, in impoverished Patterson, New Jersey, the summer school curriculum constitutes little beyond more test preparation (Glovin & Casey, 1998). In Washington, D.C., overcrowded summer school classes are short of both teachers and materials (Strauss, 1998; Strauss & Mathews, 1998). And in New York City, many students abandon plans for out-of-school experiences like summer camp or a Fresh Air vacation upon notification that they must attend mandatory summer school (Katz, 1998). Yet, such remediation seems to produce limited learning. For example, even after a summer school program that emphasized test-based content, more than two-thirds of Durham, North Carolina, eighth graders did so poorly the second time they took the state test that they were still required to repeat their grade (Hower & Kurtz, 1998).

In districts and schools that couple grade retention with high-stakes standardized testing in the name of standards, many students, especially the most vulnerable, lose more than they gain from so-called "standards-based reforms." For retained children – bored with their schooling and overage for grade, sometimes by two years by the time they leave the eighth grade – the threat of withholding a diploma rarely stimulates them to engage in school. Many of these students ultimately develop the belief that "school is not for me" and drop out; and many, under pressure of high-stakes testing, drop out earlier in their school careers (Henry, 1998; Wehlage & Rutter, 1986; Wheelock & Dorman, 1988). Indeed, being overage for grade is a better predictor of dropping out than below-average test scores (Texas Education Agency, 1996).

Current grade-retention policies may seem to be a logical outgrowth of the demand for higher standards. However, the fallout from such policies does not bode well for schools or students. In particular, with grade promotion determined by test scores, such policies deflect attention from the greater need to build schools' capacity to reform teaching and learning so that students receive the support they need to produce work that meets genuinely high standards of quality.

Standards and bureaucratic accountability. In line with new federal legislation, many states have devised standards-based policies as a way of pushing schools toward greater accountability for their performance. As policy makers reason, standards should describe exactly what all students should know and be able to do; then, assessments that match these expectations must be adopted to measure students' mastery of the standards. Each school is thereby held accountable for outcomes, with little explanation of conditions that may contribute to these outcomes. In some states and districts, principals may receive bonuses for leading schools toward test score gains or whole schools may receive monetary rewards for test-based improvements. Likewise, some states and districts list schools as being "low performing" or "under review" and slated for technical assistance or intervention from supervising authorities. Those that backslide further are declared to be "in crisis" and in need of state takeover. Theoretically, this policy framework is meant to move large numbers of schools, not simply a few, toward "meeting standards." In such a policy framework, large-scale assessments that states and districts can administer at reasonable cost become the key measure of school progress and school quality.

However, the jury remains divided about the extent to which large-scale assessments can have deep or lasting effect on practice (Mehrens, 1998). Sometimes, "new" assessments, refashioned to shift the focus away from short-answer multiple answers toward more complex and open-ended tasks, are meant to push teachers in every school toward more in-depth instruction. In some states, statewide assessments may indeed be encouraging more demanding assignments. For example, in Kentucky, where 43 percent of eighth grade teachers consider the state's new emphasis on writing to be one of the most positive features of reform, state-required portfolios of students' written work have meant that teachers are giving both more writing assignments and more diverse writing assignments (Koretz, Barron, Mitchell, & Stecher, 1996). As a result, eighth graders are using forms like persuasive letters they may never have used before, and students are being asked to polish incomplete pieces to an acceptable quality.

At the same time, even these changes may have some costs. For example, some Kentucky teachers believe they may be using too much time asking students to rewrite pieces beyond the point of instructional usefulness; and despite an increase in the amount of writing, the extent to which the quality of work has improved remains unclear (Appalachia Educational Laboratory, 1996). Moreover, a RAND report on Kentucky's statewide assessment practices found that while over half of teachers surveyed believed that increased familiarity with the tests and work with practice tests and preparation materials contributed "a great deal" to test score gains, only 16 percent mentioned such a strong connection to either increased student motivation or broad improvements in students' knowledge and skills (Koretz, Barron, Mitchell, & Stecher, 1996). In addition, careful analysis of new state assessment policies in Arizona found that instructional change occurred in response to new testing directives only in those districts and schools that already had strong capacity for change (Noble & Smith, 1994; Smith, 1997).

While some states initially hoped more complex assessments would stimulate more ambitious instructional reforms, political and technical problems with new assessments have often overwhelmed these intentions, and some states have reverted to using cheaper, more easily scored multiple choice tests deemed suitable for judging school performance. Seen as steps to ensure greater accountability, the coupling of such tests with high stakes consequences leaves students vulnerable to all the negative effects on learning long associated with such policies. These effects include time lost to real learning, a thinning and narrowing of curriculum, increased placement in special education, and deteriorating school climate and teacher professionalism (Koretz, 1988; McNeil, 1988; McGill-Franzen & Allington, 1993; Rothman, 1995; Shepard, 1991).

Without doubt, high stakes accountability policies exact the highest toll on the school experiences of poor and minority students, often reducing their schooling to little more than test preparation. For example, Smith and

Rotenberg (1991) found that time spent in test preparation reflected the degree of pressure teachers felt to raise test scores, and that such pressure was likely to be greatest in high poverty schools that already ranked low compared to other schools. Further research findings cited by Kreitzer and Madaus (1995) demonstrate that teachers in largely minority classrooms devote more than twice as much class time to test-taking preparation as teachers in largely white classrooms. High stakes are also most likely to influence how and what teachers teach in those schools where administrators are anxious about test results, when many students in the school have borderline skills, and when teachers have few resources to raise scores or improve learning beyond intensive test coaching.

High stakes accountability policies exact the highest toll on the school experiences of poor and minority students, often reducing their schooling to little more than test preparation.

Although well-intentioned policy makers may argue that test preparation helps students develop lifelong test-taking skills, in reality, students rarely transfer skills they learn in order to succeed on one test to other tests, whether the tests rely on multiple choice items or performance tasks (Koretz, 1988; Madaus & Kellaghan, 1993). For example, in Houston, officials have reported that many students passing the Texas Assessment of Academic Skills (TAAS), and attending schools rated "exemplary," scored poorly on the Stanford Achievement Test, a national assessment. In one school where 96 percent of test-taking students passed the TAAS, ninth graders scored more than two years below grade level on the Stanford test, causing some observers to ask if TAAS was over-determining curriculum (Markley, 1998).

Pressure to raise test scores to meet "accountability" goals may also mean lost opportunities to learn as teachers have little incentive to pursue more challenging content with their students. For example, in Chattanooga some middle school math teachers adopted the NCTM standards-based Hawaii Algebra Project curriculum, only to abandon it in the belief that their students' test scores could suffer on their state's more traditional standardized test. As one teacher who prepared extensively to use the curriculum noted, "The eighth grade [standardized math test] isn't going to tell us anything about Hawaii Algebra. It's like we're teaching our stu-

Pressure to raise test scores to meet 'accountability' goals may also mean lost opportunities to learn as teachers have little incentive to pursue more challenging content with their students.

dents Japanese and then testing them in French" (Focused Reporting Project, 1995). Teachers in Greenville, South Carolina, wasted valuable learning time teaching card catalog skills they knew would be included on the state assessment despite the fact that the libraries in the school and community were all automated (Rothman, 1995). Individual teachers across the country report abandoning science, social studies, art, music, and physical education to spend more time on test preparation in reading and math skills, especially in high poverty schools.

High-stakes testing for accountability can also sabotage the development of a community of learners within and across schools. "Rewards" and "sanctions" allotted in the high-stakes policy context may encourage the most competent teachers to transfer from resource-poor schools or those where large numbers of immigrant or highly mobile student enrollments make test score gains more difficult to produce (Darling-Hammond, 1996). Moreover, teachers subject to rewards and sanctions may begin to treat their students in similar coercive ways, inhibiting the development of the responsive student-teacher relationships necessary for learning (Jones & Whitford, 1997). In a 1998 survey conducted at the University of North Carolina at Chapel Hill, for example, nearly 53 percent of teachers responding from around the state described more negative attitudes toward low-achieving students among their colleagues as a result of the state's high-stakes accountability system. Large numbers of teachers also reported an increase in student anxiety about school and a decrease in students' love of learning; 55 percent said they spent more than 40 percent of their school time preparing for end-of-grade tests (Williamson, 1998).

With a narrow focus on raising test scores, educators have little incentive to engage in professional reflection and problem-solving about the school as a whole (Darling-Hammond, 1992; Ginsberg & Berry, 1991; Madaus & Kelleghan, 1993). In the North Carolina study, 68 percent of teachers surveyed believed the state's test-based accountability system would not improve their schools (Williamson, 1998). Observing the rancor that developed among schools when district "accountability" rankings of schools in San Diego became public, one parent noted, "Parents are left with the impression that [educators] have not created an environment that is conducive to [schools'] self-assessment." Moreover, pitting schools against one another discourages professionals from seeking help from one another. As one well-regarded San Diego principal of a school ranked "low-performing" added, "They've labeled you and then you have to prove you don't deserve the label. You are guilty until proven innocent. It's so divisive" (Jones, 1997).

Although accountability formulas are meant, in part, to provide parents with more accurate information about schools, the technical imprecision of measuring school performance can undermine public confidence in the validity of school rankings. In Philadelphia and Kentucky, for example, technical and conceptual flaws in accountability formulas have resulted in underestimating the progress of some schools and targeting well-regarded schools for "intervention," raising questions about the fairness and quality of the accountability system overall (Dean, 1997; Holland, 1997; Jones & Mezzacappa, 1998; Mezzacappa, 1997). Likewise, in San Diego, technical problems in ranking schools based on test scores have confused rather than enlightened the public about school quality. In that district, schools' rating could depend in part on the numbers of children tested, with percentages varying from school to school. Some schools that made dramatic gains were still labeled "low performing"; others made no improvement but escaped the cutoff score for such classification; still others were excluded from ranking altogether because of high enrollments of non-English-speaking students or because they did not include the specific grades in which students were tested. Some whose own innovations meant they did not assess students according to standard report card grades found their students' test scores were weighted twice while others escaped designation as "low-performing" by inflating grades. Under the gun to explain their ranking, some schools tried to blame certain ethnic groups or low-performing students (Jones, 1997). Perhaps not surprisingly, with millions of dollars of incentive money riding on school ratings, the top-down policing of schools may tempt increasing numbers of teachers to tamper with student results as they implement standards-based testing programs (Harp, 1997; Stecklow, 1997).

Even the use of test scores to identify schools where large numbers of students fail to meet standards has limitations. Although some schools may respond with real reforms to their appearance on a "list of shame," sanctioning such schools does not necessarily stimulate educators to develop a new repertoire of approaches so that every student will learn or build capacity of the school as a whole. More often, the actions schools take to "get off the

With millions of dollars of incentive money riding on school ratings, the top-down policing of schools may tempt increasing numbers of teachers to tamper with student results as they implement standards-based testing programs.

list" typically leaves teachers' low expectations for student achievement unchanged or principals' skills for leading a school toward a stronger learning environment undeveloped. For example, principals of schools that are under review in New York openly admitted to all-out teaching only test-taking skills or to changing the testing pool in order to raise school scores (Ascher, Ikenda, & Fruchter, 1998).

Moreover, states and districts do not always follow through with effective support for schools with persistent problems. In practice, technical assistance may often assume all low-performing schools are floundering for the same reasons, and intervention for schools "under review" may emphasize compliance over capacity-building (Ascher, Ikenda, & Fruchter, 1998). Even when intervention and consultation is of high quality, outside "coaches" may find it difficult to wear the hats of judge and helper simultaneously (Holland, 1997a). Further, in some states, technical assistance may focus more on coaching teachers on raising test scores than on improving teaching and learning. As Ken Jones, Director of Professional Development for Kentucky's Ohio Valley Educational Cooperative observes:

> Our state test and accountability system is actually restricting innovation among some schools. Having a school "change its ways" does not always mean for the better. We are learning that lesson here as the state sends more and more of its "distinguished educators" out to tell schools how to get higher test scores. It can be very reductionist and standardized.

Despite promises that top-down and bottom-up reforms will complement one another, the heavy-handed marriage of "standards" and "accountability" is ultimately a top-down strategy, forcing compliance with requirements rather than better learning. Such policies put a premium on schools *looking* better without necessarily *being* better. Tightening the screws through increased monitoring and compliance does not pave the way for real reform that addresses long-standing barriers to learning. Indeed, as long as educators at the school level experience standards as something "they" are doing to "us," the standards movement will fail to develop either the will or the skill of schools to make deep changes in the teaching and learning opportunities they offer.

Standards-based reform: Quick fix or deep change?

As long as educators at the school level experience 'standards' as something 'they' are doing to 'us,' the standards movement will fail to develop either the will or the skill of schools to make deep changes in the teaching and learning opportunities they offer.

Given policies that make testing and public reporting of test scores, not better learning, the primary focus of attention, teachers may find themselves torn between conflicting objectives. Attempting to meet established standards-based accountability goals that make schools' test scores "look good," they may put off making the difficult changes necessary for real improvements in student learning. Moreover, with public attention directed primarily toward student outcomes or results defined in terms of test scores, teachers' rarely have the opportunity to reflect on what practices are contributing to those results, whether positive or negative (Holland, 1997b). In the absence of policies that ensure stable school-based leadership and professional teaching staff, time for teacher study and reflection, and the ongoing development of teachers prepared to teach students who have traditionally been denied access to challenging curriculum, the drive for building school-wide capacity for helping students produce work that truly reflects higher standards may never even begin.

Lasting solutions to the problems of schooling and low achievement will not come from equating of standards-based reform with standardized testing, grade retention, and bureaucratic accountability. But if lists of standards pegged to large-scale testing do not contribute to real school reform, what kind of standards would serve this purpose? How can the push for higher standards translate into improved teaching and learning in all schools? Can schools extricate themselves from the

Lasting solutions to the problems of schooling and low achievement will not come from equating of 'standards-based reform' with standardized testing, grade retention, and bureaucratic accountability.

oppressive top-down models of control and standardization inherent in the use of standards for grade retention and bureaucratic accountability? Can schools find alternative models for authentic standards-based reform that will genuinely improve learning and teaching in every classroom? ◼

III. Building a Culture for Standards-Based Reform: Turning Rhetoric into Practice

If schools are to realize the promises of the standards movement, they need alternative models for standards-based reform powerful enough to generate school practices that result in all students' achieving. They need support in creating school cultures that value student work of high quality. Such a culture, founded on new habits, relationship, and routines that deepen teaching and learning, can nurture a community of learners of students and teachers alike. Establishing such a culture is fundamental to turning the rhetoric of standards into practice.

The dimensions of school cultures that foster high standards for student work are already known to educators who pursue deeper teaching and learning. Although many of these same educators remain unmoved by policymakers' calls for large-scale, test-centered, systemic reform, they do not reject standards themselves. Rather teachers who focus daily on helping students produce better work that meets higher standards of quality do assert that communities of educators, not politicians, must use their knowledge and experience to sculpt the teaching and learning experiences that will foster high quality work in each school.

Teachers working to build a school culture that supports high standards view the lists of standards that emanate from policy makers as useful only to the extent that they stimulate a deeper process for improving their teaching. As teacher Linda Nathan, Co-Director of the Fenway Middle College High School in Boston explains:

> We use the state frameworks, national frameworks, and city standards as guideposts. They are useful tools to give us an idea of what others think is important for students to know and be able to do. They are never the be-all and end-all. We firmly believe that there is no finite body of information for kids to know or finite set of skills for kids to be able to do. In this way, we run "counter" to much of the current standards movement.

Educators like Nathan do not turn to test scores to sort students who should be promoted from those who should repeat a grade, slot students into different ability levels, or lead teachers to the right page in the right textbook on a given day. Rather, these educators use standards as one lens through which they can examine their practice, help students meet learning challenges and develop stronger commitment to doing high quality work, make equal access to valued learning opportunities a reality, and open doors to future learning that matches students' own aspirations. Through concrete practice, not abstract theory, teachers in many schools are pushing for higher standards, calling for richer quality work that students and teachers do in their schools. New York City teacher Loretta Brady (1996) elaborates:

> While bureaucrats [are] making abstract lists of what students should know and be able to do and calling these curriculum frameworks "standards," we at least [understand] that far higher standards [are] achieved when the knowing is framed as a concrete task – a performance – that is personally mean- ingful and rich in the ideas at the heart of a discipline. (p. 4)

...new standards and assessments will only 'take' in a culture that fosters student motiva- tion and values a school-wide 'press for achievement.'

Unwilling to ride along as passengers on the "standards-driven" band- wagon, educators themselves are mapping their own strategy for improving student achievement. This strategy rests on a cluster of comple- mentary practices designed to improve learning. Pursuing this strat- egy, teachers are beginning to reshape what Seymour Sarason (1982, 1996) calls the "regularities" of schooling. These educators under- stand that new standards and assessments will only "take" in a culture that fosters student motivation and values what researcher Jeannie Oakes (1989) notes is a key focal point for school success, a school wide "press for achievement."

Many standards-oriented educators begin discussions about standards by focusing on the work teachers do with their students, the norms that shape the relationships between teachers, and students, and the work stu- dents produce as a result. As Joe McDonald (In Berger, 1996a) explains:

> It turns out that what we call standards are crude – albeit sometimes useful – abstractions for the culture of school. This culture is created by diverse sources: the habits and spirit of practice that characterize a teacher's intimate work and a school's collective work; the impingement of structure; the

relative openness of the school to its community; and the astounding presence of actual children with their actual attitudes and needs. (p. 8)

As these educators reorient their school culture toward standards-based work, they do not see their goals as *making the diploma meaningful again* or *producing students who can compete with the Japanese.* Instead, going beyond the abstract rhetoric of policy circles, they are embracing new norms, beliefs, and routines related to the quality of work their students do and the quality of relationships inside the school. These practitioners value the standards of their professional associations and may use curriculum frameworks developed in their own states to inform their work. But more often, it is the vision of better quality student work overall that inspires them, and to this end, they are putting new routines, beliefs about learning, and relationships into practice to develop a culture of high standards.[1]

What does school culture have to do with standards-based reform of schools? For many years, close observers of school reform have underscored the futility of any attempt to improve student learning without changing the culture and "regularities" of schooling (Corbett & Wilson, 1997a, 1997b; Dow, 1991; Fullan, 1991; Goodlad, 1984; Muncey & McQuillen, 1993; Oakes & Wells, 1996; Sarason, 1971, 1996). The rhetoric of *all students achieving* is little more than empty promise without a school culture, including the norms, values, routines, and beliefs about learning that define school practices, that nurtures that vision. If reformers fail to address the culture of schooling, the goals of the "standards movement" will remain unrealized.

What does such a culture look like? What assumptions and beliefs, school routines, classroom practices, and organizational arrangements contribute to sustaining a culture of high standards? As they work toward improved achievement of all students, standards-oriented practitioners assert that a school culture of high stan-

The rhetoric of 'all students achieving' is little more than empty promise without a school culture, including the norms, values, routines, and beliefs about learning that define school practices, that nurtures that vision.

---

[1] The author is indebted to Ron Berger, sixth grade teacher in Shutesbury, Massachusetts, whose classroom practice, first described in his unpublished paper, *Building A School Culture of High Standards,* May 1990, stimulated much of the thinking behind this paper. This paper has since appeared as a publication of the Annenberg Institute for School Reform (Berger, 1996a)

dards weaves together a set of norms and beliefs, practices, and routines so that:

- Teachers put **student work**, supported by **rich pedagogy**, at the center of teaching and learning;

- Teachers shape their **relationships** with students and among students to **nurture student motivation, effort**, and **investment** in schoolwork;

- Teachers develop their practice in the context of a **professional community** focused on improving the work all students do, coupling a "press for achievement" with standards of care.

Developing each of these aspects of school culture requires multiple changes in schools' standard operating procedures and structures. It means developing positive relationships among adults and between teachers and students. It means structuring support for students into the school day so that they will exert the effort necessary to do work that "meets standards."

THE FIRST ESSENTIAL BUILDING BLOCK:
A FOCUS ON STUDENT WORK,
SUPPORTED BY A RICH INSTRUCTIONAL PROGRAM

Schools building a culture of high standards focus on student work – portfolios, products, and performances. This work represents not only "what students know and can do" but also what teachers ask students to learn and do. Highlighting student work departs from the decades-old practice of depending on standardized test scores to depict how students are doing in school.

Why the fuss about student work?

American schools have for decades relied on test scores to portray school success. However, equating improved scores with improved learning can mislead the public about what students know or the quality of their schooling. On one hand, test scores sometimes provide an overly optimistic view of student achievement. As Ed Reidy of the Philadelphia-based Pew Foundation observes:

If you look at both the NAEP and the TIMSS data in science and mathematics, we are not doing that badly, at least not compared to other places in the world. But if you look at what our youngsters can actually do and compare their performance to what they need to do to have options as they move on, you see that we are not doing very well. (Education Development Center, 1997)

On the other hand, test scores can undervalue the sophistication of students' knowledge or skills, especially when classroom teaching has revolved around developing particular "real world" skills that tests do not assess. For example, teachers at the ALL (Advanced Learning Laboratory) Middle School in Worcester, Massachusetts, were puzzled by writing scores that appeared far below the skills indicated by students' classroom work. Working with researchers from the Center for the Study of Testing, Evaluation, and Education Policy at Boston College, they probed further and found that students who were accustomed to using technology in all aspects of their learning were dramatically disadvantaged by traditional testing conditions. In retesting their students, they discovered that those who responded to a writing prompt on a computer wrote twice as much and were more likely to organize their work into more paragraphs than a matched group of students asked to respond in longhand. They concluded that paper-and-pencil tests could substantially underestimate the competence of students who had developed the regular habit of using a word processor to execute their assignments (Russell & Haney, 1997).

In either case, tests reveal very little about the quality of work students produce. As Fred Newmann and his colleagues at the University of Wisconsin have found, even students with identical test scores can produce work that differs dramatically in quality from student to student (Newmann, Marks, & Gamoran, 1995; Newmann & Wehlage, 1995). Looking at work from students matched by social and economic background and previous academic records, researchers found some students produced well-developed, detailed essays while others produced sketchy, "bare-bones" work. Moreover, differences in student work reflected different classroom practices and opportunities to learn. For example, one student produced an essay that was the result of several drafts and multiple discussions with the teacher about those drafts; a second student produced work that included one-sentence answers to questions copied from a work sheet. Identical test scores masked these differences in learning and failed to show how well students really understood a topic or could apply their understanding to new situations.

Since test scores provide such limited information about what students know and can do with that knowledge, schools seeking evidence of how well students are developing understanding of a discipline must focus more attention on how student products, portfolios, or performances reflect their learning. As Theodore Sizer, founder of the Coalition of Essential Schools, remarks:

> We look at [students'] work, rather than tokens of their work. The 30-minute test tells us something, but not very much. The thick folder of the student's actual work, the videotaping of the student's defense of a science project – that is the evidence. (ATLAS Communities, 1997a, p. 9)

Teachers who make a commitment to guide their practice toward improving student work recognize that teaching and assignments must generate different kinds of results from those they expect when they focus only on test scores. Insisting that student work become the standard of accomplishment means that teachers must move beyond curriculum that mimics standardized tests – worksheets that require students to read paragraphs of text, fill in blanks, or complete vocabulary definitions – to assignments that help students develop thinking skills for deeper understanding: posing questions, gathering information, reasoning, synthesizing different perspectives, communicating conclusions, and applying new learning. Further, routine opportunities for teachers, students, and parents to talk about the quality of student performances, portfolios, and projects are essential to building a school culture of high standards. Without such opportunities, schools will struggle repeatedly to develop the shared sense of what work is "good enough" and what work meets "high standards."

Setting the stage: Teaching and learning for understanding.

Not all teaching and learning results in work that students can demonstrate as evidence of their learning. Depending on the school, students can spend days, weeks, or months of the school year filling in worksheets, repeating fragments of information deemed basic and fundamental for future learning. Developing a culture for standards-based reform involves challenging current norms of teaching. A shift toward good, culturally relevant teaching and authentic pedagogy sets the stage for students to create work that can demonstrate their understanding of concepts in the disciplines.

Good teaching and authentic, culturally relevant pedagogy. Good teaching is a fundamental condition fostering "good work." But in many schools, especially in urban districts, good teaching has yet to break through the constraints of what Martin Haberman (1991) calls a "pedagogy of poverty" – the ritualistic acts of giving information, directions, and tests, asking questions, and monitoring seat work and homework. In the absence of good teaching, many students lack regular opportunities to produce good work. Even when students accept the practices that characterize the pedagogy of poverty, and even when they work hard within these practices, they will be left with limited opportunity to produce work that reflects understanding of a discipline and meets standards of quality.

In contrast, classrooms characterized by good teaching are marked by opportunities students have to do good work. As Haberman explains, **good teaching is likely to be going on when students are:**

- Involved with issues they regard as vital;

- Engaged in exploring human differences;

- Planning what they will be doing;

- Applying ideals such as fairness, equity, or justice to their world;

- Doing an experiment, participating as an actor, or constructing things;

- Directly involved in a real-life experience through field trips and interactions with resource people at work and in the community;

- Actively involved in heterogeneous groups that value divergent questioning strategies, multiple assignments in the same class, and activities that allow for alternative responses and solutions;

- Pushed to think about an idea in a way that questions common sense or a widely accepted assumption, compare, analyze, synthesize, evaluate, and generalize;

- Redoing, polishing, or perfecting their work;

- Accessing information;

- Reflecting on their own lives and how they have come to believe what they do.

If the features of good teaching stand in contrast to the pedagogy of poverty, these same features complement practices that characterize *authentic pedagogy*. As described by University of Wisconsin researchers Fred Newmann and Gary Wehlage (1995), authentic pedagogy engages students in work that develops in-depth understanding of concepts in a discipline. Rather than covering facts or topics in list-like fashion, students produce work that requires them to organize information and consider alternatives, engage in disciplined research and elaborate their findings through extended writing, and connect their work to a concept, problem, or issue similar to one they might encounter outside the classroom. In classrooms where authentic pedagogy is the norm:

- Students are involved in higher order thinking – synthesizing information, generalizing, explaining, and hypothesizing in ways that lead them to new understandings;

- Students are pursuing deep knowledge by engaging in the central ideas of a concept and exploring connections and relationships of ideas within the topic;

- Students and teachers have substantive and extended conversations about the subjects that build on and develop shared understandings of ideas and topics;

- Students make connections between their classroom learning and problems or experiences they might encounter in the real world.

Whether called good teaching or authentic pedagogy, these practices embrace the kind of learning anticipated by the standards of the professional associations. For example, the *Standards* of the National Council of Teachers of Mathematics call for students to work in small groups, discuss ways to solve problems in student- and teacher-led discussions, make conjectures and explain problems that may have more than one correct answer, use hands-on materials, calculators, and computers, and work on individual problems and group investigations (NCTM, 1989). These practices have implications that go well beyond matching discrete skills to "Students will...." statements. They anticipate learning generated through the process of producing work that has significance in the world beyond the classroom.

Most important, these practices have demonstrable effects on student achievement. As the University of Wisconsin researchers learned when they reviewed student work in 24 study schools, students in classes where teachers employed authentic pedagogy were more likely than their peers in more conventional classrooms to produce high quality work independent of their scores on standardized tests. Further, they found that these effects appeared for all students regardless of social or economic background (Newmann & Wehlage, 1995). Likewise, a carefully designed study of the effects of NCTM standards-oriented classrooms on student achievement as measured by standardized tests found that middle school students' knowledge of algebra increased at a greater rate in classrooms characterized by greater use of practices recommended by NCTM. Again, the effects were positive for students with both high and low Grade Point Averages (Mayer, 1998).

Middle school students' knowledge of algebra increased at a greater rate in classrooms characterized by greater use of practices recommended by NCTM.

Teachers further enhance good teaching and authentic pedagogy by adopting "culturally relevant" practices that boost their effectiveness with diverse student groups, including African American, Latino, and new immigrant students (Ladson-Billings, 1994; Lipman 1998, Nieto, 1992). Culturally relevant pedagogy includes teaching students what Delpit (1995) calls "codes of power," the skills to take on the challenges of the dominant culture, especially those practices like testing and ability grouping that have historically served to curtail opportunity for poor and minority students. But culturally relevant practice benefits all students because it pushes teachers to individualize teaching to account for the normal diversity in any given classroom. As Gloria Ladson-Billings (1994) explains, culturally relevant pedagogy means drawing on students' culture itself so that students will both succeed in school and also think critically about their role in the larger democratic society. Likewise, Sonia Nieto (1994) explains, such pedagogy means accepting that "equal is not the same;" rather teachers recognize and use differences in learning styles, social and communication styles, and language differences to engage and motivate students. In this sense, culturally relevant pedagogy supports a culture for standards-based reform that embraces all students. Nieto adds:

33

High standards can be achieved in a great variety of ways and through a multitude of materials. Multicultural education means finding and using culturally, multiculturally, and linguistically relevant materials in developing students' basic skills. It also means using a variety of approaches, from peer tutoring to dramatizations, in instruction. Raising standards and expectations does not mean homogenizing instruction but creating new and different opportunities for learning for all students. (p. 282)

A school culture that sets the stage for standards-based learning by incorporating good teaching and authentic, culturally relevant pedagogy into students' regular opportunities to learn offers students multiple ways to be smart. These pathways may reflect notions of multiple intelligences (Gardner, 1993) and lead to work that reflects diverse, but equally high standards of quality. By allowing students to become smart in diverse ways, teachers can motivate students to succeed academically without forcing them to sacrifice their personal or social identity. Culturally relevant pedagogy is key to creating school cultures where students feel "safe to be smart" and can demonstrate their accomplishments through diverse pieces of work.

By allowing students to become smart in diverse ways, teachers can motivate students to succeed academically without forcing them to sacrifice their personal or social identity.

Curriculum for good student work. Good teaching and authentic, culturally relevant pedagogy put student work at the center of learning. But students must also be learning about *something,* and for most schools, that something lies in the core subjects of language arts, mathematics, science, and social studies. Many teachers, especially new teachers, look to an articulated curriculum in these content areas for guidance in making decisions about teaching and learning, and sometimes miss finding it. As one teacher describing her situation on the Middle-L listserv (16 July 1998) queried:

I'm going to be teaching 6th and 7th grade language arts. The problem that I have is that my school doesn't have a curriculum for those grades. If anyone could help me with what should be taught in those grades, I'd be forever grateful.

Curriculum that supports good student work must go beyond the basic expectation of telling teachers what to teach. In addition, curriculum must weave the *content* of guiding documents like the standards of professional associations or curriculum frameworks together with principles of authentic pedagogy and good, culturally relevant teaching. It must support assignments that challenge students to develop reasoning and problem-solving skills as they delve into the big ideas of the disciplines. In this light, assigning eighth graders to trace a cross-section of the human skin can no longer be called "learning" in science; and requiring seventh graders to stretch rubber bands on geo-boards to match the triangles, squares, and octagons printed on photocopied worksheets can no longer substitute for real learning in mathematics. Likewise, testing how well students can match Civil War generals with the battles they fought, or overseeing students as they place question marks in isolated sentences for three days in October fit neither the standards of the professional associations or the criteria for authentic pedagogy in social studies or language arts. Such assignments do not allow students to demonstrate complex thinking – comparing, dissecting, analyzing – in the content areas. Lacking any focus on learning for understanding and demanding little in-depth thinking, these assignments do not generate student work that can help teachers identify gaps in understanding or guide them in teaching and re-teaching concepts. Indeed, the work students produce in response to such assignments will be connected to little more than discrete facts or skills which students will, in all likelihood, forget shortly after they satisfy the demands of their teacher for completed work.

...students need access to the 'new content' that includes thinking skills and content derived from diverse traditions.

As much as good teaching, students also need a curriculum that pushes them to produce high quality work. This means students need access to the "new content" that includes thinking skills and content derived from diverse traditions. This access is still largely lacking, even in otherwise responsive middle grades schools. As Douglas Mac Iver of the Center for Research on the Education of Students Placed at Risk (Education Development Center, 1997) notes:

> [Schools] are discovering that they are far away from the standards that are being set as acceptable standards of performance.... What you find so often is that seventy-five percent of the learning time in these schools, which have made great strides otherwise, is spent in content that is really old content, rather than introducing students to new content.

Standards from the professional associations sketch out the new content students need to support learning for understanding and for future success.

However, in the belief that students must master "basic skills" before moving on to grapple with the concepts of the disciplines, many teachers still put off teaching recommended new content, choosing instead to repeat old content over and over. For example, in contrast to the suggestions for curriculum embodied in the NCTM *Standards*, some 40 percent of all mathematics lessons taught to U.S. eighth graders include arithmetic topics, three times the amount taught to eighth graders in Germany, while math textbooks include a decreasing amount of new material every year through the eighth grade (Flanders, 1987; U.S. Department of Education, 1997). Moreover, as the Third International Mathematics and Science Study (TIMSS) has reported, most eighth graders in the United States are enrolled in a math curriculum that is typical of the seventh grade curriculum in other countries, and much science learning concentrates too much on memorization and less on understanding (U.S. Department of Education, 1997; Woodhams, 1998).

Curriculum that supports learning for the kinds of understanding that support good student work requires more than moving a traditional course of instruction into the earlier grades or increasing the amount of old content required for mastery. Such a strategy may even cloud what is required for real reform. For example, in a study of nine Michigan districts working to match math and science teaching more closely to reforms called for by the National Council of Teachers of Mathematics and the National Science Association, researchers found that some local leaders misinterpreted the NCTM's standard for problem solving, which assumes that students will think about one problem for a long period of time, to mean merely that students would work on an increased number of story problems (Spillane & Thompson, 1997). In the same vein, learning algebra in the eighth grade clearly has positive effects on learning in mathematics (Smith, 1996); however, simply moving the traditional ninth grade algebra course into the eighth grade does not alone constitute standards-based reform in mathematics. What students need, to play out the example from mathematics, is a standards-based curriculum that develops students' familiarity with concepts of mathematics, including algebra, engages them in investigations of those concepts, and fosters students' use of mathematics as a language for describing science and the world.

What students need is a standards-based curriculum that develops students' familiarity with concepts of mathematics, including algebra, engages them in investigations of those concepts, and fosters students' use of mathematics as a language for describing science and the world.

New content must also go beyond the traditional to draw from diverse sources, including students' communities themselves, if curriculum is to engage all students and meet the criteria of authentic, culturally relevant pedagogy. As Sonia Nieto (1992) explains:

> Children who are not in the dominant group have a hard time finding themselves or their communities in the books they read or the curriculum to which they are exposed. When they do see themselves, it is often through the distorted lens of the dominant group. American Indian children read about themselves as "savages," who were bereft of culture until the Europeans arrived; African Americans read sanitized versions of slavery; Mexican Americans read of the "Westward expansion," with no indication that their ancestors were already living on the land onto which Europeans were expanding; and working-class children learn virtually nothing of their history except perhaps that the struggle for the eight-hour day was a long one. Little wonder, then, that school curricula and real life are often at polar extremes. (p. 76)

New content drawn from multicultural sources is critical if students are to connect their learning to the world. Multicultural content that allows all students to "see themselves" in what they are studying allows students to bridge the worlds of school and home, helping students who are not from the dominant culture feel safe to be smart. But because multicultural content reflects the larger world as it is, it also enhances learning for understanding of all students. As Georgia State University's Asa Hilliard (n.d.) notes:

New content drawn from multicultural sources is critical if students are to connect their learning to the world.

> When I think of pluralism in the curriculum, I first and foremost think of a truthful curriculum that paints an accurate picture of the total human experience, no matter what events we choose to [focus on]. A truthful portrayal of human events will force a pluralization of the curriculum instantly.

As young adolescent students seek to find their place in the larger world outside of their families and schools, they need honest information that satisfies their curiosity about that world. With residential segregation increasing across the country, students' best source of information about an increasingly interlinked world – and opportunity to make sense of it – is the school curriculum. Teachers who want every student to succeed in an ever-changing society work to help young adolescents develop the cultural knowledge and skills necessary to negotiate their way in the larger world and at the same time deepen their understanding of their own community and its role in that world.

Clearly new standards call for new pedagogy. Building a culture for standards-based reform means reconsidering old assumptions that ground effective teaching and learning. If every student is to create work that meets standards, educators must reconsider how curriculum and instruction allow every single student to develop thinking skills, practice them, and learn for understanding. Educators must assess their pedagogy to determine how all students can find an entry point into the learning process. They must hold traditional assignments up to the light of standards from national professional organizations and against the criteria of authentic pedagogy as a way of assessing ways existing curriculum assignments meet or fall short of those standards.

Using principles of authentic pedagogy to guide curriculum selection. Adopting curriculum that incorporates content, assignments, and assessments developed to reflect the standards of those professional associations can ratchet up teachers' expectations for all students. Far from being scripted or teacher-proof, these curricula involve students and teacher in thoughtful discourse about problems presented through literature, science, and mathematics using content highlighted in the professional standards. They frequently include lessons concentrated on exploring subjects in depth through hands-on assignments. Many new curricula also have the advantage of having been piloted and field tested in a variety of schools with diverse students, then refined for improvement, and evaluated independently.

But how do teachers begin to assess new curriculum packages now available? Principles of authentic pedagogy and good, culturally relevant teaching can help educators as they select new curriculum from available packages of materials. For example, teachers selecting new curriculum may ask:

■ *Will this curriculum engage students in the 'big ideas' of a discipline?*

- *Will this curriculum allow students some choice over the work they do to learn content in depth and some control over the resources they will use to understand those ideas?*

- *Will this curriculum involve students in in-depth Socratic discussions in heterogeneous groups?*

- *Will this curriculum require students to develop critical thinking skills by gathering information, posing questions, synthesizing data and ideas, solving problems, and communicating?*

- *Will this curriculum involve students in creating products much as real scientists, historians, social scientists, mathematicians, and authors create a product?*

- *Will this curriculum support diverse learning and allow students opportunities to see themselves in their learning?*

- *Will this curriculum encourage students to seek feedback on, reflect on, and refine their thinking and work?*

- *Will those in the world outside the school use or value the products students create through this curriculum?*

- *Will this curriculum encourage teachers' own development as learners?*

Using these questions as a guide, educators find that, unlike many textbooks, some new packaged curricula reflect standards of authentic pedagogy in their focus on learning for understanding. Those that match schools' efforts to build a culture for standards-based reform include materials that stimulate in-depth understanding and engage students in hands-on learning and serious conversation about the subject matter. Four examples follow.

- Language arts teachers focused on improving students' critical thinking skills through Socratic discussion about text may consider such literacy and discussion programs as *Junior Great Books*. This program engages students and teachers in extended "shared inquiry" discussions about literature from a variety of traditions. Students learn to read for meaning and draw on evidence in the text to support their views, deepening student comprehension and teacher respect for students' opinions in the process. *Junior Great Books* complements other literature-based reading approaches, including literature circles (Daniels, 1994), which encourage student choice of reading, and *Accelerated Reader,* which motivates students to expand their reading beyond assigned test. *Junior Great Books* also engages students in writing and arts-related work so that they delve deeper into the themes of the literature, creating theater and visual arts pieces for production and display (Wheelock, 1998a).

■ Teachers seeking curricula that opens up opportunities to think about high quality literature through reading, writing, and probing discussion may also consider *Reading for Real,* a program developed by Oakland, California's Development Studies Center. Students listen to and discuss whole books read aloud, and they discuss books, short stories, and poetry in pairs. Follow-up conversations about particular questions at home with their parents engage students in academic conversations with adults outside the school. Students choose books to read on their own and read at least 20 books a year. Writing assignments stress revision for quality. Like the approaches developed by Harvey Daniels (1994) and Nancie Atwell (1992), the program reflects principles of cooperative learning and the value of developing work for different audiences. Like *Junior Great Books,* it puts critical thinking skills, including recognizing different viewpoints and modifying ideas in the face of new evidence, at the center of learning for understanding (Schaps, 1994).

■ Science teachers may consider new National Science Foundation-sponsored programs that engage students for understanding the "big ideas" in physical life, and earth/space sciences, science and technology, science and personal/social perspectives, the history and nature of science, and unifying concepts. Reviewed by the National Science Foundation for opportunities to pose questions, gather information, weigh evidence, make arguments, and communicate findings, curriculum materials may be comprehensive like the *Middle School Science and Technology* materials of Colorado's Biological Sciences Curriculum Study Group or the *Science 2000* materials developed by Decision Development Corporation of San Ramon, California; single-year focused like the *Event-Based Earth Science* program developed by Montgomery

(MD) County Public Schools; or supplemental and technology-driven, like the National Geographic *Kids Network*, developed by TERC and the National Geographic Society (National Science Foundation, 1996). Still using the same criteria, teachers might also choose older curricula like *Foundational Approaches in Science Teaching* (FAST) from the University of Hawaii, a curriculum that does not require extensive laboratory facilities to execute (Epstein and Salinas, 1990).

■ Middle grades mathematics teachers may consider curriculum like Michigan State University's *Connected Mathematics Project*, the University of Wisconsin's *Mathematics in Context* curriculum, the *Middle School Mathematics Through Applications Project* (developed at the Institute for Research on Learning, Palo Alto, California), *Seeing and Thinking Mathematically* (developed at Education Development Center, Newton, Massachusetts); and the University of Montana's *Six Through Eight Mathematics* (STEM) all set the stage for learning mathematics in greater depth, with learning benefits for students of all backgrounds (Viadero, 1996).

In some states, high quality packaged curricula, like these math programs, closely parallel state curriculum frameworks. In others, educators alter them to fit more closely with state parameters. For example, Julia Hankins, principal of Grant Middle School in Corpus Christi, reports that when she and the math teachers at Martin Middle School where she was formerly assistant principal adopted the *Connected Math Program* (CMP), the acclaimed three-year NCTM standards-based math curriculum, they had to move some *CMP* content from one grade to another so that the work parallels the Texas Framework of Essential Skills. For Martin's math teachers, this effort meant that, while acknowledging the parameters of traditional frameworks, students would still have access to curriculum that would offer opportunities for problem solving, communicating, and reasoning in mathematics regardless of their scores on tests of computational skills.

Designing new curriculum for good student work. Schools that are building a culture for standards-based reform may also choose to develop their own curriculum to reflect principles of authentic pedagogy as well as standards of the professional associations of their own state. In some schools, teachers are mapping existing curriculum to identify overlaps or gaps in study units and provide greater curriculum coherence. As teachers hold their school curriculum up to the expectations of professional standards, they may eliminate, shift, or add concepts to reflect more closely the expectations of those standards. For example, as teachers realize that the unit eighth graders are doing on the rain forest repeats what they have done in the sixth or seventh grades, they can, perhaps for the first time, make decisions together about what content belongs where in their school's overall curriculum. Standards from the professional associations can help identify the substantive content teachers want students to understand; from this foundation, teachers can then structure assignments around tasks that require researching, reasoning, and analyzing information, and they can focus these assignments on helping students produce written work, products, performances, and portfolios that meet standards of high quality.

Because developing new assignments that lead students to quality work is new for many teachers, many middle schools draw on support from national school reform groups that work with whole schools to develop a set of procedures for planning curriculum. One of these groups, Expeditionary Learning, has been especially successful in identifying "design principles" that teachers can use to boost students' learning through "expeditions" (Academy for Educational Development, 1995). As Amy Mednick of Expeditionary Learning explains, "learning expeditions" are in-depth, thematic investigations that involve students in real-life projects, fieldwork, and service. Teachers planning learning expeditions use guiding questions and learning goals that are aligned with district and state standards. The investigations they design inspire and compel students to achieve academic skills and habits, think critically, learn subject matter, and accomplish high levels of work through critique and revision. As a result, students become more motivated in their academic work, develop perseverance and self-discipline, and excel on the standardized measures of achievement.

Although teachers at individual schools design learning expeditions that connect with their own diverse communities, teachers in participating schools all draw on common "design principles" that reflect core values and a shared understanding about how students learn (Campbell, Leibowitz, Mednick, & Rugen, 1998). These principles value students' self-discovery, the "having of wonderful ideas," and student responsibility for learning; they also assert the value of learning that balances intimacy and caring, success and failure, collaboration and competition, diversity and inclusion; and they reflect the belief that students learn from interaction with the natural world, from reflection in solitude, and from service. Teachers keep these principles in mind as they develop their expeditions using a structured process that guides teachers in considering how a topic connects to content standards, identify guiding questions that will focus the learning, and learning goals that describe what students will know and do.

Learning expeditions in the middle grades are consistent with middle schools' traditional commitment to develop students' thinking skills through interdisciplinary learning. For example, at Fulton Intermediate School in Dubuque, Iowa, teachers Angela Budde and Sarah Johnson designed a four-month "Investigations Expedition" centered on a study of birds. Beginning with district expectations that all fifth graders would practice the scientific method, teachers fashioned lessons so that all their students, many from low-income families, would develop observation and recording skills by using microscopes to describe a cell. Working in groups, students made observations, formed hypotheses, gathered data, tested predictions, and summarized and recorded their observations in lab reports. Although some experiments were flawed, student mistakes opened up opportunities for discussing variables and invalid conclusions. Students further practiced writing skills in field notes based on their work as naturalists counting bald eagles with experts from the state's Department of Natural Resources, and they developed research skills as authors of illustrated books on a bird of their choice, ranging from backyard birds to the Hoopoe, Japanese crane, Adelie penguin, and Toco toucan. Writing to specifications of a rubric they designed, students critiqued one another over several drafts; working to blueprint specifications, students also designed and built birdhouses. As a culminating project, students designed replicas of different bird habitats, developing a classroom sanctuary full of papier-mâché birds in their appropriate setting for an audience of student, parent, and community visitors. Students "staffed" each corner of the sanctuary, prepared to explain the habitat and answer questions. Throughout the project, students also wrote weekly letters to their parents to provide them with up-to-date information about what their classroom work involved (Budde & Johnson, 1998).

This and other expeditions from schools as varied as the Martin Luther King, Jr. Middle School in Portland, Maine, and the School for the Physical City in New York City demonstrate how teachers *begin* their planning by examining district or state curriculum standards and using the standards to provide a rational for diverse activities that focus on in-depth learning goals. Then, as teaching helps students to connect learning in one discipline to learning in other disciplines, new possibilities for student work unfold, allowing the expedition to remain dynamic. For example, as teachers Budde and Johnson report, after the initial expedition at Fulton Intermediate School, students' own questions played into implementation in subsequent years, as students, for example, became engaged in watching and documenting chicken eggs hatch into chicks. At this point, the expedition helps shape the culture of the entire school. Younger students who have seen "the bird thing" enter Budde's and Johnson's classroom ready and willing to do the work necessary to meet high standards.

Ultimately, standards-based pedagogy should involve students in projects that require them to hone basic skills and develop thinking skills in the context of creating real work. It should result in students' deepening content understanding so they can connect that understanding to the world outside their classrooms. As the work of Expeditionary Learning has evolved, it has demonstrated how teachers can develop curriculum that reflects broad standards, fits criteria for authentic, culturally relevant pedagogy, and results in students creating high quality work that meets standards without being standardized.

Standards-based pedagogy should involve students in projects that require them to hone basic skills and develop thinking skills in the context of creating real work.

Developing and implementing standards-based curriculum is not easy. As educator Jane Pollock of the Mid-continent Regional Educational Laboratory (ASCD, 1997) warns, teachers working to develop standards-based units run the risk of reducing curriculum to a set of "neat activities." Even when teachers focus on standards-based content and monitor the steps students take toward producing quality work, good teaching and strong curriculum in individual classrooms is not necessarily enough to boost the achievement of all students. Also essential is school-wide academic coherence that reinforces learning for understanding in every classroom in every grade.

Academic coherence. In many middle schools, students' academic experiences are often fragmented and lacking in coherent instructional focus. In some schools, inconsistency is readily apparent in the different and conflicting expectations, curriculum, textbook series, and teaching strategies of different classrooms. In other schools, educators may embrace so many extra programs, often in response to perceived student deficits, that the school becomes a "Christmas tree school" (Bryk, Easton, Kerbow, Rollow, & Sebring, 1993). Such schools are so laden with programmatic ornaments that their core academic mission collapses under the weight of their "add-ons." Building a culture for standards-based reform means rejecting the Christmas tree model and establishing an academic program that is coherent across the whole school. Schools develop such coherence in different ways.

Curriculum mapping. To promote greater coherence, some schools go through a process of curriculum mapping, systematically identifying the content different teachers are highlighting in each grade. Using the map they develop, teachers then beef up, abandon, or shift their content for better learning. For example, at Broad Meadows Middle School in Quincy, Massachusetts, this process began when the school's seventh grade teachers, demoralized in the face of budget cuts, decided that they would either "give up or team up." Then as teachers teamed up to plan for a better curriculum, they moved from a program that encompassed hundreds of topics to one that highlighted several themes in-depth. As social studies teacher Ron Adams explains:

> We met in the home economics classroom with the principal, special education teacher, all Grade 7 academic teachers, the shop teacher, and the home economics teacher. We were going to team together, but around what? Out of all the hundreds of topics in math, science, language arts, social studies, and reading, what one, two, or three things did we believe our students should know in-depth, on many levels, for the rest of their lives? If we could answer that one question, we would discover the themes around which our seventh grade team would be anchored.

Although the teachers were a team on paper, with 120 students in common, each knew next to nothing about what the others were teaching. Adams elaborates:

> We got out blank sheets of large newsprint. We each took a page and we each listed on our own sheet the topics, skills and units which we would teach over the school year. We taped them on the wall. In a glance we saw for the first time the hundreds of topics which we would parade before our students over the course of the school year. We looked at the list from our students' point of view. There were an overwhelming number of topics.

From the list of topics, the seventh grade teachers realized that three stood out. So, as Adams relates:

> We agreed that for seven months during the school year, we would teach our respective curriculum, perhaps in isolation. But for a month in October, we would team our talents and community contacts to "teach the hell out of the Industrial Revolution." How did the farming United States become an industrialized giant? In December, we would team around the Civil War and its causes and its effects today. In May, we would team around the biggest threat to the survival of democracy and freedom: World War II.

At Broad Meadows, the process of establishing a stronger content focus also resulted in building greater instructional consistency. As teachers identified how the curriculum they had been teaching in isolation overlapped and intersected, they also realized that individually they had similar beliefs about instruction. This realization crystallized for them when science teacher Harold Crowley pointed out, "We know how to teach," then asked, "So what have we noticed about effective teaching and learning over the years?" As they described their most positive experiences, teachers realized they shared a belief in student learning for understanding through "hands-on" projects and role play, field trips, opportunities to "make the abstract concrete," and studies that connected academic learning to the wider world. Then, over multiple planning meetings, as they identified the most important concepts their students needed to learn, they designed a unit based on a single question: "How did the United States transform itself from a nation of farmers where things were handmade into a nation of factory power where things were machine made?" They decided that students would answer this question through reading of related literature, performing a play about the early Lowell textile mills, studying New England rivers and the principles behind the powering of the turbines and water wheels, candle making, and contra dancing.

For teachers at Broad Meadows Middle School and others, grade level curriculum mapping was the springboard to more lively and connected curriculum, and key to raising teachers' awareness of how they could pare down their curriculum in the interest of learning for greater depth and understanding while still working within district-mandated curriculum. This process can have similar benefits at the district level. For example, Rupi Boyd of San

Diego's Taft Middle School (San Diego City Schools, n.d.) reports that when middle school science teachers from across the district met to map the content of their teaching from month to month, some were dismayed at the prospect of giving up some of their units, complaining that although particular topics like weather were part of the elementary curriculum, students arrived in the middle grades without knowing it. But as teachers compared their curriculum map with district and professional standards, their facilitator pushed them to reframe their views of "knowing" content:

The TIMSS Report, which compared American student achievement in math and science with students all over the world, told us we have to teach fewer things in more depth. We can't go on teaching everything every year!

The TIMSS Report told us we have to teach fewer things in more depth. We can't go on teaching everything every year!

At both school and district levels, then, aligning school-based curriculum to standards requires teachers' discussing existing content, reorganizing content according to the most essential themes, and identifying teaching strategies that promise the most impact on learning for understanding. Content is not separate from teaching; both weave together to reinforce a coherent academic purpose.

Whole school reform models. While some schools begin to build a culture for standards-based reforms within their existing framework, others take a different tack. Since the mid-80s, a number of whole school reform models have helped schools establish a common sense of purpose across all grades. For example, the Accelerated Schools Network at Stanford University helps schools across the country reorganize all aspects of school life, including curriculum and instruction, around the commitment to "accelerate, not remediate." The Co-NECT (Cooperative Network for Education Community for Tomorrow) Project, located at Bolt, Beraneck, and Newman in Cambridge, Massachusetts, and sponsored by New American Schools, promotes greater coherence in teaching and learning through school-wide use of technology of all kinds. Members of the Coalition of Essential Schools achieve coherence by putting nine common principles into practice in ways that highlight students as workers.

The Paideia School model, based on principles espoused by Mortimer Adler in his Paideia Proposal (1982), represents another model that fosters academic coherence school wide. Paideia's focus of reform is primarily on teaching strategies. For example, Chattanooga's School for the Liberal Arts, one of several Paideia Schools in Hamilton County (TN) Public Schools, organizes learning around a single-track, liberal arts curriculum designed to prepare every single student for work, citizenship, and lifelong learning in a democratic society. The school's academic program realizes Adler's vision of instruction that is 80 percent "hands-on," supplemented with didactic teaching, and offers coaching to students who need it. In addition, once a week, all students participate in a heterogeneously grouped Socratic seminar. In a 90-minute period, every teacher in the school, including the librarian, counselor, and physical education teacher, leads small Socratic discussions on text selected for each grade level. A seminar committee of teachers in the school develop discussion questions for literature and periodicals selected from suggestions of teachers, students, and parents; and writing assignments are tied to discussions. Over time, the strategies of open-ended questioning and careful reading of text have spilled over into all the school's classrooms, and teachers' expectations for thoughtful student participation spread school wide (Wheelock, 1994).

Coherence based on shared pedagogy. Sometimes schools introduce greater academic coherence not through interdisciplinary teams or national reform models, but by adopting specific curriculum approaches that are congruous with good teaching and authentic pedagogy. Middle schools adopting three-year curricula in math or science benefit from pulling their teachers together around the common assumptions about learning and pedagogical approaches that add consistency across several grades. Such an approach means that students can experience consistent expectations as teachers implement a curriculum based on common assumptions about learning over several years.

For example, since 1993, twenty elementary and middle grades schools in several urban districts have pursued greater instructional coherence through school-wide implementation of the *Junior Great Books* Program, a reading and discussion program that involves all students in close reading of literature and extended "shared inquiry" discussions about that literature. As teachers across all grades consistently teach students skills in approaching literature and discussing ideas from that literature, schools gradually develop a culture in which all students learn and practice the skills of thinking about literature through questions that invite multiple answers, seeking for evidence to support their responses to the text, and listening to their peers' views with an open mind. Such common understanding cannot develop if only a few classrooms or teachers in one grade use the approach. As one Chicago principal explains, "Everyone had to agree that we were going to do it. I wanted it school wide so that everyone would be accustomed to the approach and have the same expectations" (Wheelock, 1998a).

When teachers communicate shared expectations through a common methodology that values thinking and understanding, students develop new habits for learning that reinforce a larger school culture that supports learning for high standards. As one teacher in a Chicago school using *Junior Great Books* school wide reports:

> By the second year, students will sit and listen. They've matured in terms of listening, waiting for the other person to finish the comment. They sit, listen, think before making a comment. And they come up with new slants to the stories.

Another teacher elaborates:

> The students are different now. This year with the ones who've had it before, I didn't have to explain over and over what an interpretive question is. At this point in the year, I'm getting interpretive questions from *them*. Their writing is a lot better too, more on target. And their discussions over all... they get it! They are much better!

Using new curriculum to build a new culture for standards-based reform has a number of advantages. Often, teachers benefit from materials that push them to try new practices and go against prevailing norms and assumptions about learning. For example, teachers used to asking questions that presume one right answer can benefit from lessons and materials that reinforce norms more compatible with inquiry-based learning for understanding. Teachers used to delaying units that push students to develop reasoning, communicating, and problem-solving skills until students have mastered the basics may find the encouragement they need in packaged lessons that push them forward and provide materials to diversify their instruction. Finally, packaged curriculum can establish common ground for teachers to move forward together to try new strategies. As students become accustomed to these strategies, coherence becomes easier to achieve.

Coherence based on valued "habits of mind." Curriculum is more than academic content. Students also learn from schools' "hidden curriculum," the norms and values of the school that are translated into "the way we do things around here." These norms and values themselves reinforce academic coherence across whole schools.

Curriculum is more than academic content. Students also learn from schools' 'hidden curriculum,' the norms and values of the school that are translated into 'the way we do things around here.'

Some schools build academic coherence around a set of questions that stimulate discussion about what students are learning and to what end. For example, from among many questions that might generate such discussions, Clifford Weber, Associate Superintendent in Arizona's Yuma School District #1, selects three that have helped develop coherence in the schools he works with. Weber begins the process in conversations with students on visits to classrooms where he routinely asks: "What are you doing?," "How are you doing [with it]?," and "Why are you doing it?" Weber says, "The answers tell you a lot about students' experiences in schools." He explains:

> Let's say you ask kids, "What are you doing?" and they tell you they are graphing the angles of a set of triangles. Well, then you ask, "How well are you doing?" They might say, "So far, I haven't gotten it," or "I really don't understand it yet," or "I think I'm beginning to get the idea," or "I've got the idea. It's better now than the first time." This tells me the kids are self-assessors. Finally you ask, "Why are you doing this?" and they say, "Well, if I can do this, I can be an architect." This tells me that they understand how what they're doing connects to their real world, that it has some meaning for them.

As Weber explains:

> All this tells me what kids understand. When you get good answers to these questions, you know things are going well, they're going to be eager beavers, they're motivated. But if I ask the first question, and the kids say, "I don't know," this tells me life at school is not good for these students.

Weber insists that adults must build opportunities for such conversations with students into every school classroom. Thus, Weber describes how teachers in the Bloomfield, Colorado schools, where Weber was superintendent for many years, took these three questions and turned them into building blocks for classroom instruction. Provoked by Weber's questions to students, teachers in the Bloomfield schools created their own guide to building student reflection and self-assessment into all their lessons. In addition to Weber's three questions, all teachers also press students on a regular basis to answer the questions "What do you already know about [a topic]?" and "When are you going to use it?" Teachers see these questions as a means for helping students continually connect current work with past learning and future applications. With all teachers basing their teaching on these questions, students come to understand the value their school places on their purposeful work and the process of reflecting on that work.

In other schools, as teachers spend time together examining student work and discussing teaching and learning, they identify the habits of mind they value most. Making these habits of mind explicit can affect the entire school culture. For example, over many years, educators at Central Park East Secondary School (CPESS) in New York City have developed their school's culture around the belief that certain "habits of mind" should permeate the work produced by students and teachers alike and their interactions in a democratic society (Meier, 1995). As CPESS teachers view them, these valued habits of mind involve:

- *Looking for evidence: How do we know what we think we know? What's our evidence? How credible is this evidence?*

- *Identifying viewpoint: Whose perspective are we reading, hearing, and seeing? What other perspectives might exist if we changed our position?*

- *Making connections: How is one thing connected to another? Is there a pattern in the evidence?*

- *Considering alternatives: How else might it have been? What if...? Suppose that...?*

- *Assessing importance: What difference does it make? Who cares?*

With these key questions posted prominently in every classroom, students and teachers use these habits of mind as reference points for everything they do. Sometimes the questions serve as prompts for thinking about "essential questions" in the humanities, math, or science. Educators and students may call on these habits of mind as they work through various disciplinary situations. In addition, the school's guide for assessing students' final portfolios rates students' work on criteria reflecting these habits of mind.

In large and small ways, the habits of mind that CPESS stands for represent "standards" for how students will live out their role as learners and members of a school community. Moreover, they provide a common language that allows students and teachers to talk together about their work and relationships. As former co-director of CPESS Deborah Meter noted in an *Education Week* on-line roundtable (23 April 1997):

> Schools like Central Park East are arguing that learning how to take responsibility for one's ideas is what schooling is for; and it starts with the grownups. It can only develop (and then thrive) in schools that are obliged to defend their habits, and thus also in a position to change them. That means school folk have to look the kids (and their parents) in the eye and say, "This is what we have decided it means to do good work."

With "habits of mind" articulated as values shared by every adult at CPESS, students' orientation to the school culture becomes self-perpetuating. Entering seventh-graders become acculturated to the expectations of the school and understand the rationale for school routines that are part of the daily life of the school. As they progress, they take on the role of helping younger students understand "how we do things around here." When they graduate, these habits of mind have not only shaped their school lives, but their orientation to the world and their role as citizens in a democracy.

Whether through mapping of existing curriculum, adopting whole school reform models, implementing new curriculum, or identifying valued habits of mind, schools' work to develop greater academic coherence is essential to building a culture for standards-based reform. In addition, schools must promote a set of classroom practices that reinforce the overall academic mission of the school and that focus on student work that reflects standards of quality.

Classroom practices supporting high-quality work

Standards developed by the professional associations envision complex learning. They envision learning that "sticks" because students have explored a topic in depth and can pull together information to communicate new learning to others. Such learning depends on high content and authentic pedagogy. But it also depends on a set of classroom practices, habits, and "things we do around here" that help students develop the work habits that lead finally toward finished products that meet standards of high quality. Many of these practices coalesce as students engage in pursuing projects that combine the practice of skills with in-depth understanding of selected topics.

Schools that are developing a culture of high standards may turn to "project work" as an effective vehicle for learning, one that both allows students to demonstrate what they know and helps students develop the habits that support high quality work. As sixth grade teacher Ron Berger (1996) explains, project work has many features that help students learn about standards for quality work. In Berger's classes, projects that create work for a "real world" constituency build standards of quality into the work itself. One year, for example, Berger's students orchestrated a study involving the testing of radon in the community's homes. This undertaking required students not only to learn about radon gas, but also to master skills in data analysis and the use of tables and graphs, employ experimental techniques used by testing professionals, practice scientific writing, and prepare a final report for use by their own neighbors in their own town. With town residents and officials as their audience, students' work *had* to meet high standards of quality. Berger (1996) elaborates:

Schools that are developing a culture of high standards may turn to 'project work' as an effective vehicle for learning, one that both allows students to demonstrate what they know and helps students develop the habits that support high quality work.

> There would be no test on the concepts. The stakes were much higher: the students would themselves be teachers of children and adults in town, and if they didn't understand this stuff perfectly, the consequences were obvious. Students knew that families could be nervous and even perhaps quite upset during the testing process and results. They themselves had to be calm, clear, and informed. (p. 14)

The radon project is one of many that have allowed Berger's students to generate work that has currency with audiences outside the school. Over the years, Berger's sixth graders have engaged in a yearlong study of water, executing student-run, professional-quality testing of the water from their town's private wells, with results produced for individual households and the community's board of health, newspapers, and conservation commission (Berger, 1996b). His students have also studied the history and politics of deaf culture, explored the physics of sound, and learned American Sign Language, all in preparation for developing successful school exchanges with two neighboring schools for deaf students. They have written biographies of senior citizens in their town, providing elders and their families with a concrete testimonial to their lives. They have analyzed census data and town records, turning raw numbers into percentages they then used to graph changes in their town's voter registration patterns and occupations for a report published in the town newspaper. They have written, illustrated, and bound their own chapter books, which the school library catalogs and circulates among students. In each case, students know that people outside the school will be using their work. They know their names will be on their work for years to come, and that their work will be valued, not because of the grade it receives, but because it will affect the lives of others in thei community and beyond.

As one of two teachers responsible for the learning of his school's exiting students, Berger employs many routines and practices that build students' skills, develop their confidence as learners, prepare them for the demands of their next school, and allow each one to produce work of high quality. As part of any project, students view exemplary work from their field of study. They present drafts of their work, whether an architectural blueprint, a report, or a plan for a field trip, for critique from their peers and experts from the community. They have opportunities to rewrite and redo work. They reflect on their own work through self-evaluations, and they present final products to a panel of outsiders.

In Berger's classes, these processes and routines work together to help students develop their own judgment for establishing when their work meets standards of quality. Thus, when Berger asks his novel-writing students, "Are you ready to turn in the final draft of your chapter books?," three students speak up: "No way!" says one. "Not in *this* class!" says another. "Maybe last year, but not this year!" says a third. Likewise, when "outside reviewers" question graduating students about the whole of their year's work, asking, "How do you know when your work is good enough as a finished product?," one student responds, "When it looks like the articles I've seen that real writers do for newspapers," while another answers, "When I can't get anyone to give me any more suggestions for making it better."

The routines that characterize Berger's classroom are key to developing a culture of high standards. As standards-oriented teachers talk about their work, they, like Berger, highlight a cluster of practices that are key to fostering a culture of high standards. These practices:

- Make expectations for work concrete and understandable;

- Engage students in improving their work;

- Focus on work that must satisfy standards of a "real world" audiences of parents, professionals, and community members.

Making high expectations concrete and understandable

Talk about high expectations for all children is hardly new. Across the country, schools have, for years, mounted banners proclaiming, "**All children will learn.**" Such slogans, however, do not begin to map out how teachers will embrace the set of beliefs necessary to drive and sustain a vision of students learning for understanding through work that engages students' intellects. In fact, teachers' personal beliefs may directly contradict this vision. For example, Mary Lee Smith and her colleagues in Arizona (1997) found that two-thirds of teachers surveyed believed that students needed to master basic skills before progressing to problem solving. In a similar vein, Carol Ann Tomlinson (1998) and her colleagues report, "[In a stratified random sample of 1,988 middle schools] only 29% of principals and 21% of teachers agreed or strongly agreed that their students were able to think at high levels of critical thought" (p. 5). Building a culture for standards-based reform requires challenging and changing these patterns.

High teacher expectations for better learning are already manifest in some classroom interactions with some students in some schools. For many years, good teachers have pursued specific questioning strategies with students that communicate high expectations. These teachers know that "wait time" is essential to allow students to think about their answers. They know they need to probe beyond one-word answers to get students to clarify the reasoning that supports their views. They know the importance of making sure every student has a chance to participate, leaving no student "invisible," and returning student work with specific comments rather than generalized praise, a single grade, or no mark at all (Mid-continent Regional Educational Laboratory, 1984-85). From these and other practices, young adolescents can readily distinguish those teachers who have high expectations for their work from those who do not. For example, asked to describe teachers who helped them learn, Philadelphia middle school students reported they knew that teachers had high expectations for student success when teachers insisted that students complete assigned homework, offered constructive critique, and made specific suggestions for how students could correct mistakes (Corbett & Wilson, 1997a).

Schools can begin to make high expectations the norm for all students by clarifying for students and teachers alike exactly what good work looks like.

Schools can begin to make high expectations the norm for all students by clarifying for students and teachers alike exactly what good work looks like. In these schools, teachers study curriculum standards in different content areas, improve the quality of learning assignments to reflect those standards more closely, develop guidelines and rubrics describing different levels of quality for student work, and make these rubrics available to students and parents. Schools that are developing a culture of high standards also make sure that every student has regular opportunities to see "exemplars" – samples of excellent work in the area of study – that make expectations for excellence concrete.

Rubrics guide teachers and students toward high quality work. To make expectations explicit to every student, teachers increasingly create opportunities for students to review clear-cut descriptions of the qualities of excellent work and view examples of that work part of their teaching. In some schools, these descriptions, or rubrics, evolve from teachers' discussions about student work and their shared expectations for quality. In other schools, teachers coach students through a process of thinking about the qualities of good work, so that, as they design their own rubrics for assessing their work, students develop the habit of continually asking themselves, "Is this good enough?"

Rubrics are valuable tools for making expectations clear to students who ask, "What do I have to do to get an 'A'?" and for nudging students toward becoming more self-directed learners. As teacher Jo Anne Wang of Bangkok's Ruamrudee International School notes:

> Rubrics communicate to students what is expected of them; they take the mystery out of grading. Using rubrics in the classroom encourages students to excel and become self-directed

learners..... Rubrics are a good starting point for teaching students self-assessment.

Middle school students agree. When Long Beach, California, seventh grade teachers Lorrie LaCroix and Karen Maine asked their Cubberly Middle School students how rubrics had improved their learning, they learned that rubrics were most important for helping students comprehend the expectations of new assignments (Focused Reporting Project, 1997a). Said one, "Before I knew about a rubric, I was terrible. Now I kind of understand." A second noted, "Rubrics help you improve your work because you are told right away what is expected of you." Several added that rubrics helped them think through their work from the beginning to the end. One explained:

> When you are given an assignment, you need to look at its requirements. Sometimes there are things on the rubric that I have overlooked. I can change, and know what to change, by the rubric guidelines.

For some students, their appreciation for the power of rubrics was grounded in an awareness that their use of rubrics had translated into improved grades. As one noted: "You can go back and make your work better if you haven't completely followed the rubric. It lets you know exactly what you need to do to get an A."

Students' comments, however, go beyond noting how rubrics contribute to better work for individual students. Rubrics are also part of a shift toward a culture for standards-based reform, a culture that balances a "press for achievement" with an ethic of fairness and support. Indeed, some students resist the push toward achievement and high expectations that rubrics represent. For example, several Cubberly Middle School students admitted that even with the promise of better grades, the rubric's "press" and the implication that students could all turn in work of better quality if they focused on the standards it set made school life less comfortable for them. As one reported: "[The rubric] has brought my grades up on Problems of the Week, but what bothers me is that most of them require a lot." Another added: "For me [the worst thing about rubrics] is that you have everything the rubrics ask you to put on your paper, but it has to be almost perfect and fully explained."

Rubrics also provide a push for students who might otherwise settle for just "getting it over." As one explained: "I think the worst thing about rubrics is that maybe you're at a level 3 and maybe it makes you feel bad because you feel you have to push yourself harder to get to a 5 or 6." Added a classmate: "When I use a rubric, I don't always get a [perfect score]. True, it's right there, but you really think you got it all, and you don't. Your teacher may disagree."

Yet rubrics also temper resistance to high expectations and the push to meet standards by also introducing an element of guidance and fairness into classrooms so that every student can see that it is both possible and safe to be smart. As one Cubberly student notedt: "I like the way [rubrics] word the scores and also how they show you to get that score. The guidelines are right down to the point and are precise to what you need to get that score."

Rubrics reduce the potential for teacher subjectivity and favoritism in grading that has sometimes made 'being smart' unsafe for young adolescents.

Equally important, rubrics reduce the potential for teacher subjectivity and favoritism in grading that has sometimes made "being smart" unsafe for young adolescents. And they give students a sense of efficacy in relation to how their work is assessed. As one student put it, "There is less guilt, favorites, or decision. This is a more 'fair' way of grading. Also you can see why you got that grade." Another elaborated more fully:

I think if teachers used rubrics instead of oral directions, students would get better grades because they could just look at the rubric instead of keeping asking the teacher. Also, it would be better with teachers if they had a rubric because if they liked you, they could give you a better grade, and if the teacher didn't like you, they could give you a bad grade, and the student couldn't do anything. But if they had a rubric, they couldn't because they would have to point out what you did wrong.

Busy teachers do not develop a new rubric for every new assignment. Some use rubrics developed in collaboration with other teachers in their school, grade level, or department that connect to the broad presentation or performance skills embedded in their district's or state's content standards. Others turn to published sources of sample rubrics, such as the Chicago Public Schools *Performance Assessment Idea Book* (Perlman, 1994), Association for Supervision and Curriculum Development guides to alternative assessment (Herman, Aschbacher, & Winters, 1992; Marzano, Pickering, & McTighe, 1993; Hibbard,1996), "tool kits" designed for specific subject areas like math and science (Northwest Regional Education Laboratory, 1994), or publications of independent networks of reforming schools like the National Center for Re-structuring Education, Schools, and Teaching (Darling-Hammond, Einbender, Frelow, & Ley-King, 1993). Still other teachers gather ideas about performance tasks and rubrics posted on internet sites of organizations like Vermont's Exemplars (http://www.exemplars.com). Sometimes school districts make public their own rubrics used to guide teaching and learning in general skills. For example, the Toronto, Canada, School District posts rubrics for reading comprehension, writing performance, language usage, and mathematics pro-cedures, reasoning, conceptual knowledge, and communication, all available for teachers, parents, and community members to learn what good student work looks like(http://www.ebe.on.ca/Depart/resear/rubric.htm).

Professional sources like these can offer guidance for teachers who want to build understandable assessments into their daily instruction, but used to this end, rubrics are best seen as a "first step." As teacher Jo Anne Wang explains:

> These rubrics are very good as models for designing your own. However, I've found that rubrics designed by other teachers don't work as well for me in my classes. This is because the standards of evaluation are particular to a certain class or set of circumstances and are not applicable across the board. Some-times, the standards in a generic rubric can be ambiguous.

Moreover, all rubrics are not of equally good quality, and some may even discourage good work. For example, relating what they did not like about rubrics, Long Beach's Cubberly Middle School students complained that some rubrics "don't fully cover all the situations" and wished they were not re-quired "in stories or anything creative." They also portrayed some rubrics as "kind of confusing" with "too many rules" and described some language as "hard to understand."

Poor-quality rubrics serve neither students or educators well. As Ray Fenton of Anchorage Public Schools cautions:

> If [rubrics] are vague and general they do not help us recognize the qualities we wish to achieve. Bad rubrics or descriptions are less than useful and may confuse us about the qualities of good work and cost us credibility with ourselves and the com-munities we serve.

Researchers who have followed the growing use of rubrics to improve student work echo these observations. As UCLA professor W. James Popham (1997a, 1997b) notes, rubrics can be useful tools, both for teachers as they plan instruction, and for students as they learn about what constitutes good work on assignments that require constructing a product. However, he also warns that rubrics that are too general and vague, too connected to a single specific task, or too lengthy and complex will ultimately be useless for guiding instruction or learning.

Rubrics are key to fostering a learning culture that conveys the expectation that every single student can meet standards by producing work of high quality.

Still, rubrics are key to fostering a learning culture that conveys the expectation that every single student can meet standards by producing work of high quality. As one Cubberly Middle School seventh grader concluded:

> Rubrics improve my work because it gives me guidelines on what I do. If I was supposed to do a project without a rubric, my grade would definitely be lower. My classmates feel the same.

Building a standards-based culture means making expectations for students concrete. With rubrics posted on classroom walls, distributed to parents, and clipped into students' notebooks and binders, students are always aware of what it means to "be smart."

Exemplars make "what good work looks like" explicit. Getting students accustomed to doing work that meets standards of high quality also means providing them with opportunities to study exemplars, sample pieces of work representing *good* and *excellent* standards of accomplishment. These exemplars make the definitions spelled out in the rubrics real to students. As one seventh grader from Cubberly Middle School asserted, "The best rubrics show you each step to complete your work. Also, they give some examples of how you should do it so you can follow them" (Focused Reporting Project, 1997a).

Exemplars that accompany rubrics can be helpful to teachers as well. As Ray Fenton of Anchorage Public Schools explains:

> We all need to know at every level of the educational system what we are willing to call *good* or *bad*, *better* or *worse*; or what we say meets the standard or is substandard work. The

best way to make these hard comparisons is through comparison of our work, either work that we feel represents the standard we wish to meet or the ideal we wish to achieve..... If
[rubrics] help us understand the qualities of good work or be
more consistent in the recognition of good work, they are a
help.... [But] two people may use the same rubric and come
to quite different conclusions about the quality of a given product.... It makes a lot more sense to think in terms of examples
of quality work which illuminate and give meaning to a rubric
than it is just to think about rubrics without work samples.

Part of the challenge of building a culture for standards-based reform,
then, involves saturating each classroom with examples of high quality work
that match the rubrics so that students and teachers alike have before them
images of excellence. These images of excellence can help guide students
and teachers alike toward what they hope to achieve. If some of these examples surpass what is possible for most learners, that is in the nature of
"standards." As Grant Wiggins (1993) insists:

Standards are always out of reach; that is the point. The standards of performance and the standards of self-discipline in
one's work are always "ideals" for all but the world's best
performers in every field. Thus I do not "expect" most people
to meet the standards set by the best. My "expectation" is that
everyone will strive to improve his or her work by studying
what is best and work continuously to narrow the gap between the current level of performance and the ideal level of
performance. (p. 285)

How do teachers expose students to examples of excellence? Sometimes,
these examples are part of the curriculum itself. For example, all students at
Chicago's Amelia Earhart School and other schools implementing the *Junior
Great Books* Program school wide regularly read high quality literature and
engage in discussion of that literature. On top of that, students routinely
view, study, and discuss works of art that echo the themes of that literature.
For example, along with their reading and Socratic discussion of the William
Saroyan story, "Gaston," students work with a practicing photographer to
examine and discuss family portraits, paintings, and photographs depicting
family relationships. The close reading of both text and artwork helps students develop a sense of the standards that define quality in both literature

and the visual arts; by the time they are ready to write their own stories and take photographs to portray their own family connections, standards for excellence are firmly established in their minds (Wheelock, 1998). In other schools, experts may visit schools to introduce students to their professional-level work or invite students to their workplace so that students can view expert work. Opportunities to view the work of local book authors, illustrators, house builders, quilters, jewelery makers, bakers, horticulturalists, journalists, architects, or others who "work to standard," combined with the chance to discuss the work processes that nurture quality work help standards become real to students.

Teachers building a culture that supports high quality work also draw on students' own work samples to illustrate work that meets different levels of quality. For example, San Diego's Carol Barry, a middle school teacher for many years before becoming a principal, pulls her students' best portfolio pieces into a "library of exemplars" with sample pieces representing the different abilities she expects her students to develop as they prepare written work through the year. Then students who follow them the next year can study these exemplars to understand how well they are developing those abilities themselves, adding their own examples to the pool of student work (Barry, 1995).

Other teachers help students understand the meaning of quality by showing work from the real world that represents standards of excellence. For example, in the process of coaching her seventh and eighth graders as they researched and wrote books for third graders on topics of their choice, humanities teacher Kathy Greeley (1996) of the Graham and Parks School in Cambridge, Massachusetts, introduced her students to a variety of examples that represented excellent work. They examined published nonfiction books for young readers and discussed what made different kinds of writing successful. They also met with a professional illustrator who spoke with them about how art differs from illustration, how different media suit different moods, and how he himself prepared to begin illustrating a book. Then based on the professional examples they had seen, and in response to the question *What makes a good book?*, students developed their own criteria for producing their own book covers, text, and illustrations.

Providing students with rubrics and exposing all students to examples of excellent work are the first steps schools can take to developing a culture to support standards-based reforms. In addition, as students have more opportunities to examine and discuss exemplary work, teachers can use that work – from professionals, experts, or students themselves – to help students articulate criteria for"good work." In the process, students begin to learn the "language of standards," and this language opens up new ways of improving their work through critique, revision, and self-assessment.

Engaging students in improving their work

Building a school culture that supports all students' doing work that meets standards means introducing new routines that give students the time and attention necessary for producing work that meets expectations and new norms that encourage students to seek help for revising and polishing their work on a regular basis. Currently, a variety of school regularities and beliefs about learning work against giving all students opportunities to revise their work. For example, curriculum objectives or frameworks that emphasize covering many topics encourage teachers to rush through the curriculum and contribute to learning that is a "mile wide and an inch deep." In this context, schools may confuse pace of instruction with real learning, and may mistake "getting it the first time around" for "smartness." To keep the pace, students may slide along, settling for first-draft work over work that "meets standards." They may learn to hide any sign that learning is sometimes difficult or requires effort. Or they may refrain from asking for help if it means looking like "a loser."

Yet, in real life, how many us approach any new task worth doing well and produce quality work the first time we take it on? Are we really so sure that those who complete work ahead of others necessarily come up with work of the highest quality? Are the quickest solutions to any problem always the best solutions? And how are we to learn that our mistakes – and the process of trying, not "getting it" quite right, and trying again – are ultimately among the best sources of learning for understanding.[2]

In many schools now, teachers often require students to do the assignment; then students turn in that assignment to the teacher for a grade. Often, students receive grades without comments, a practice that the National As-

---

[2]The author is indebted to John D'Auria, principal of the Wellesley Middle School, Wellesley, Massachusetts, for his articulation of the connection between students' attitudes and beliefs about learning, student work habits, and school routines and practices.

sessment for Educational Progress (NAEP) reports limits achievement. For example, according to NAEP reports on reading, higher literacy achievement is associated with teachers' commenting on student ideas, noting mistakes on student work, or highlighting what students do well. Yet many teachers provide no comments at all or comment only on how well students have followed directions or on the amount students write, neither of which is associated with higher achievement (Wheelock, 1995).

In schools that are developing a culture to support standards-based reform, teachers provide students with time to rewrite and revise work to produce an accomplished product.

Teachers' focused responses to the content of student work is essential to learning. But equally important are routines that allow students to continue to improve a piece of work so that it "meets standards." In schools that are developing a culture to support standards-based reform, teachers provide students with time to rewrite and revise work to produce an accomplished product. In addition, processes for students to receive continual assessment of their work in progress, combined with opportunities for peer critique and self-assessment, help students develop skills for making their own judgments about when work is "good enough" to call "finished."

Feedback from teachers and peer critique help students rewrite and revise papers and projects

Perhaps it is not surprising that, while young adolescent students talk a great deal in social groups, these same teenagers rarely have conversations about their work among themselves (Corbett & Wilson, 1997a). Such conversations may not be compelling when the assignments themselves do not engage students' passions and interests or when they do not lead to products that have meaning to anyone beyond their classrooms. But when teachers require students to learn by applying skills and creating a performance or product, they must also build in opportunities for conversation about that work as it develops.

Time for revision and peer critique go hand-in-hand as essential elements in developing a culture that encourages students to persist in producing work that meets high standards. Different teachers build opportunities for revision and peer critique into their classes in different ways. For example, middle school teachers like Lorrie LaCroix and Karen Maine of Long Beach increasingly ask their students to pair up to critique each other's work, using rubrics to guide conversations. According to their seventh graders, these sessions benefit both students in the giving and receiving of feedback. As one noted, "It's fun looking at our fellow students' papers. Grading them is also fun because then you get ideas from each other to make your paper better" (Focused Reporting Project, 1997a).

In other schools, "peer critique" involves the entire class. For example, at the Francis W. Parker Public Charter School in Devens, Massachusetts, young adolescent students routinely present work at various stages of completion to their classmates for scrutiny. Because the work is eventually to be shown at an assembly of the entire school, students want to be sure that their projects, say, those based on their study of the Civil War, will be as good as possible. To this end, teacher Michael Mann gathers his students into a circle, and as each student comes forward to present, perform, or otherwise explain his piece – an original poem, a built-to-scale diarama of the slave quarters described in the book *Incidents in the Life of a Slave Girl*, or an original ballad based on the history of the 54th Regiment – his classmates examine the work and ask questions. Some want to know how the presenter solved particular problems of execution; others query their classmates about content, accuracy, or the"message" they are trying to convey. Finally, three students, specifically designated by Mann to provide feedback before each presenter begins, respond to Mann's request for comments, both warm and cool. Mann's purpose is to be sure that students hear something from their classmates about what they like about the piece, but he also wants them to provide some guidance for revision, so he opens the question up to the whole class: "What could she do with this piece so that people who don't know much about this period will understand it better?" Over the course of the morning, every student participates, and every student leaves with ideas for making his/her piece better in some way.

For schools like Parker, the opportunity for students to present their work and receive feedback from their peers is not a one-shot event. Rather it is a normal routine in a "culture of revision" that pushes students to think continuously about improving their work. Because peer critique is part of the "Parker way," students understand that giving and receiving peer feedback is meant to help everyone, that everyone can learn from letting others view work with a fresh eye, and that everyone has something to contribute to the process. Peer critique complements, not substitutes for, teachers' assessment of student work; and from students' perspective, it can be at least as effective for learning as adult feedback. As one of Parker's middle graders insists,"Feedback is important. When it's someone my age who's giving me feedback, I really listen. I can identify with them."

Young adolescent students do not come to the skills of peer critique by accident. In classrooms where peer critique works well, teachers like Ron Berger teach the skills of critique explicitly. For example, in Berger's classroom, students may display a draft blueprint or illustration, or read from a larger piece of work they are writing, then explain what they are trying to achieve, what they like, and what they are having trouble with in relation to their work. Only then do their peers respond, following steps Berger has taught them: To comment on something positive using "I like..." or "I notice...." statements; to make specific comments that refer to particular parts of the work; and to avoid accusatory "put-downs." Students rehearse the critique process at the beginning of each year when Berger himself presents a piece of his own work, then presents the work a second time, incorporating the comments students have made and reflecting on how those comments have made his own work better.

The impact of these routines is as varied as the personalities of young adolescent students. For some, these routines free them from having to turn in work they themselves are not satisfied with and give them the satisfaction of knowing that, with time and support they can accomplish things they didn't think they could do. As one of Berger's students acknowledged: "When I get frustrated now, it's not like it used to be. I used to turn something in angry at it. Now I don't. I wait out my frustration. I organize my thoughts. I went through so many drafts of the blueprint that I got to find out I could do this." Another described how revision and critique helped her become more sure-footed as a learner. She recalled: "At the beginning of the year, I was quite shy. Then I got more used to my class. I knew they wouldn't make fun of me. I got a lot of critique from my friends, and everyone was helping me."

Revising work in a climate of support, then, teaches persistence and develops confidence, and these traits reinforce one another as students see changes in their work. As a third student summarized his work on one project:

> I progress a lot in drafts. I take things out, add things in. The
> final draft of my work had almost no resemblance to the first.
> I use the critique of my classmates really well. I took their
> critique and made it a lot less busy.

Ultimately, the test of practices of revision and critique is that the work of every student meets standards. When these practices become classroom regularities, this is precisely the effect, whatever students' past experiences. As one student reflected on her "blueprint project" in Berger's class:

> At first I thought, "I can't do this!" From the rough draft to the final draft is quite a long way. It went from wacky to realistic. But in this class, even if you can't draw that great, everyone comes up with a beautiful drawing in the end.

Creating a culture that encourages all students to do work that meets standards means involving students in their learning and building students' capacity to direct their own learning. Opportunities to revise work and give and receive feedback as the work proceeds equip students with the tools they need to participate in a community of learners, improve their own work, and support their peers in meeting standards.

Self-assessment of work. In addition to teaching students to use rubrics and exemplars to improve their work, schools can also develop a culture for standards-based reform by teaching students to reflect on their work habits and learning processeS. In these schools, teachers orient students to the value of reflecting on what works for them as they approach new tasks. They also teach students to assess their own work habits, learning styles, and approaches to new tasks in the belief that these skills will contribute to successful lifelong learning. Providing students with opportunities to assess not only what they are learning but how they are learning helps students further internalize standards for good work.

Providing students with opportunities to assess not only what they are learning but how they are learning helps students further internalize standards for good work.

Teachers introduce students to self-assessment by building time into the schedule for regular review of students' work samples, giving students regular practice in discussing and reflecting on their work. For example, Chris Stevenson (1997) suggests that teachers foster young adolescents' willingness to put forth the effort necessary to meet new challenges by asking students to reflect on such questions as:

What have I learned about myself as a learner?

What have I learned about my abilities, aptitudes, and interests?

What have I learned about what is good work? excellent work?

What have I learned about how I can produce excellent work?

What have I learned about how to organize my learning to be successful?

What have I learned about what is most difficult for me to learn?

What have I learned about more effective ways for me to learn challenging things?

What have I learned about how I can get help from others? be helpful to others?

What have I learned about the kinds of teaching that help me learn best?

What have I learned about how to adapt to teaching that doesn't work well for me?

What have I learned about working with other students? working alone?

What have I learned about what I can do to be more successful?

What have I learned about how I am growing? changing? improving?

These questions, argues Stevenson, focus students on how they can change their habits to improve learning. Taken together, they communicate the message that success depends more on students' effort than ability and that students have control over the quality of their work.

Classrooms where students practice skills in self-assessment help students internalize an appreciation for high quality work and develop good work habits that form the foundation for lifelong learning. For example, at the Portsmouth Middle School in Portland, Oregon, math teachers who introduce students to algebraic thinking using the NCTM standards-based "Math in the Mind's Eye" materials, use several self-assessment tools to promote learning. To help students become accustomed to thinking about the quality of their work as a matter of course, students keep a generic rubric for their class – what they call a "problem solving guide" – in their notebooks at all times. This four-point rubric describes criteria for:

1. **Exceptional work**: 1. I gave valid mathematical explanations for what I did. 2. a) I discovered more than one appropriate answer for the problem, or b) I found more than one way to

solve the problem. 3. I shared my thoughts and observations about the problem. 4. I extended the problem by one or more of the following ways: a) developing and testing new conjectures, b) making generalizations, c) explaining a math idea new to me, d) making connections to other math ideas or other subjects).

2. **Quality work:** 1. I gave valid mathematical explanations for what I did. 2. I found an appropriate answer for the problem. 3. I shared my thoughts and observations about the problem.

3. **Work requiring revision:** 1. I showed an understanding of the problem, but I need to revise to: a) give valid mathematical reasons for what I did, b) find an appropriate answer, c) share my thoughts and observations about the problem... or 2. I'm on the wrong track and I'm stuck. My plan for getting on the right track is... and...

4. **"OOPS!** I didn't try to do it. My plan for getting it done is...

This rubric applies to class problems and homework and builds in accountability by including a place for a parent's or guardian's signature. In addition, math teachers want students to learn that success requires effort as well as math performance. So printed on the other side of the problem-solving guide is a checklist that spells out the criteria for effort. Students thus consider whether, on a regular basis, they take responsibility for learning (attempting all assigned activities, exploring math concepts using a variety of materials, and seeking help when they're stuck); participate in cooperative groups (by solving math problems, considering ideas of others, and questioning others about their thinking); and communicate about mathematics (explaining thinking in writing and orally). Finally, students evaluate their effort, mathematical performance, and their overall striving for excellence in conference with their teachers. As teachers report, "For so many years in education, assessment was synonymous with grading. Assessment now is helping students assess themselves as learners."

'For so many years in education, assessment was synonymous with grading. Assessment now is helping students assess themselves as learners.'

When teachers talk about helping students become lifelong learners, the dispositions that allow learners to persist in the face of obstacles are at the top of their list. Developing students' skills of self-assessment to reinforce the importance of effort and persistence is a key practice in school cultures that support standards-based reform.

Creating work for the "real world"

A third dimension of making student work, not test scores, the focus of learning involves putting an emphasis on student work for the "real world." Practices that that put student work before audiences outside the classroom for examination, comment, critique, appreciation, and use by definition incorporate standards of quality into the execution of that work. These practices include school displays of work, student-led conferences, presentations and exit exhibitions, and extended projects that have a real world audience.

Displays of student work. In many American schools, the habit of posting student work for display on bulletin boards and in administrative offices is a time-honored practice. How and whose work is displayed, however, can reveal particular norms about the expectations schools hold for the kind of work that all students can produce. Some schools, for example, display only the work of "top" students, so that some students never have the opportunity to show their work for others to see. Other schools, interested in expanding the number of students whose work has a wider audience, may allow unfinished or incorrect work to be posted; but in doing so, they may convey that such work is *acceptable*, reinforcing the impression that standards are lax.

Some teachers address the tension between their desire to encourage reluctant learners and the desire for higher standards through the posting of incomplete work, noting that it is "work in progress" and inviting critique for further improvement. But schools that focus on student work of high quality ultimately insist that every student must produce work that can stand up to outside scrutiny and meets standards of excellence. As Berger (1996a:38) explains:

> We are obsessive about detail in my classroom and proud of it. If that means we are small-minded, so be it. To create beautiful fiction without concern for spelling and grammar makes a lot of sense to me. When the fictional piece reaches final draft, however, and is bound as a book and put on display for the community, spelling and grammar make a big difference, and obsessing about it is crucial. When students show me a technical diagram they've drawn that has graphic balance and artistic flair but is inaccurate in some of its technical detail, I don't accept it on effort. It goes back for another draft.

Building a culture to support high standards means embracing a set of routines and practices that push students to meet standards because their work will be seen by those outside the school who "matter" – parents, community members, trades people, and professionals – who themselves carry expectations for good work. When all students know their work will be seen outside the classroom walls, the choice between showing the work of only some students who produce excellent work and showing the work of all students while sacrificing quality is moot. Among Berger's students, for example, one out of five has a special education plan; yet because he makes sure that all students see exemplary work, have time to rewrite and revise, and develop the habit of giving and receiving thoughtful critique, every one of his students produces work that meets standards on many dimensions, both conceptual and technical.

The practice of using student work for display has particular benefits for developing school-wide cultures to support high standards. When the work of every student is posted in public places, younger students have before them concrete examples of the kind of work expected of them in subsequent grades. In some schools, this is reinforced when students are asked to create work that will be used by younger students. For example, ninth graders at Fulton Valley Prep in Santa Rosa, California, make books on Latin America for fifth graders; and fifth graders at Fulton Intermediate School in Dubuque make books on different birds for younger students in their school who then understand that their own work will become public when their reach the middle grades.

Finally, schools that are developing a culture of high standards are pushing the display of student work beyond school walls and into the world via the Internet, allowing for a continuing examination of work by outsiders. For example, Santa Rosa, California, teacher Kathy Juarez assigns her Fulton Valley Prep ninth graders the task of writing book reports for posting on the Internet. She also regularly arranges for her students to discuss autobiographical stories with adult key pals identified through several list-serves who comment on students' work according to guidelines she suggests (http://metro.net/kjuarez/Grow_Up/email.html). Such connections let students know that the audience for their work includes adults who, although they may be only names in an e-mail address, care that they produce high quality work.

Student-led parent conferences. Among those in the outside audience for students' work, the most important are parents, and many middle schools annually afford parents the opportunity to meet in conference with individual teachers or with teacher teams to discuss student work. But schools that seek to develop a culture of high standards, where students learn to articulate what they have learned and what they have yet to learn, are beginning to rethink the routine approach to parent conferences. Instead of the typical approach in which teachers talk and parents listen, these schools are working to expand students' opportunities to explain their learning in a dialogue with the adults who care about them. To this end, some are adopting student-led conferences that push students toward accepting personal responsibility for academic performance, develop self-evaluation, organizational, and oral communication skills; and encourage students, parents, and teachers to engage in open dialogue (Hackmann, 1997).

Student-led conferences put students actively in charge of communicating what they are learning and how well they are learning it. For example, at Springfield Middle School in Battle Creek, Michigan, one seventh grade team is finding that when they ask students to lead conferences with parents about their work, students begin to take greater responsibility for their own learning. Special educator Kim Roy first learned about this strategy when she attended a conference looking for ways to help students assess their learning. When she presented the idea to the other teachers on her team, they were enthusiastic. "We hoped we could get more kids more involved in learning," she recalls.

When students lead conferences with parents about their work, students begin to take greater responsibility for their own learning.

After planning in their team meeting over the summer, teachers introduced the idea to their students, and by the end of October, classes were making preparations that would allow students the opportunity to discuss their work with their parents at the regular November conference. Students created folders, carefully decorated to impress their parents. They also used district-wide writing and math rubrics, along with rubrics developed to match particular school projects, to help them select the work they would include. In their teacher-student advisories work, students also reviewed the work they had selected – two projects each in math, English, and social studies – and discussed why they thought particular projects were their best work. With the school year still in its beginning months, and with some students struggling to complete some assignments, teachers pushed every student to prepare, asking questions like, "What are you good at, and how do you know?" Teachers also helped students practice leading the conference and responding to practice questions they thought parents might ask.

As students prepared, teachers also thought through how to generate interest on the part of parents. Teacher Kim Roy explains that although teachers had always made themselves available to parents for conferences during afternoon and evening hours, turnout was feeble, a pattern familiar to many middle grades schools. So Springfield teachers worked hard to maximize parent attendance for the new student-led conferences. The team met with the school's PTA prior to the conferences. The school sent letters to parents. Students themselves wrote invitations to their parents. Teachers made necessary arrangements to take a photograph of every parent and child.

Laying the groundwork in these ways paid off. When the date arrived, parents of 69 of the team's 72 children showed up during the 3:00-to-8:00 allotted time block. Roy describes what happened:

> We set up our tables in the library, with chairs for parents and students next to each other. We scheduled students for a half-hour each, four to six kids at a time. We set out a sheet of paper with a few questions that we thought might spark parents' interest, and we had all the teachers there, but off to one side. The students escorted their parents to the assigned tables. We could see that some parents were focusing on their child, and really listening. Sometimes they would start out sitting across from one another, but as they talked, the parent would come around and sit next to the child.

The outpouring of support from parents relieved anxious teachers who had been unsure of how many parents would show up. Roy elaborates:

> Initially we had comments that this would be a waste of time. Parents wanted us to tell them about the problems we were having with their child. They were worried they wouldn't have time to talk with us alone..... In fact, on the first evening of the conferences, several parents appeared without their children. When they saw what was going on around them, one said, "I'm going to reschedule this." Another mom got the dad to stay and watch, and she went home and got the child.

When the students finished describing the work in their portfolios, showing parents what they had learned and what they needed to learn, students would call the teachers over to join in. Roy continues:

> *Then* we would bring over the report card, not before. And it really made a difference. By the time the kids got through explaining what they were good at and what they needed to learn, and had gone over their attendance and behavioral records, the report card grades made sense to the parents. We didn't have any arguments.

The connections between student work and report card grades are now more understandable not only to parents but to students themselves. As a result, teachers have greater leverage to push students to achieve. As Roy explains:

> We've had quite a few kids who will ask what they have to do to make their work better. At the beginning we were looking at kids who didn't complete their assignments. Now, we can say, "Look, how many math assignments have you handed in?" and "What are you going to do to improve?" You can challenge them to do more. They're beginning to internalize the idea that if they work at something, they'll get better.

Indeed, developing skills of self-reflection is an ultimate goal of this effort. "This is not about test scores or grades," Roy insists. "It's about communicating about what your learning, taking pride in your work." Parents also understand this well. As Roy explains:

> When we got done with this, most parents said they saw things about their kids' ability and potential through the conference that they never would have seen through a grade. They were impressed their child could demonstrate and talk about the work.

While they could return to traditional teacher-led conferences if they chose to do so, Springfield teachers see too many positive outcomes they believe will only grow over time to abandon the practice. In particular, teachers are impressed with the impact on students' motivation and effort, especially that of discouraged learners. Roy observes:

We didn't leave it up to the kids. Everyone had to do this. Even the kids who hate school and did not have very good work had to do this. And not one of them was resistant. If we weren't giving kids a chance to share their work, we wouldn't even get some work turned in.

Over the next rounds, teachers hope to take advantage of students' new motivation to develop more "showcase" pieces based on projects, and combine displays of the work with student conferences. They are also considering facilitating three, rather than two, conference sessions to keep students motivated. As Roy sees it, "We've got some kids working now because they know there's this opportunity to share coming up.... Kids like the fact that, for once, they get the chance to sit down and share what they can do with their parents."

Nancy Fenton, principal of Springfield Middle School, emphasizes that the seventh-grade team's use of student-led conferences is just "one part of the total picture" of a school-wide focus on student achievement. She says students are learning to take academics more seriously and become more self-critical. She explains, "Students have to explain their work's strengths and weaknesses. When you understand these things, you have more ability to correct what you're not pleased with, and you do better quality work."

As students move out of the elementary grades, parents often have less and less contact with their schools about student learning. For example, a recent Rhode Island survey found that one quarter of middle grades students never spoke with their parents about their school work, and only one-quarter of parents with children in high school had contact with their school's teachers (Krieger, 1998a, 1998b). Student-led conferences are key features of a school culture that puts student work front and center as the goal of learning, and trains the lens of students, teachers, and parents alike on that work.

Student-led conferences are key features of a school culture that puts student work front and center as the goal of learning.

Exit projects and presentations. In many schools, often only the most polished students have the opportunity to demonstrate mastery in public, whether through science fair projects, public speaking, or publication of prize-winning essays. Teachers working to develop a culture of high standards, however, extend these opportunities to every student. As part of developing a culture in which students know they are preparing work that will be reviewed by others, standards-oriented schools are developing new rituals that require every exiting student to summarize the work completed over the year or sometimes over the course of his/her time in school.

In some schools, "exit projects" that pull together learning from different subject areas constitute the final requirement before students move out of the middle grades and into high school. At Chattanooga's School for the Liberal Arts, for example, teacher Jeri McInturff has spearheaded the practice of requiring all eighth graders to compile a magazine on the subject of their choice as a condition of graduation. As she explains, "I wanted to do something to culminate the eighth grade, but I didn't want to have a final exam." Working with other core subject teachers, along with the librarian, guidance counselor, and technical education teacher, McInturff devised the notion that students could present their work in magazine format, based on their researching a topic of their choice in depth, writing and formatting text, incorporating illustrations, and presenting the highlights of the topic on an original cover.

Initially, the effort seemed overwhelming. Without previous student work to guide them, teachers struggled to create a rubric that would capture the most important qualities they hoped to see in finished work, and they ended up with "too many gray areas," too many choices, and too much subjectivity. Moreover, students were not used to projects that extended over several months, and helping students organize their work proved challenging. Not surprisingly, with the guidelines for good work unclear, student products were spotty and many required rewriting. Still, teachers could see the germ of potential for this new ritual, and the following year, they drew on their initial experience to alert students of pitfalls and guide them toward better products.

Over several years, as teachers have learned what the project requires of them and their students, expectations for the project have clarified among teachers, the school's middle grades students, and their parents. Teachers have learned, for example, to buttress the project with a variety of supports, beginning with a letter to parents signed by every eighth grade teacher. Teachers explain that the project will extend over the last quarter of the school year and will involve a field trip to the state library. They describe the project's requirements, alerting parents that students must complete the project to attend the graduation celebration; they note that students can approach any one of the teachers for extra help, and they include a rubric that clarifies standards for the finished product, with reference to expectations for research, use of multiple sources, writing, and art work.

During the last nine weeks of school, then, CSLA's eighth graders are hard at work on their magazines, consulting the librarian, using traditional and electronic sources. Students' topics of choice have included sports, crime, animals, rock and roll, Plato and Aristotle, and architectural design. Students carry a "working notebook" with them at all times. Class time and homework all focus on the project, and many stay late into the afternoons to type their work into the school's word processors. As McInturff emphasizes:

> It's extremely hard work. Our students were scared at first because when they got the information about what they had to do, it seemed overwhelming. But we work with them from the very beginning to the end. We spend time in class and also turn the work they have to do into homework assignments.

Finally, students, parents, and teaches examine the magazines together at the year's end conference. This is the chance for students to reflect on both the quality of the final product and their skills in planning and organizing. Magazines are also displayed for the entire school community. As McInturff notes: "Seeing the work is powerful! Parents see this wonderful work. They're in awe. They can't believe it. We put them out in the library for the PTA. We have held kids from going to private school."

After five years, McInturff is convinced that the exit project is critical to preparing all students for the challenges that await them in high school. She reports:

> These kids have never produced anything of this quality in their academic lives before. This is a stepping stone to prepare them to handle hard work. I am stretching them to their limits. It should not be easy.

As word about the eighth grade assignment has gotten around the school, the effect has been to boost the anticipation for challenging assignments among younger students as well, and according to McInturff, "Our kids are coming in now asking, "Are *we* going to do an exit project?" What's more, the standards for the projects themselves become higher every year. As McInturff uses the projects from students of previous years as exemplars, students consider how their peers turned their ideas into accomplished products, and overall quality improves as students apply those insights. As McInturff explains:

> It's a combination of learning for the kids and the teachers. The magazines our eighth graders are doing are getting better and better. Partly that's because we as teachers know more, but it's also because the magazines the kids see are better. The eighth graders have better and better examples to look at.

While CSLA's exit project is an innovation at the school, it is not incompatible with the district's curriculum standards. In fact, McInturff explains, "If you go through the standards, we find these projects meet them all."

In some schools, the exit ritual takes the form of a year-end presentation to other students and parents. For example, at Hill Middle School in Long Beach, California, ESL teacher Juli Kendall prepares her sixth graders – none English-proficient at the beginning of the year with her – to explain their work to a panel consisting of their student peers and adults from outside the school at an annual community portfolio day. To help students prepare, she develops tools so that students can talk about their work with one another, explain how they decided on one piece of work that represents their best work of the year, and explain the relationship of this piece of work to the district standards. For example, students use a "Writer's Workshop Scoring Guide" to explain how their written work has improved from first draft, through revision, to preparation for publishing. Further, they might assess the organization, interest, logic, variety of style, and use of conventions in the work.

Kendall also involves students' peers in assisting at the presentation where classmates provide feedback to one another about their work. Using Kendall's guidelines, students complete sentences such as "My favorite piece in your portfolio was..... because.....;" "I like the way you.....;" and "One thing I want to tell you is......" on a form that students add to their portfolios. Likewise, participating adults are asked to complete sentences like "I noticed that.....," "I liked.....," "I wonder....," "I was surprised by....," and "This reminds me...." Adult participants are also provided with guidelines designed to engage students in conversations related to district standards for students learning English in Long Beach. For example, adults may query students about what they find easiest or most challenging about learning a second language and ask them to discuss the areas of English in which they would like to improve.

Across the country in Massachusetts, young adolescent students at the Francis W. Parker Public Charter School are also required to present the work they select as their best and most representative and discuss their work publicly with peers, parents, and teachers before moving ahead to the school's high school grades. Students "gateway," as Parker calls this process, when they have pieces of work that "meet" or "exceed" standards in six skill areas, including reading, writing, research, oral presentation, listening, and art. Students are not on their own in this effort. Teachers help students prepare to gateway by coaching students in selecting work that meets or exceeds standards, writing a cover letter, and scheduling the presentation for invited teachers, classmates, family, and guests. This coaching takes on an individualized focus depending on the students. One day, for example, teacher Mike Mann might tutor 13-year old Anna in rehearsing the original writing piece she will read aloud at her gateway. Another day, Mann might nudge special education student Mark toward re-doing a written piece that needs work. Meeting standards is not so easy for Mark who recalls, "In my old school, they'd just give you a C +. Here you have to do it over 'til you get it right." Still, Mark knows that a successful gateway will let him keep up with his age-mates, so he sets to work under Mann's watchful eye.

At Parker, a member of the Coalition of Essential Schools, teachers see the gateway as an opportunity for students to practice reflecting on their own learning in a public forum. At the presentation, students introduce themselves and discuss work they are especially proud of and reflect on the assignments that have been most difficult for them. Finally, students respond to questions from the audience. Unlike a parent conference, students present their work much as they might do in a job or college interview. At the same time, the gateway affords students an opportunity to speak openly about learning challenges, and students may reveal fears about the years ahead. Anna, for one, admits, "I find research boring, especially things I don't care about," adding, "And I'm probably going to get a couple of 'Just beginnings' in Division II. I'll have to get used to that." Yet, the climate of the presentation, while formal, is also celebratory, and students, all of whom know they will be asked to rise to the same occasion, find cause to provide support and praise. On the occasion of Anna's gateway, classmates honor her with such comments as, "You really help people and give really good advice," and "You're really hard-working. I see how hard you work in Spanish," and "I have to admire your ability to stand up and say what you're thinking."

Exit projects and presentations in the middle grades include a variety of approaches. Overall, teachers who engage students in such "graduating projects" look for projects that ask students to demonstrate both knowledge of content, personal interests, and habits of lifelong learning: persistence, awareness of strengths and weaknesses, organization, and independent effort. Like the practices of revision and peer critique, exit projects and presentations offer students places where all feel safe to be smart. At their best, they also affirm the pleasure of accomplishing work that meets standards of excellence in a supportive environment.

Meeting real-world standards of citizenship and community service. When students' school work has value to the community outside the school, students can immediately understand the answer to a perennial question: "What do we have to do this for?" When work is of value to audiences outside of school, "standards" become part of the learning process from the beginning. The results must "work" in the real world. Students understand that what they are doing is "for real," not just to "get a good grade" for throwaway work.

When work is of value to audiences outside of school, 'standards' become part of the learning process from the beginning.

To communicate that being effective in the real world means "meeting standards," some schools organize all student learning around projects that have an immediate impact in their local community. For example, at the Bluebonnet Applied Learning Academy in Fort Worth, Texas, some middle school students work as horiticulturalists on a propagation project at the city's botanical gardens; others work as docents at city museums, a role that requires them to understand the content of current exhibitions and to explain it to museum-goers. Students write proposals to do work for city departments, and as part of a partnership between the school and one of the city's improvisational theater troupes, students apply to write plays under the supervision of a professional playwright.

At Bluebonnet, students view basic skills as tools essential to accomplishing tasks in the real world. One year, in one high-stakes project, students had complete responsibility of planning for a visit to Fort Worth schools by a delegation of Japanese teachers. Students prepared for the visit by tackling a study of Japan's history and current affairs, customs, and approach to schooling. Then, meeting professional standards of the travel industry, they laid out an itinerary for their visitors from the moment they stepped off the plane until the moment of departure, including visits to schools, evening entertainment, meals, and lodging. They prepared all materials to orient their guests, and they arranged for greeters to escort the delegation from the airport. Knowing any flaws in the planning could inconvenience or discomfort their visitors, the project itself built in standards of accuracy in all their work, from writing background materials to making hotel reservations. Not surprisingly, asked about the school's expectations for homework, students shake their heads and roll their eyes, explaining, "We don't have homework at this school. We have deadlines!"

Sometimes students and teachers happen onto a project requiring students to meet standards of effectiveness because the lives of others may depend on it. For example, at Broad Meadows Middle School in Quincy, Massachusetts, students' study of labor conditions during the industrial revolution and the history of slavery in the United States coincided serendipitously with a call from the human rights program director of the Reebok Corporation who had heard that the school's young adolescent students had developed a reputation for their project work. She wanted to know if Broad Meadows students would be interested in a guest speaker about their age, who, although sold at the age of four to a rug maker in Pakistan, had escaped at age ten and was speaking out across Pakistan against child slavery. His name was Iqbal Masih.

Iqbal Masih translated Broad Meadows students' study of past child labor and slavery conditions into the present. Students connected Iqbal's experiences with those of Harriet Tubman, his words with those of Abraham Lincoln. The class studied excerpts from *Oliver Twist,* read Katherine Patterson's *Lyddie,* and discussed the decision made in Lowell in the 1820s to forgo child labor in the first textile mills. Students wondered if Pakistan was just now having its own industrial revolution and why was it repeating the mistakes made in other countries in another century.

After Iqbal's visit, students wrote 670 letters to the heads of governments where child labor is legal, and to corporations that employ children in agriculture. Then, four months later, on Easter Sunday in 1995, Iqbal Masih was shot to death riding a bicycle near his grandmother's house in Pakistan. Shocked at the news, remembering Iqbal's dream that all children would be free and in school, and determined to show that the bullet that killed Iqbal could not kill his dream, the Broad Meadows students decided they would respond to Iqbal's murder by organizing other middle school students across America into "The Kids Campaign to Build A School for Iqbal." Students identified news sources and wrote press releases, all to inform middle school students in all 50 states about their plan to pursue Iqbal's dream. Forming a partnership with the Pakistani human rights group SUDHAAR, they opened a bank account, set up a trust fund, and managed donations, eventually raising $147,000. They prepared background papers, and traveled to Washington to testify on child human rights before Congress. In November 1996, SUDHAAR and Broad Meadows successfully established and opened "A School for Iqbal" in the Punjab Province of Pakistan. Today, 278 children ages 4-12, boys and girls, Muslims and Christians attend the school, 252 who never attended school before, because of the work started by Broad Meadows seventh graders.

For schools seeking to focus their students' learning on creating work that has currency in the real world, projects oriented to community service learning present unique opportunities for teaching students that doing work for real audiences means paying attention to doing work that meets standards. Through such projects students learn firsthand that the more the work meets standards of quality – for precision, neatness, and accuracy – the more professional it will appear and the more powerful its effect. Schools that are building a culture that values high quality work need not design such projects as "add ons," separate from the disciplines. Rather, teachers can build them into the academic curriculum, applying learning in the core subject areas to problems in contemporary society, both local and global, so that students learn content in-depth and for understanding.

Using SCANS standards to guide work projects. Projects that meet standards of the outside world may also involve students in using skills that are valued in the world of work. These skills, as defined in 1991 by the Secretary of Labor's Commission on Achieving Necessary Skills (SCANS), include "workplace competencies" such as managing time, money, materials, space, and staff; using interpersonal skills, including working in teams, leading others, and negotiating; managing information by acquiring, organizing, evaluating, interpreting, and communicating information and complex ideas; understanding and manipulating systems including monitoring and designing social, organizational, and technological systems; and using technology. Some schools, as part of their strategy for improving student work, are using these skills as a way of organizing student projects that have a distinctly real world flavor. The motivation for doing a good job lies in the fact that what students produce has a real world audience.[3] For example:

- At the Mandalay Middle School in Broomfield, Colorado, 140 heterogeneously grouped seventh grade students studied homelessness in the Denver area over a three-week period. During school time, students read current articles on the status and causes of homelessness in the United States and Denver. They used a computer network to compile data on the problem, created pie charts describing the homeless population, and prepared bar graphs describing the reasons for homelessness. They also compared the amount of money spent on services to the homeless with the money spent on other social services. Students gathered information about the service system for the homeless, and each student volunteered at a local service, interviewed someone at the service, and wrote about that experience in a journal. Then, teams of five students each presented the information they had gathered to over 20 Denver-area businesses focusing on the problem and what each person could do to help the homeless, raising $1,300 in the process. Ultimately, students worked together to decide how to allocate this money.

- At the Gleason Lake School in Plymouth, Minnesota, 25 sixth grade students work for four weeks to take over and run the local "Countryside Cafe," a restaurant in their community. In small groups, students investigate the tasks related to the restaurant business including incorporating as a business, writing a business plan, and tallying profits. Students interview professionals who explain each aspect of their role in detail – a lawyer who explains the incorporation process, a banker who assists students in taking out the loan they need to run the restaurant, the health inspector who certifies the restaurant's compliance with regulation, and the restaurant's real-life owner who details advertising, purchasing, cooking, serving, hosting, and cleaning

---

[3]In 1993, Arnold Packer of Johns Hopkins University Institute for Social Policy placed an announcement in *Scholastic Magazine* inviting middle schools (grades 5-8) using SCANS standards to design learning activities to submit descriptions of such projects in competition for 15 awards of $1,000.00 each. The projects described here are drawn from the award-winning submissions he received.

responsibilities. Based on these interviews, students prepare job descriptions, develop an advertising campaign, and observe in the restaurant. On opening night, students executed all these roles. Later, they tallied their gross income, repaid their bank loan, assessed their earnings, and determined how they would spend their profit.

■ At the White Oak Middle School in Cincinnati, 125 eighth graders perpetually asked their physical science teachers "What do we have to know this for?" So teachers answered by designing a project that involved students in a school-based "corporation," with students assuming roles of research scientists, engineers, inventors, accountants, sales and advertising personnel, and patent attorneys as they designed, produced, and kept financial records of their inventions. In the classroom, students selected a product they want to produce based on principles derived from physics and chemistry. They then developed a market survey, gathered and presented data, developed a product prototype, wrote sales and advertising copy, and kept financial records. Then, students displayed prototypes for such products as "Student Stress Balls"(oobleck-filled balloons to be squeezed under stress); student-designed key chains (made from clear polystyrene salad containers, drawn with markers, and placed in an oven to shrink them to one-third of the original size); wave density bottles; and permanent foaming pop cans. After four days, students had orders for $500.00 worth of products priced up to $.50. Students then organized a production line to make enough for the demand, with some teams making a profit.

SCANS standards can enliven teaching and learning in all subject areas.

While some reformers have dismissed SCANS standards as irrelevant to the standards movement, preferring to focus solely on subject area standards, experiences from schools illustrate that, in fact, SCANS standards can enliven teaching and learning in all subject areas. By challenging teachers to design academically rich learning activities in which student work counts – sometimes in terms of money, but also in terms of pleasing the customers of that work, in their communities and among their peers – SCANS standards can shape learning in mathematics, science, social studies, and literature to put students' work as the central indicator of learning for understanding.

Talking about standards with students. As schools grapple with the implications of the standards movement for their practice, they must assess the extent to which every classroom provides opportunities for students to engage in conversations about their work and understand what constitutes quality work. Ultimately, the evidence that schools have created a culture that encourages all students to do work that meets standards lies in the extent to which student talk reflects greater student commitment to direct their own learning and produce high quality work (Corbett & Wilson,1997a). Only through such conversations can students gain understanding of what meeting standards really means.

Schools that use rubrics and exemplars to make standards concrete, develop positive dispositions for learning through peer critique, revision, and self-assessment, and offer students opportunities to create work for audiences beyond the school walls also open up opportunities for "student talk" about standards. These rituals help students articulate, then internalize, standards that define good work. In addition, sometimes students need specific instruction so that they can learn the language of standards and break what Lisa Delpit (1995) calls schools' "codes of power."

Demystifying official standards. Regular conversations, formal and informal, between teachers and students about work that meets standards are key rituals of a school culture that supports standards-based reforms. In addition, some middle grades educators also teach students to understand the formal standards of the larger system. These teachers begin by acknowledging that these standards are often full of jargon, difficult for adults, let alone young adolescents, to decode. Then they figure out ways to make those lists of "Students will...." statements real to their students. For example:

■ While working as a teacher at Muirlands Middle School in San Diego, Carol Barry (1995) decided that she would ask her sixth graders to examine the standards she was using to assess student portfolios and re-write them in "kid-friendly" language. Confronting such expectations as "Demonstrates analytical capabilities" and "Makes reasonable inferences," students rewrote these standards so that they could be understood by in-coming sixth graders to prepare them for more challenging learning. Students assured Barry that the re-written definitions were far easier for them and their schoolmates to understand, stimulating Barry to assign old students to work with new students entering into their class to explain the specific knowledge and skills the portfolio writing process aims to develop.

■ At Hill Middle School in Long Beach, California, ESL teacher Juli Kendall uses a similar approach. Knowing her students need to understand what the district's standards mean to them, Kendall uses district content standards as part of her reading and study skills lessons. Reading policy statements regarding district standards, sixth graders highlight key statements about what students will be able to do at different levels of English proficiency. As Kendall's students begin to understand exactly which skills make for fluent readers and fluent writers, they also begin to speak the language of standards.

Behind Barry's and Kendall's efforts is a commitment to fostering a sense of efficacy that all their students need as they encounter challenges defined by the outside world. In their San Diego and Long Beach classes, these teachers seek to help students use and negotiate "codes of power," the language of those with status in society. Other teachers approach the same task by preparing students for standardized tests, acknowledging how scores are used to distribute opportunities, and preparing students to do their best on required tests, without designing their entire curriculum to achieve this end. The understandings students gain from these exercises helps demystify the language of standards and reduce it to terms students can apply in their work.

Developing a mindset for continuous improvement of student work. The public implicitly expects school improvement to be constant and ongoing. Newspapers routinely announce test score improvements or declines, with the assumption that the numbers should rise indefinitely. But test score gains alone explain nothing about the conditions that contribute to the increase, and they rarely provide clues for ways to improve teaching and learning. In contrast, a collection of student work executed in response to meaningful assignments can offer more concrete evidence of what students have really understood and what they have not learned well. When judged against rubrics developed for self-assessment and viewed in light of critique and feedback from peers and outsiders, relentless attention to student work provides clues as well to where teaching and assignments themselves have improved or fallen short of standards.

Teacher Linda Nathan explains that no single routine that focuses on student work has significant effect on its own. Rather, the collection of processes and routines that make student work the key indicator of learning act together to raise standards continuously for high quality work. In the process, standards themselves remain dynamic, ever-changing, as teaching and learning benefit from reflection and revision. As Nathan notes:

> Schools that believe in standards emanating from the schoolhouse start from a messy place. That is, we firmly believe that standards are not something fixed.... In other words, the "good" paper from last year is not the "good" paper from this year because each year we improve as teachers and so can coach better work from our students. We have outsiders inside the school all the time.. That is how we improve and gauge whether what we are doing is "good enough." Teachers and students are always talking about high quality work and revising work until it meets the standards. Teachers and students together design most rubrics. Students are involved at all levels.

Nathan concludes, "The kids are right when they say school gets harder each year. It does!" But when a school's culture provides structure and support through rubrics, exemplars, peer critique, and self-assessment strategies, and in a climate of supportive and inclusive relationships, students can experience the satisfaction of meeting the challenges of doing "harder work" in a climate of support.

What's more, students themselves come to understand that learning is always continuous, and that working to "meet standards" is an ongoing process. When presented with assignments that are difficult for everyone, the young adolescents in Ron Berger's classes, for example, initially feel unsure of their capacity to meet Berger's challenging assignments. Yet as they work toward completed projects, they learn that their study of exemplars, peer critique, and time for revision, and the support of their classmates work together to make the notion of ongoing improvement basic to their learning. As one student reporting on the process of creating a house blueprint reflected, "I sort of didn't do so well at first. Then I got better and better."

In a climate that values continuous improvement, even the most confident students learn that they can make good work better. As another of Berger's sixth graders related:

I thought my work was pretty good, but when we talked about it, I found there were a lot of problems. Now I go home and think about how am I going to make it work. What helps me is doing the project, finding my mistakes, and doing it over again.

For these young adolescents, continuous improvement is an expectation that touches all learning, providing students with the dispositions essential for future work and learning success.

New rituals, new conversations, new lessons. In the day-to-day life of schools, the practices and rituals that put student work at the center of teaching and learning – the use of rubrics and exemplars, peer critique and revision, and the application of work for audiences outside the school – are the practices that stimulate and sustain student talk about standards. Yet most middle schools may still have a long way to go before they reach all students with these practices. For example, summarizing a district-wide teacher survey on standards implementation in the classroom, teacher Art Indelicato (1998) of Minneapolis Public Schools reported that although teachers' responses indicated a trend to displaying more student work, only about one-quarter always displayed student work that met standards, and of those, only half always provided rubrics with which to judge that work. Further, while one-third of the teachers reported they always encouraged students to "discuss with one another acceptable work that meets standards," less than one-quarter of students "always" talk about the quality of their work, and only 12 percent critique that work.

The practices that focus on students' work, developed through a rich, coherent academic program, are fundamental to a school culture in which it is safe for all students – those who think their work is pretty good at first, and those who have a lot of doubts – to produce good work. Such a culture makes being smart the norm by offering support from all quarters for all kinds of work that meets standards. This is the most immediate benefit of these practices. But as students assume more adult roles as citizens, workers, and learners, they are also likely to remember the lessons these practices teach: *Everyone experiences learning challenges at different times and in different ways. There's always room for improvement. It's smart to ask for help. When it gets too hard, take a break for a while. Persistence pays off.*

THE SECOND ESSENTIAL BUILDING BLOCK:
A MOTIVATIONAL CLIMATE FOR HIGH STANDARDS

Current standards policies rest on several assumptions: *Hold students accountable, and they will work harder. Let students know there are consequences for failure, and they will perform. Communicate higher standards, and students will rise to your expectations.* Guided by these assumptions, and seeking greater student investment in learning, policymakers and educators often fall back on old-fashioned tactics of rewards and threats, including practices like grade retention that actually undermine achievement and motivation. But in practice, although some individual students put forth greater effort in the face of threatened penalties or promised rewards, "raising the bar" alone does not stimulate students to apply themselves to succeed academically. As Blythe McVicker Clincy (1997) points out, the claim that "Students will learn more when more is expected of them" is a "facile and misleading half-truth" (p. 68). As hard as students may work, if they are working in settings devoid of intellectual stimulation, meaningful relationships, and support structures, it is unlikely they will produce work that meets standards of excellence.

Likewise, the claim that a set of consequences and rewards will best serve those who have historically been most disenfranchised in our schools is, at best, naïve. Punitive policies not only fail to motivate many struggling students; they also contribute to students' disengaging from school (Wehlage & Rutter, 1986). When the novelty of pizza parties for improving attendance or a new pair of sneakers for meeting honor roll standards wears off, the reality remains that four out of ten students "feel bored" as often as "every day" or "almost every day" while only one in four "gets excited" that frequently by something they study in school (Farkus & Johnson, 1997). When a system of incentives and consequences fails to change student performance, educators are still left with persistent questions of how to help struggling students meet standards: How do we motivate students who already appear uninvested in schoolwork? How can we reach apathetic students who now fail to turn in even the minimal amount of homework and push them to respond to higher standards?

> *Punitive policies not only fail to motivate many struggling students; they also contribute to students' disengaging from school.*

These questions cut to the core of teachers' day-to-day work in schools. And as teachers find that practices that focus on student work – the use of rubrics and exemplars, opportunities for peer critique and revision, and projects executed for a real world audience – can themselves enhance student engagement, they also know that the focus on student work is only one dimension of a culture that supports standards-based reform. In addition, student investment in schooling has to do with the human relationships students experience in schools. As New York City teacher Christine Cziko (1996) points out:

> For a teacher, it is easy to become overwhelmed by the growing number of approaches to assessing student work – from the standards movement to calls for alternative assessment, from rubrics to test scores, from outcomes to portfolios. I sometimes worry that what gets lost in the conversation is what actually happens between young people and the adults who care about them in places called schools. (pp. 87-88)

"What actually happens between young people and the adults who care about them" is at the center of student learning. Moreover, young adolescents are the first to describe what individual teachers do that matters. For example, Dick Corbett and Bruce Wilson (1997b) found "pockets" of good practice in urban middle schools that prodded students into sticking with difficult work and achieving at levels higher than their peers. Students in these settings reported that they worked harder when teachers made an effort to engage students in interesting activities, made sure students understood what they were supposed to be learning, and refused to allow students to give up or turn in incomplete work. In a study that produced parallel findings, middle school teacher Monica Richards (1987) also found that what motivated students was not, as she expected, a reward-centered bonus-point system but rather teachers who cared enough to use multiple resources to teach a concept and who connected with students' families through positive notes to parents.

What motivated students was not a reward-centered bonus-point system but rather teachers who cared enough to use multiple resources to teach a concept and who connected with students' families.

Establishing a motivational climate in which every student feels safe to work with diligence, tackle new learning, learn from mistakes, and do work that meets standards – the essence of being smart – begins with individual teachers who care enough about students' success that they repeatedly probe for clues that will help them understand how to best help each student to meet standards. Making student investment in school a norm school wide means taking individual teachers' practices and beliefs about learning and structuring them into the daily life of all classrooms to create a "press for achievement" and a climate that motivates every student to learn. Such a climate depends on:

- Caring relationships between teachers and students;

- Beliefs and routines that value effort, risk-taking, and opportunity, including detracking and heterogeneous grouping;

- A diversified curriculum and instructional program that ensures that every student has opportunities to learn for understanding;

- Challenge, cooperation, and participation;

- Concrete support for students who need it through extra-help opportunities that convey a commitment to helping every student achieve;

- Flexible scheduling;

- Counseling and mentoring to match students' aspirations.

Caring and optimistic relationships

For many young adolescents, motivation to learn and work hard depends in part on being part of a caring community of peers and adults. Yet the notion of schools as caring communities of learners is often easier to talk about than to realize. For a variety of reasons, including high teacher-to-student ratios, poor teacher attendance, and fragmented schedules, many schools fall short of the ideal community of learners. Yet, for many students, the opportunity for consistent, personalized relationships is essential for learning. As Luis Garden Acosta, founding educator at El Puente's Academy for Peace and Justice, a small theme school in New York City, insists:

For many students, the opportunity for consistent, personalized relationships is essential for learning.

> What's needed in schools are human relations. People must realize these are our children. We're all one family and that transcends our homes, the street, and the public institutions. When we bond with each other and build the realization that nurtures our humanity, that is when education happens. (Steinberg, 1996)

That such relationships are essential nutrients in students' schooling is perhaps most apparent in schools that enroll large numbers of poor students. Over and over, struggling students in inner-city schools report that "nobody cares," that they feel "bored," "ignored," and "invisible;" that school "hurts [their] spirit," and that they encounter racial and ethnic prejudice on a regular basis (Darling-Hammond, 1997; Farrell, 1990; Fine, 1986, 1991; Institute for Education in Transformation, 1992; Nieto, 1992).

Caring is not the same as hand-wringing about students' circumstances. Rather, caring that motivates is intimately tied to actions and decisions to ensure that all students do good work. In fact, even when schools "restructure" to change their organizational arrangements, teachers' beliefs and actions that contribute to a hostile learning climate, especially for poor, African American, and Latino students, may remain unchanged. As Pauline Lipman (1998) found in her detailed ethnography of two junior high schools, despite intensive reorganizing, many teachers' view of African American students as being "at risk" set the stage for pervasive labeling, lowered expectations, and limited opportunities to learn for those students. Seeing their students primarily in terms of perceived deficiencies, teachers had little sense of responsibility for their students' academic success. In response, many African American students withdrew from any engagement in real learning.

Our most disenfranchised students are not the only ones who need a "safer" school culture free of prejudice and stereotyping. Middle class students also describe school conditions that undermine their sense of emotional "safety." Mary Pipher (1996) introduces us to one such student:

> Aubrey had a litany of familiar complaints about her junior-high days — lots of name-calling and teasing, girls hurting each other, boys being too sexual and aggressive, a rape in the school bathroom, and guns in the parking lot. And she had complaints that were her own. She hated 'titty twister days' and flip-up days when boys flipped up girls' skirts. Two boys who were failing English destroyed her creative writing project. Someone drew a swastika on her friend Emma's locker. Aubrey hated the pain that racism caused her friend. She and Emma talked about dropping out together. (pp. 184-185)

Students and schools pay a high price for tolerating the interpersonal hostilities that undermine human connections within schools. Even apart from other harmful social or economic factors, encounters with prejudice significantly increase students' vulnerability to personal problems. In a recent analysis of findings from the National Longitudinal Study of Adolescent Health, researchers found that students who experienced prejudice at school were at greater risk of emotional distress (Blum, R.W. & Rinehart, P.M., 1977; Resnick, et al., 1997; Vobejda, 1997). This same study found that "school-connectedness" could protect young adolescents from academic, social, and health risks; it noted specifically that positive relationships between students and teachers were even more important than smaller classes for learning.

Positive relationships between students and teachers were even more important than smaller classes for learning.

This should not surprise those who know teenagers well. Young adolescents seeking to expand their horizons beyond their family and neighborhood circles look not only to their parents but to adults beyond their family for ways to experience and understand the world. Many count on their teachers to make schools better places than the society in which they live. They need places where teachers take conscious steps to ensure they are safe to succeed academically and socially. Students' knowledge that the adults in their school care about them as individual learners and people helps make that success possible.

Teachers first communicate that they care when they treat students as individuals. For example, students interviewed by California's Institute for Education in Transformation (1992) reported they knew teachers cared when teachers "laughed with them, trusted them, asked them or told them personal things, were honest, wrote them letters, called home to say nice things, touched them with pats, hugs, handshakes or gave them the 'high five,' or otherwise recognized them as individuals" (p. 19). Echoing these findings, educator Lisa Delpit (1995) describes how teachers make personal contact with the young people in their charge while also communicating that every single student must achieve. As she explains:

> In many African American communities, teachers are expected to show that they care about their students by controlling the class; exhibiting personal power; establishing meaningful interpersonal relationships; displaying emotion to garner student respect; demonstrating the belief that all students can learn;

establishing a standard of achievement and 'pushing' students to achieve the standard; and holding the attention of the students by incorporating African American interactional styles in their teaching. Teachers who do not exhibit these behaviors may be viewed by community members as ineffectual, boring, or uncaring. (p. 142)

Students do their best work when they believe they have some support to fall back on, and when they know they are "visible" to others who will speak honestly to them about matters of school and life. In the absence of such caring, students are unlikely to make the extra effort to produce anything of quality. And when the absence of caring goes beyond indifference to subtle or overt racism, some students, whose intelligence may shine outside school walls, may explicitly choose to "not learn" in school. Educator Herbert Kohl (1992) explains:

Not learning tends to take place when someone has to deal with unavoidable challenges to her or his personal and family loyalties, integrity, and identity. In such situations, there are forced choices and no apparent middle ground. To agree to learn from a stranger who does not respect your integrity causes a major loss of self. The only alternative is to not-learn and reject their world. (p. 16)

While it is tempting to succumb to the magical thinking of those who assert that simply raising the bar will result in better student performance, students' motivation is at least as dependent on immediate relationships in a fair and inclusive climate as on abstract promises of future rewards for harder work. Higher standards will make most sense to students when teachers' actions are consistent with their words. As Lorraine Monroe, an acclaimed middle school principal notes, "When you are a superb teacher you work from the heart, take children's pain seriously. When you work with children, you have to watch what you say and do" (Hart, 1997, L6).

Schools that are places where students are motivated to create work that meets standards practice what Theodore Sizer (1994) calls "rigorous caring" and "caring rigor." Rigorous caring defies formula. Teachers who practice rigorous caring respect students' individual integrity, comment directly on academic strengths and weaknesses, and insist on students' capacity to do better work. Confronted with students who have been getting by for years, have chosen to "not learn," or have learned patterns of helplessness that interfere with their achievement, teachers can best inspire students to work harder when they approach students as individuals who bring unique interests, aspirations, life experiences, and values to the classroom. Examples of the effect of such caring follow.

- Teacher Loretta Brady (1996) relates that she needed to follow her students from seventh into eighth grade before she discovered that Alfredo would finally put forth exponentially greater effort for learning when he could write authentically about his own life and find readers among the school's adults who would provide feedback for improvement. She tells too how she endured months of Hannah's resistance to producing more proficient written work before she discovered that Hannah's resentment would melt away when given the chance to deliver her words in dramatic form before a live audience.

- Herbert Kohl (1992) describes how, by offering ways for Barry, one of his students, to "save face," he made it possible for Barry to maintain his role as classroom rebel and also learn to read. He also tells of how he shaped his student Akmir's daily encounters with racism to become the driving force behind Akmir's careful and analytical reading of text, thinking about "big issues," and developing evidence he could use to challenge the political status quo.

- Sara Mosle (1995) reports that when her contrived writing assignments failed to hook New York City students, it occurred to her that young people, like adults, would write more if they had a real audience. With this realization, she began to correspond with individual students. As students wrote about their lives in their notebooks, Mosle responded with a few sentences, enough to provoke more writing. As the dialogues developed, Mosle picked up clues she could use to motivate her students to push ahead in their learning: that one of her Dominican students had memorized the witches' spell from *MacBeth* and wanted to know more about *Romeo and Juliet*, and that another would willingly stay after school to write long letters to his father in jail.

"Rigorous caring" balances nurture and "press" so that ultimately students learn to act on their own behalf. It includes support tailored to students' individual strengths and needs. It depends on teachers' making personal connections with students so that they can coax, cajole, trick, and entice reluctant students into habits of working hard, revising, rewriting, and daring to care about producing high quality work.

Structures that support caring and enhance teachers' knowledge of how individual students learn become even more important when schools' expectations for students include learning for understanding as evidenced by better student work. As founder of the Coalition of Essential Schools and co-director of the Devens, Massachusetts, Francis W. Parker Charter School, Theodore Sizer (1996) explains:

> One cannot teach a student well if one does not know that student well. If the task is the mere memorization of simple lists, maybe, or the development of a routine skill. Serious understanding of an important and complex issue, the stuff of good secondary education? Rarely, if ever. (p. xiii)

Schools striving to create a culture of high standards expand opportunities for better human relationships through a variety of organizational structures and routines including teaming and looping, teacher advisories, and smaller learning communities.

Teaming and looping

For many years, advocates for middle grades students have promoted the practice of in-school teaming, the assigning of 40 to 100 or more heterogeneously grouped students to a regular pair or group of teachers with expertise in different disciplines (Carnegie Council on Adolescent Development, 1989; George & Alexander, 1993; Lipsitz, 1984). Common planning time scheduled for each teacher team allows teachers to get to know students' strengths, identify problems, and plan coordinated and consistent teaching and learning strategies to support individual students. Team planning time also provides space for teachers to hammer out expectations for students and review student work in light of those expectations. In some middle schools like the Parker School in Devens, Massachusetts, teachers team in two-member teams. With one teacher responsible for the humanities, including social studies and language arts, and another responsible for math and science, teachers have half the students they would in a departmentalized school and can develop stronger relationships with students.

In recent years, some schools have boosted the effectiveness of teaming through "looping." This practice matches teacher teams with a cluster of students over several years, so that teachers who begin working with students in the sixth grade "move up" with these same students through the eighth grade. This arrangement allows teachers to get to know the learning strengths and needs of students as they grow and develop through early adolescence, and it is especially compatible with learning goals that emphasize reasoning, problem-solving, and communicating through in-depth projects. Echoing Sizer, middle grades consultant and Shelburne (VT) Community School's former principal Carol Spencer asserts, "It takes more than one year for teachers and students to find ways for students to achieve the larger outcomes we are looking for."

'It takes more than one year for teachers and students to find ways for students to achieve the larger outcomes we are looking for.'

Educators report a variety of advantages to looping. Looping adds time to learning that would otherwise be lost to familiarizing students to new routines at the beginning of each school year, and some see the practice as a springboard to summertime learning since teachers can assign in-depth reading or vacation projects and pick up on them immediately at the beginning of the next school year (Burke, 1996). In a study of looping in the middle grades, Paul George found that three-quarters of the teachers surveyed reported they were more aware of students' academic needs, with many also describing huge benefits in classroom management (Pyle, 1997). In this vein, for example, teachers at Detroit's Hutchins Middle School say that because they are more aware of students' social and academic needs, they can intervene before problems reach a crisis stage. As they explain, "When students get into 'he said-she said' situations, we know them well enough that we can mediate the problem right away." Moreover, because all teachers work with students over three years, teachers share responsibility for boosting students' achievement on state tests. With the burden of high-stakes testing no longer resting entirely on the eighth grade teachers, looping may also foster stronger professional collegiality.

Clearly, multi-year looping has obvious positive effects on teachers' *caring* for students. In addition, looping enhances teachers' *daring* as teachers build on better relationships with students to organize learning in different ways. For example, results of recent surveys of Philadelphia seventh and eighth graders assigned to teams that had looped for at least two years pointed to

Looping enhances teachers' 'daring' as teachers build on better relationships with students to organize learning in different ways.

looping as enhancing students' feelings that their teachers wanted them to do well. What was of greater surprise was that "looped" students were more likely than "non-looped" students to describe their teachers as moving away from traditional "chalk and talk" approaches toward more innovative instruction, with teachers grouping for cooperative learning and asking students to explain their math work (Mac Iver, Ruby, Balfanz, Plank, & Prioleau, 1998). This diversification of instruction can itself contribute to boosting students' engagement.

Teacher advisories. Advocates for successful middle schools have long recommended teacher advisories, the practice of allowing regular time for adults in the school to meet with small groups of teachers, as a way to enhance and personalize teacher-student relationships. Advisory groups play a role in ensuring that every student has at least one adult who knows her well enough to be an advocate, and overall teacher advisories can increase students' sense of belonging and membership in the school. As Mac Iver (1990) reports:

> Based on principals' estimates, a school that provides students with extensive social support and frequent opportunities to discuss topics that are important to them by means of a regularly scheduled group advisory period is more successful than other schools in increasing the proportion of its students who stay in school until high school graduation. (p. 464)

Advisories can contribute to student motivation in a number of ways. Small group discussions can become places where teachers can directly confront self-limiting beliefs about intelligence and concerns about "appearing too smart" (Midgley & Urdan, 1995). In some schools, advisories can specifically teach students how to assess their interests and goals, provide them with information about careers and higher education, and walk them through a decision-making process that can help them realize a future course of study that matches their aspirations. In others, advisories help students develop the study skills necessary for doing better work. While the program focus varies, what remains the same is that advisories are the basis for ensuring that every student has

Advisories are the basis for ensuring that every student has an adult in the school who knows him well enough to be the person in his corner, his cheer-leader, coach, and booster.

an adult in the school who knows him well enough to be the person in his corner, his cheerleader, coach, and booster.

Smaller learning communities and schools. In part as a result of a trend toward consolidating small schools into larger ones, average school enrollments in the United States now stand at 635 students, with some middle and high school enrollments reaching several thousand. But as school size has increased, a growing number of educators have rebelled against the "shopping mall school," arguing for smaller schools as an alternative. Although "smaller" is a relative concept, those who advocate smaller schools define "small' as an enrollment of some 300 students (Klonsky, n.d.).

Reviewing literature on school size, Kathleen Cotton (1996) found a number of indications that small schools offered a climate that would motivate students to engage in academic learning. Students in small schools tended toward more positive attitudes toward school in general, and student attendance and suspension rates were typically more positive than in larger schools. Caring, interpersonal relationships among students, teachers, and administrators also set the stage for a strong motivational climate. Moreover, in smaller schools participation in extracurricular activities is much higher among all student groups, including minority and low-income students. Students' expression of greater satisfaction from their extracurricular participation further signals enhanced identification and engagement with school.

Small school size also allows for professional relationships that focus on core issues of instruction. As Deborah Meier, founder of New York City's Central Park East Secondary Schools, explained at a 1993 Philadelphia conference on small schools:

> To find the necessary time for thoughtful discussion [of higher standards], we need to create schools in which consensus is easy to arrive at, argument is encouraged, even fostered.... For teachers to truly start thinking through the task before them – not merely individually but collectively and collaboratively – for this to happen, schools must be so small that governance does not become the topic of their discussion but issues of teaching and learning do.

Reports on smaller school sizes suggest that building large new structures may be misguided, and they trumpet a warning that further consolidation of existing schools may have educational costs that outweigh any apparent financial savings. More important, lessons emerging from "small schools practice," along with findings on the benefits of teaming and advisories, should bear on the restructuring of middle schools and highlight the importance of consistent, supportive student-teacher relationships that allow students to feel that they have an advocate at school who knows and appreciates them as individuals. These relationships are key to maximizing student motivation and investment in schooling.

Structures for caring are only the beginning. Experience from exemplary middle schools clearly indicates that as teachers and students develop stronger relationships, teachers can more effectively "reach" students and establish caring connections that can stimulate and sustain student engagement. Teachers working in smaller learning communities can prod young adolescents to persist in creating better work, based on what they know about individual students, not in response to a rule-driven, one-size-fits-all policy. Yet many schools remain mired in traditional organizational forms. For example, despite the promises of teaming for strengthening teacher-student relationships, this approach, although gaining momentum, is still not widespread. As Mac Iver (1990) found in a survey of middle school principals, most middle-grades schools (63%) did not use interdisciplinary teaming at any grade level, and those that did rarely coupled teaming with sufficient common planning time. However, data from the 1993 NMSA study (McEwin, Dickinson, & Jenkins, 1996) show marked increases in the percentages of schools using teaming, particularly at the sixth grade level where teaming is now predominant.

Moreover, even when teams do exist, teachers do not always focus on developing new ways to motivate students academically or on ensuring that all students are known well as *learners* by at least a few adults in the school. For example, in the two junior high schools Pauline Lipman (1998) studied over several years, teachers' awareness of African American students' *social* needs increased when they organized into teams. However, this awareness did not translate into higher expectations for students' academic potential or increased professional commitment to take steps to close existing gaps in opportunities to learn or achievement.

Structures that foster consistent, caring relationships are necessary but not sufficient for developing student motivation to do better work at more challenging tasks more of the time. Teaming, looping, advisories, and smaller learning communities are all desirable. These structures, however, deliver a payoff only in tandem with a larger set of beliefs and actions that shape a school culture for standards-based reforms.

Beliefs and routines focus on effort, risk taking, and opportunity

Many current beliefs about learning undermine attempts to develop schools in which every single student can produce work that meets standards. Consider for a moment the value many schools put on getting the *quick* answer *right away,* or *getting it* almost *without thinking.* This attempt to save minutes may result in mistaking an accelerated covering of content with more challenging learning, leaving many students with little to show for their time spent in school. Middle grades educator Nancy Doda tells how a visit to a suburban middle school revealed the ways in which the emphasis on speed in learning shortchanges students:

> I asked the students, 'It's January and I'd like to know more about what you've learned so far this year. Can you tell me?' The students paused and pondered. They chuckled, and then one said, 'How about this week?' I said, 'Sure but can you tell me more about the big picture?' Then the student said, 'We are in the accelerated group.' I said, 'Yes I have been told that,' and he said, 'Well, I guess we went too fast 'cause I hardly remember much.'

Certain school practices place high value on completing assignments quickly over producing work that reflects effort, care, and quality. Thus, many schools elevate students who quickly complete assignments to the rank of "fast learners." At the same time, some routinely relegate students who try harder to master school tasks to the "slow" group regardless of whether the work they produce could ultimately, with time and support, be comparable to that of other students. Many schools allot grades not on students' most complex work or work that represents the culmination of learning, but on the average of all graded assignments. Thus, students who get a slower start or must progress a greater distance to catch up ultimately rank below their peers, even if their final work products are identical. In these and other ways, schools convey the message that "getting it right from the beginning" counts for more than effort, improvement, and final

Building a culture for standards-based reform means uprooting many old assumptions about learning to make way for new beliefs about how students 'become smart.'

work quality. In this context, students can easily believe that teachers value work done quickly more than work done well. Not surprisingly, many internalize a view of themselves as slow and do not learn strategies that can see them through challenging assignments. Building a culture for standards-based reform means uprooting many old assumptions about learning to make way for new understandings about how students "become smart." In addition, new beliefs set the stage for new practices that foster motivation through valuing of effort, risk taking, and opportunity.

Student beliefs about intelligence, learning, and effort

For decades, we have assumed that if we could only get the rewards and consequences "right," we could motivate students to work harder and improve achievement. The "right" incentives must be worthy of students' aspirations and dignity, however, if they are to motivate students to work harder academically. As Milbrey McLaughlin and Shirley Brice Heath (1993) note, "More incentives to achieve, such as promises of support for college attendance, can activate youngsters to take school and their achievements seriously" (p. 212). In fact, programs that combine future financial scholarships for post-secondary education with structured tutoring, mentoring, and peer support effectively motivate many middle grades students to persist in school (Wheelock & Dorman, 1988).

More recently, cognitive psychologists point to a set of more complex factors that contribute to students' investment in learning. These researchers tell us that, as much as any system of rewards, students' motivation is strongly tied to their beliefs about intelligence and learning. As Valanne Henderson and Carol Dweck (1990) explain:

> In fact, a student who is less bright than others but who has an adaptive motivational pattern – that is one who is persistent, is able to maintain effective learning strategies and a positive attitude toward academic tasks – may turn out to be a high achiever. In contrast, some of the brightest students who have maladaptive motivational patterns – the ones who give up easily, do not use good learning strategies, and do not enjoy academics – may fall considerably behind and fail to fulfill their potential. (p. 309)

In turn, students' beliefs about intelligence shape their feelings and behavior in relation to achievement. For example, as Henderson and Dweck (1990) have documented, students who believe that intelligence is inborn and who view ability as fixed may succeed as long as they master tasks easily and win positive attention from others. Confronted with more challenging tasks, however, these same students may fall short of success, and when they do so, they may see failure as a sign of limited ability and may avoid taking on future challenges that will "expose" their inadequacy. In contrast, students who view intelligence as flexible and expandable are more likely to tie increased competence to their own effort, approach problems with a sense of excitement, learn from mistakes, and persist in the face of difficulty.

These different belief systems have a clear effect on student achievement in the middle grades. Henderson and Dweck (1990), for instance, describe one study that followed sixth graders as they moved into seventh grade in a new junior high school. Regardless of prior achievement, students who believed that intelligence was malleable and viewed their studies as a way to increase their capacity received better grades than those who approached junior high believing that intelligence was innate and fixed. Moreover, students who were less confident of their intelligence but still believed that they could learn to improve their competence did much better than expected; at the same time, students assessed as highly confident but who believed that intelligence was inherent and depended on others to validate their ability did much worse than predicted.

In related work, researchers have further delineated how the kinds of comments adults provide students in school can contribute to students' effort and motivation to tackle new problems. For example, in one study, Carol Dweck and Claudia Mueller (Dweck, Kamins, & Mueller, 1997) offered fifth graders a set of problems to complete. All students were praised for success, but some were told "You must be smart at these problems," while others were told, "You must have worked hard at these problems." Then researchers observed how students responded to subsequent sets of problems, including self-selected problems. The results were striking. Of the students praised for their intelligence, 67 percent chose to work on "Problems that I'm pretty good at so I can show I'm smart." In contrast, of those praised for their effort, 92 percent selected "Problems that I'll learn a lot from, even if I won't look smart." Students in a control group who were praised only for their initial success chose both kinds of problems equally. Subsequent studies replicated these results with racially and demographically diverse sample groups.

Of additional interest was further research that found that after students praised for their "smartness" confronted failure, they began to demonstrate a greater sense of helplessness over their learning, enjoyed new tasks less, and were less likely to persist in mastering skills by taking problems home. In short, praising students for success rather than for their effort, the strategies they use to learn, or the product of their effort can result in students' feelings that they must *look smart* to continue to receive recognition. As a result, many such students may circumvent situations, including opportunities for learning new skills, that present a risk of their failing.

Motivating young adolescents depends in part on helping them understand learning in terms of 'expandable intelligence,' effort, and risk taking rather than inborn ability.

The work of Dweck and others makes it clear that motivating young adolescents depends in part on helping them understand learning in terms of "expandable intelligence," effort, and risk taking rather than inborn ability. And while all students need to learn about new ways of thinking about intelligence and effort, minority and female students may need to do so most of all. How so? As Stanford psychologist Claude Steele (1997) points out, students' motivation to achieve depends on their belief that they will prosper and belong in school; they must identify with school to think of themselves as scholars. However, when minority or female students set out to succeed in some settings – in mathematics or science classes, for example – they do so in the context of unspoken but prevailing societal notions that they are not adept or competent in certain academic settings. As a result, many experience what Steele calls "stereotype threat." Fearing that they will fit the expectation of the stereotype regardless of their competence, students' back away from challenge, even when they are fully capable of mastering required tasks. When this happens at school, academic performance suffers, and many students may retreat from school learning, snubbing their nose at any rules that demand any effort to achieve.

The work of such researchers as Dweck, Mueller, and Steele highlight the ways in which the interplay of beliefs about intelligence, effort, and learning – whether held by teachers, students, parents, or in the community – and responses to achievement together play a huge role in student motivation in school. What are the implications of this research? What actions can schools take to circumvent students' self-limiting beliefs and support in their place beliefs that will empower and motivate all students to expend the effort necessary to learn?

Teaching students about effort, risk taking, and cooperation. Educators who want to make sure that school is a place where it is safe for every single student to be smart act explicitly to counteract students' beliefs that learning depends on inherent ability. Sometimes, these actions evolve from teachers' thinking about their own beliefs about learning, including how some might limit students' success, then structuring into their classroom new routines that are more closely aligned with new understandings about learning. For example, when Susan Ray (1996), eighth grade teacher at Kentucky's Mt. Washington Middle School, considered the challenges she faced as she learned statistics in her own graduate program, she began to wonder how she could ensure students enough learning time to develop new skills. She did not want to slow the pace of instruction, nor did she not want to give in to a "coverage model" of learning. Most important, she realized that if her students were to learn to value effort, risk initial failure, and learn from their mistakes, she would have to let them know that in her classroom, success was not "excellence on demand" or "getting it right the first time." She knew that if her students feared taking risks, they would give up on "hard" challenges and resist learning.

As she thought about how to encourage her eighth graders to take more risks as they faced tougher learning situations, Ray identified four key beliefs that would guide her as she helped her students push their limits. Once she identified these beliefs, certain teaching strategies followed to match them. For example:

■ **Believing that her students take unnoticed risks every day** and believing that she needed to understand better the difficulties they faced in learning math, Ray now asks her students to write a short math autobiography which they present to their classmates in timeline format.

■ **Believing that her students need encouragement to persist beyond initial failure**, time to practice new skills, and explicit guidance on how to tackle projects that allow them to see the "end point" of their work, Ray involves students in designing checklists and rubrics for portfolios, group tasks, and investigations so they can see what they have to do to create exemplary work. She also tells her students stories about adults – both famous and ordinary – who made mistakes in the pursuit of knowledge.

■ **Believing that students' learning depends on their understanding that they can improve their work over time**, Ray makes sure her students will have both the opportunity to do first drafts and the time to revise, correct, and polish work on long-term investigations before she begins the assessment process.

■ **Believing that students learn from what the adults around them do as much as from what they say**, Ray takes risks herself in front of her students, talks about her own failures and fears and how she overcomes them, and about the mistakes that have helped her learn.

Clearly, how teachers think about learning can influence how they shape classroom practices to foster greater student motivation. In addition, schools can counteract adolescents' views of ability as fixed by speaking directly to students about recent research on intelligence. For example, teachers from the Middle School of the Kennebunks in Maine visit feeder elementary schools to present information about Howard Gardner's research on multiple intelligences, then return several weeks later to talk with each incoming seventh grader about not how smart they are but the ways they are smart. By the time they enter the middle school, not only do teachers know incoming students well but students have a mindset that they can "be smart" in different ways.

Even more explicit guidance in rethinking assumptions about learning is built into particular teaching strategies, especially strategies for "complex instruction," a form of cooperative learning pioneered by Elizabeth Cohen (1986) of Stanford University. Alert to the potential of differential teacher expectations getting in the way of effective teaching with heterogeneous groups, Cohen's research highlights the importance of speaking to students specifically about the assumptions about learning and success. For example, her research demonstrates that cooperative groups with diverse students work best when teachers explicitly instruct students in two rules: "You have the right to ask anyone else at your learning center for help," and "You have the duty to assist anyone who asks for help." In tandem with challenging multifaceted assignments, Cohen also urges teachers to tell students, "No one person is going to be good at all the skills necessary to complete this task, but everyone will be good at at least one." Cohen's research also identifies the power of identifying successful learning strategies of low-status students and remarking favorably on these strategies within hearing distance of other students. These interventions have implications for ways any teacher using cooperative learning as an instructional strategy can heighten motivation and achievement.

Finally, schools can communicate new perspectives on effort and ability to students by building new norms into all aspects of school life. They may do this, as Steele suggests, by fostering "optimistic" teacher-student relationships and by ensuring all students opportunities for challenging work in heterogeneous groups, teaching that encourages multiple perspectives on problems, and access to role models who demonstrate multiple ways of achieving academic success. They may introduce students to testing situations in such a way as to communicate that tests do not reflect inherent ability. They may create settings that counteract prevailing stereotypes and avoid labeling, and as the research (Dweck, et al., 1997) suggests, they may explicitly teach students that corrections or negative comments on work are not judgments of innate ability, but instead a source of help and information for improving future work.

Teachers' rethinking school norms about effort and risk taking. Middle grades educators who pay attention to recent research on motivation are working to devise ways to communicate the value of effort and risk taking so that students will persist in working toward success. Reframing notions about risk taking and effort may begin in individual classrooms, but those building a culture for standards-based reform also work to infuse entire schools with these values. At the Wellesley (MA) Middle School, principal John D'Auria describes how he and his teachers have slowly developed a school-wide climate that values effort, risk taking, and learning from mistakes. For example:

- In the school's annual family orientation and in regular issues of the principal's letter to parents, D'Auria directly informs parents of recent research on motivation, effort, and school success. In particular, D'Auria emphasizes Dweck's findings that praising students for their success on the basis of ability can set students up for self-limiting behavior. He explains that when such students run into later setbacks, they may conclude that if their ability accounted for successes, their lack of ability must be the reason for their failure. D'Auria suggests that parents apply this research at home by connecting their children's success to effort, thoughtful problem-solving, and commitment.

■ In English/language arts, Wellesley teachers put in long hours writing extensive feedback to students about their writing with suggestions for improvement. Then, before handing back papers to students, teachers explicity say to the class, "Now I know some of you are going to see this feedback and think, 'I'm not a good writer,' or 'Mr. Mitchell doesn't think I am a good writer.'" He explains that good writing *always* takes work, critique, and revision, and explicitly talks with students about getting to the next stage of their writing.

■ In mathematics, if students do not do well on an exam, teachers build in opportunities for students to examine and analyze their errors, requiring them to produce extensive explanations of their mistakes. This provides teachers with a window into students' thinking processes so they can offer individualized feedback to students; at the same time, students can earn points back as they correct errors and learn from their mistakes.

When students see the quick completion of their work as a sign of inherent ability, they may also believe that any task requiring effort is "too hard," a sign that they must be "too stupid" to make it worth their while to persist. With this in mind, D'Auria has explicit discussions with students about how their desire to appear cool can undermine not only regular class work but also performance on state-wide standardized tests. He relates:

[During the state-wide testing of eighth graders], I speak to each homeroom about taking their time. I acknowledge explicitly how hard it is to notice that others have finished the test when they are still working. We wonder together, "What does that say about you as a student?" We had a great discussion where kids could name the feelings about feeling dumb because they were not looking like they had a lot of ability if they took too much time. Generally, my eighth graders hung in there and took their time for most of the exam.

Adults at Wellesley Middle School themselves learn from discussions about effort and learning. For example, in one discussion about reading, many teachers recalled growing up with the belief that good readers read "effortlessly." In examining that assumption, a science teacher related that he never understood a science article the first time around, and that he always reread it several times for meaning. Another teacher brought up recent research pointing to findings that good readers do not skip words, but ask questions, make predictions, notice their feelings when they read, and make connections with other information they have. By the end of the conversation, teachers were wondering if reading is ever "effortless" for anyone and pondering what that might mean for their teaching.

Detracking and heterogeneous grouping. Regardless of what teachers tell students about effort and ability, however, it unlikely that students will believe that they really mean what they say without parallel changes in the ability grouping practices that sort young adolescents according to perceived intelligence. The practice of categorizing students into "high," "average," and "low" groups and offering them a differentiated curriculum is a well-entrenched tradition in schools at all levels across the country, but this practice accelerates, in particular, during the middle grades years (Braddock, 1990). Sensitive to the way others see them, young adolescents are well aware that different placements reflect teachers' views of their ability, and these understandings threaten to undermine the motivation of all students.

Indeed, as research psychologists point out, the decline in motivation to engage in academic activities in middle school is strongly related to classroom and school environments. For example, describing how young adolescents increasingly view "ability" as a fixed trait, Anderman and Maehr (1994) report:

> As the child moves to the middle grade years, he or she is likely to experience a school context that stresses the importance of relative ability. As a result, a situation arises in which putting forth effort may be problematic. To put forth effort and fail means one is "dumb." This is likely to cause motivational problems in the case of students who, for a variety of reasons, may not be able to compete favorably for grades and other types of academic recognition. (p. 290-291)

As schools make greater use of ability grouping and tracking as students move from the fifth to ninth grades, students risk not only depressed achievement but also reduced motivation to learn.

Thus, as schools make greater use of ability grouping and tracking as students move from the fifth to ninth grades, students risk not only depressed achievement but also reduced motivation to learn. In fact, the greater use of tracking and ability grouping through the middle grades coincides with the period during which students' can develop some of the self-limiting belief systems about intelligence, learning, and effort that Henderson and Dweck (1990) describe. The specific placements students encounter in the middle grades may further reinforce mistaken beliefs about ability that undermine student motivation and engagement in learning. Children placed in "gifted" classes, for example, may come to identify their ability with their label, understand that label as a form of "ability praise," and back away from challenges that might risk failure (Dweck, Kamins, & Mueller, 1997). Students in low groups may also "accept and internalize the stigma, coming to view themselves and their potential much as society and its agent, the schools, view them" (deLone, 1979:111). Moreover, in racially diverse schools, where ability grouping contributes to in-school segregations and "top" groups are disproportionately White, ability grouping ensures that African American and Latino students will encounter the harmful effects of what Steele calls "stereotype threat" every day, further undermining confidence of even those students who believe they could succeed in such settings.

On the face of it, ability grouping and tracking are incompatible with standards-based reforms. Standards of the professional associations assume that all students can achieve at high levels, learn from a challenging curriculum, benefit from work that requires reasoning, communicating, and problem solving. In contrast, tracking assumes that intelligence is inborn, that only a few can achieve at high levels, and that schools must differentiate curriculum so as to match teaching to measures of "ability." If the movement for higher standards is to succeed, existing tracking and ability grouping practices, along with the beliefs about intelligence and learning that support these practices, must change.

If the movement for higher standards is to succeed, existing tracking and ability grouping practices, along with the beliefs about intelligence and learning that support these practices, must change.

Despite the widespread use of ability grouping in the middle grades, a number of pioneering schools are detracking, setting the stage for a positive motivational climate and standards-based reforms (Oakes & Wells, 1996; Wheelock, 1992). The experiences of these schools underscore that the process of detracking requires not only regrouping students into heterogeneous teams but also establishing new norms, routines, and relationships that make the most of the diversity of regrouped classrooms. Grouping for diversity is essential if students are to learn multiple modes of creating good work, benefit from diverse perspectives on that work, grapple with the complexities of divergent thinking, and expand their definition of "being smart" to include making an effort, making mistakes, and seeking help. However, just as detracking depends on reducing the separation of groups of students from one another, it also demands that all students have equal access to challenging, diversified curriculum and instruction. Without detracking, executed through a review of all the ways in which schools distribute opportunities to learn then, the effort to develop a strong motivational climate school wide will be less than complete, and the majority of young adolescents will continue to resist doing work that meets standards.

Grading practices and second chances. In the explosion of conversations about "standards-based reform," the one topic that crops up over and over is the topic of student grades. Pointing out that A-work in one classroom can translate into C-work in another classroom, some critics decry grade inflation and call for more standardized grading practices within schools. Raising similar concerns of unequal expectations from school to school, others call for more reliance on standardizing testing as an apparently more "objective" measure of student achievement.

At the same time, some classroom teachers admit that grading depends on a variety of factors, not the least of which is their wish to use grades to motivate students. These good intentions can lead to substituting a "standard of effort" for a "standard of quality." For example, in a qualitative evaluation of standards-based reform in one large district, Barbara Neufeld (1996) found that most middle school teachers considered *effort* first, *completing work* second, and *quality of work* third in their grading decisions. But, in the absence of clear standards for student work, made concrete through rubrics and exemplars, grades based on effort only reinforce a climate of low expectations in the suggestion that effort is the *only* thing that can be expected from students. Grades for effort in the face of low quality work may even contribute to students' beliefs that, like their work, their effort too is inadequate, counting for little in producing competent work.

Grading for effort suggests that schools see effort as an end in itself. In contrast, a culture for standards-based reform views the cultivation of effort as the *means* to improved achievement and student work. So how can teachers use grades to motivate students without compromising the goal of better academic work? For starters, teachers who use rubrics and exemplars to establish clear standards for *good* and *excellent* work establish a motivational climate by clarifying standards for student work within classrooms. These teachers communicate that all students are expected to do quality work, and they back up this expectation by using *rewrite* or *incomplete* comments to give students additional time and opportunity to meet established standards.

Some teachers who focus on helping all students meet standards of quality also acknowledge that sometimes producing such work requires extra time. For example, in Peterborough, New Hampshire, Corval High School teacher Mike O'Leary (n.d.) allows students to request more time on projects using a formal "Extension Request Form." This form represents a contract between O'Leary and his students. It establishes the new due date for the project, and students must explain in writing the reasons for their request. If the project is turned in late beyond the second date, students lose points. As O'Leary explains, this system enhances student responsibility, planning, and motivation to complete work they feel proud of.

In addition, whole schools can motivate students by building opportunities for "second chances" and improving work into their regular school routines, including report card grading practices. Concerned that too many students settle for C or D grades, some may change their report cards to include *Honors*, *Pass*, and *Rewrite* grades to push students to work to revise inadequate work. At Battle Creek's Southwestern Junior High, for example, grading practices now offer A-grades only to students who do extra-credit projects, and students with grades that indicate work is incomplete receive regular reteaching and extra support to re-write and re-do low-quality work. The effect of these practices is evident in new student habits. As one student reports, "I do three 'extra credits' for A-level work in most of my classes now. Once you get into the hang of doing it, you just keep doing it!"

Ultimately, grading systems in a culture for standards-based reform should be multi-faceted and designed both to reach and motivate students. Practitioners and researchers alike offer a variety of approaches, some of which take into account the role of grading for motivating all students. For example, some propose systems for reporting on student progress that may be especially effective for discouraged students whose past failures leave them with little motivation for new challenges (Mac Iver & Reuman, 1993/1994). If

anything is clear, it is that one single letter grade without narrative explanation
is hardly adequate for meeting standards
of honesty and fairness that are themselves essential for sustaining teacher-student relationships and motivating stu-

*One single letter grade without narrative
explanation is hardly adequate for meeting
standards of honesty and fairness that are
themselves essential for sustaining teacher-
student relationships and motivating students.*

dents. Teachers developing grading practices to enhance student motivation
to meet standards must do so in collegial conversations within each school,
and in conversations with their students, as they develop shared expectations
for learning.

Challenging, diversified curriculum

Schools that are building a culture for standards-based reform know that
they cannot motivate students to produce good work when curriculum is
presented as the "same old thing." Students who, year after year, are presented with lists of arithmetic problems, worksheets, paragraphs to read and
summarize, and dates to memorize ultimately become what Shirley Fox, assistant principal of Howard Middle School in Orlando, Florida, calls "curriculum casualties." As Fox says:

> I've never met a student who didn't want to learn. Children
> love to learn. But we have children who are failing, acting out,
> unsuccessful. They're "curriculum casualties." We expect them
> to come in, sit down, and learn everything the way we present
> it. It should be the reverse. We need to diversify the curriculum
> to match different children.

The practical wisdom of Fox and others echo research findings on authentic pedagogy that emphasize the importance of hands-on, in-depth curriculum that pushes students to do good work that meets standards without
being standardized. By offering students a variety of routes into a particular
focus of study, students can become hooked on that study and motivated to
pursue learning in depth as they produce work that meets standards. For
example:

■ Teachers surveyed, interviewed, and observed as part of a ten-
school study of Expeditionary Learning reported that learning
expeditions increased students' motivation to participate and work
hard (AED, 1995). Students reported they were taking more re-

sponsibility for their own learning through collaborative group tasks, and that they had discovered they could succeed at intellectual challenges they thought were beyond their limits. Four-fifths of sixth graders expressed the belief that how much they had learned depended on their own efforts.

■ *Immigration 1850*, a challenging interdisciplinary curriculum developed at Project Zero draws on multiple ways of understanding 19th century immigration using primary sources and data, literature, and hands-on activities. Students may analyze family budgets for the period in relation to those of the 1990s, compile graphs and charts based on the data base of employment opportunities of the period, or write and produce plays based on newspaper accounts of the period. This wide range of ways of learning opens up possibilities for students to be smart in a wide variety of ways.

■ *The Human Biology* ("HumBio") Middle Grades Life Sciences Project based at Stanford University includes 24 interdisciplinary units to be used over a two-year period and is designed specifically to motivate students of various backgrounds and interests. Students learn through lab work, writing, role-playing, debates, and small groupwork. Student motivation benefits from the varied activities and peer assistance strategies of Elizabeth Cohen's work in complex instruction.

■ *The Connected Mathematics Project* (CMP), a comprehensive NCTM standards-based curriculum for grades 6-8, organizes learning around the "big ideas" in mathematics while requiring students to practice skills through projects, investigations, and extended problem solving. Many students arrive in the middle grades unfamiliar with curriculum that encourages them to reason carefully, explore ideas, and consider mathematical questions that may have more than one right answer. Within a few months, they become fully engaged. Thus, the Project notes, by the second year, "students start the year expecting to tackle more challenging problems and to construct arguments to justify their thinking and reasoning. They understand the demands of working in pairs, in groups, and individually. Establishing the expectation and pattern of classroom discourse is much easier" (Connected Mathematics Project, n.d.). In an independent evaluation of the curriculum, researchers found that CMP students did better on challenging open-response items that emphasize reasoning, communication, connections and problem solving compared to students in other curricula. In addition, CMP students seemed to retain more learning momentum over the summer months than other students (Hoover, Zawojewski, & Ridgway, 1997).

Diversifying curriculum is key to communicating to students that learning benefits from multiple perspectives on solving problems, whether in mathematics, science, literature, or social studies. In turn students demonstrate competence in a variety of ways and learn that success does not depend on behaving or thinking according to "one right way;" they can choose to be smart in a variety of ways. This effect is especially important for stereotype-threatened students (Steele, 1997). Student motivation further benefits when a diversified curriculum also includes multicultural content that connects them with the real world. As Asa Hilliard explains:

> Children, no matter what their racial or ethnic background, should be presented with pictures of the real world.... This is how we assure that children from every group will find themselves at the center of materials that they study. Motivation and self-esteem are deeply affected by the topics that we choose to present and by the coverage we choose to give those topics from a pluralistic perspective.

Provided a richer curriculum, students who have typically received only a basic skills curriculum may excel in ways that change teachers' expectations about these students.

A more multi-faceted, motivational curriculum also implies a curriculum that goes beyond the basic skills work characterized by worksheets and short-answer quizzes to include more opportunities for students to engage in reasoning and problem solving. Provided a richer curriculum, students who have typically received only a basic skills curriculum may excel in ways that change teachers' expectations about these students. For example, urban teachers implementing the *Junior Great Books* Program found that as they engaged students in challenging literature and implemented shared inquiry discussions in heterogeneous groups, their expectations of students changed (Wheelock, 1998a). As one noted:

The Program has given me a chance to see students in a different light. I've been impressed with some of the students. They thought up a lot of things I didn't think of. I could see a positive effect on some students who already had a lot of potential, especially with shared inquiry where they could form their own opinion.

Another added:

I was amazed with the answers of the lower-ability students. It made me ask what we are missing. After I did *Junior Great Books*, I had a little round-robin group reading a chapter book, and I heard these kids say, "I agree..." and "I disagree...."

Student investment in learning also improves when students can make choices within the curriculum. Teachers who begin to diverge from traditional teaching to allow students themselves to choose a subject to study in depth note that students who seem disengaged in "regular" classes begin to create work that reached beyond what teachers expected of them. For example, after Chattanooga's School for the Liberal Arts started requiring all eighth graders to produce a magazine on a subject of their choice, teacher Jeri McInturff reports:

Kids that I have to push on other things are constantly working on this. They ask for help, they ask to go to the library. It's the kids who need a push who really start to shine.... One overage child did his exit project on gangs in high school. His magazine was not very sophisticated, but his cover was a huge canvas painting he had photographed. He produced!

In many middle schools, "challenge" is often reserved for certain students selected for particular qualities, while others are left to experience the traditional fare of schooling. Challenge is seen as something valuable only to those with particular abilities, and often as something to pursue in settings where students are separated from others. However, in reality all students grow from challenge in teaching and learning assignments. Building a motivational climate means presenting meaningful challenges that are hard for every single student in ways that are as diverse as the learning styles of young adolescents, then building in the support to make meeting those challenges within everyone's grasp.

Extra support to help students meet standards in a challenging curriculum

Schools that are developing a culture of high standards communicate "caring rigor" by making sure that every student receives the support needed to meet standards for grade promotion. Educators in such schools know that grade retention undermines achievement and is a poor substitute for good teaching and learning. To avoid grade retention and ensure that students are prepared for the next grade, these schools offer every student effective help *early* and often during the school year, *before* rather than after students fail. Moreover, they see academic failure as evidence that they themselves have failed to provide students with the support they need to do better work.

Schools that assert that every student can learn take concrete steps to saturate school life with opportunities to access the extra help they need to succeed in their age-appropriate grade. The steps they take vary from school to school, but effective approaches have several characteristics in common: they are offered early and often as a normal part of the school routine; and they are often multi-dimensional, with supports for academic achievement made available in a variety of ways. Effective solutions are school-based solutions, designed and owned by each individual school. Schools that practice "caring rigor" and "rigorous caring" *anticipate* that students will need extra help to achieve. In these schools, teachers take responsibility for the success of every student. Their commitment reflects Sizer's observation (1996) that "the new assumption, which has emerged in the past fifteen years, is that if a kid does not get it in the usual way, the school should try to help him to get it in another way. Everybody has to get it. No one can be sorted out" (p. 35).

Schools that operate on the assumption that "everybody has to get it" recognize that some students whose work lags behind acceptable standards need numerous opportunities for extra help in order to succeed. For example, Jon Bennett, principal of Bluffton-Harrison Middle School in Indiana, explains that his school employed multiple approaches to increase the number of students leaving eighth grade who were prepared to succeed in high school. In its first year this strategy reduced the number of students who could have failed from 70 to 8. What's more, his school initiated efforts to reduce the numbers of students at risk of failing before the crisis of non-promotion became imminent. He reports:

> We started early in the year giving these students the support
> they needed. My assistant and I came in on weekends to help

students during Saturday School; we stayed after school to help kids who were struggling; we set up an after school tutoring program where students could receive additional assistance,from the teachers (who received their regular hourly rate of pay). Our school social worker met frequently with the at-risk kids to help them with study skills [and] went to homes weekly to visit with parents to offer suggestions on study skills. If the parents couldn't be reached at home, he visited them at work. We developed learning contracts with students who were failing classes to help them develop a plan for improvement, and we regularly called home with positive news for students who improved. We always followed up a postive phone call with a letter to the parent. We met with failing students either at grading time or mid-term time and explained that they needed to pass their classes and offered any assistance they desired to help them pass.

Bluffton-Harrison's story illustrates the features of an approach that produces success. First, a multi-faceted strategy attends to both academic and social needs and provides support at the time of need, not after failure occurs. Next, opportunities for second chances are part of the school culture, and even up to the last grading period, students know they will be supported in completing unfinished assignments. Third, support is intensely personal, with teachers monitoring progress of vulnerable students so that no one can fall between the cracks.

With these principles in mind, schools mix and match a variety of interventions to fit the conditions, resources, and the needs of their students. While supports take various forms – sometimes in-school, sometimes out-of-school – these are not add-ons provided to special students. Rather, extra help is a norm, a regular routine in the school's culture, a "regularity" that supports the larger culture of high standards and reflects the shared belief of school faculty that it is their primary responsibility to see that every student meets standards. For example:

- At New York City's School for the Physical City, humanities teachers persuaded all the school's teachers and support staff to contribute to making audio tapes of chapters of the challenging novel that launched their unit on the Great Depression so that under-prepared students could read along to borrowed tapes. In addition, teachers offer read-aloud session three times a week, with a schedule of chapters to be read on each day posted as an invitation to any student or teacher who wishes to attend (Cziko, 1996).

- At New York Prep, a middle school in East Harlem where fewer than a quarter of students were at grade level in mathematics, the principal established a math laboratory to give students in small groups three additonal periods a week of enrichment to supplement their regular course work, an action resulting in dramatic gains in math achievement scores (Steinberg, 1996).

- At Southwestern Junior High in Battle Creek, Michigan, Principal Steve Hoelscher says, "If you were to come into our school any day after school, you would see about 50 students working away to re-do unfinished or sub-standard work." At Southwestern, college students and a para-professional supervise this after-school time. In addition, Southwestern sets aside one period daily for reteaching and extension, a time for students to re-work assignments (and for teachers to re-teach concepts in new ways) or to extend learning in specific areas of the curriculum. Teachers also offer before-school tutoring for any student who needs it. In addition, given the school's commitment to heterogeneous grouping and inclusion of students with disabilities, special education teachers are co-teaching with regular teachers to provide extra help to students who need it in all classrooms.

- Two U.S. Department of Education Blue Ribbon School finalists in Michigan found different ways to provide extra help for students who needed it. At Highlander Middle School in Howell, a peer tutoring program trains 50 eighth grade students to spend time after school to help students in the sixth and seventh grades. "The older students volunteer their time, one-on-one, to help a younger student whose grade may have slipped below a C in reading, writing, or math," Principal Charles Kraeger reports. At the Mary Thompson Middle School in Southfield, Principal Michael Horn reports that the school's assurance of transportation home is a key part of an after-school tutoring program designed to help students improve their understanding in science (Ilka, 1997).

■ South Hadley (Massachusetts) Middle School encourages every single student – whether in danger of failing or in need of help with organizational or study skills – to join a one-hour daily after-school homework help program. As Principal Richard Sawyer explains, "Sometimes parents are working two jobs, one in the day and one at night, and no one's able to make sure they've done their homework. Or sometimes parents find they have problems supervising, because they get into disagreements about which work will be done, or how it will be done." The program is informal and run like a club. Dues are $12.00 a week for those who can pay, with scholarships available. A teacher's aide confers with regular teachers about specific students' needs and also offers help to all students. The program is part of a school-wide effort to offer extra help to students, including one-to-one tutoring for students with disabilities (Aguilar, 1997).

■ Ninth graders at Montclair (New Jersey) High School benefit from the extra support provided by community volunteers who are trained as writing coaches by professional writers and who staff the school-community writing center. Coaches provide on-the-spot help to any student working in the school's writing lab, so that five adults may be available to support 25 students at any given time. In addition, coaches ease teachers' workload, and allow teachers to use the writing process to its fullest extent, by reading early drafts of papers assigned in tandem with challenging readings in ninth grade World Literature classes.

■ In order to support every student in a challenging standards-based college-preparatory curriculum developed by the Interactive Mathematics Project, Boston's Fenway Middle College High School enrolls all ninth graders in an additional twice-weekly math course where students review math operations and practice test-taking. Teacher Linda Nathan explains, "Our purpose is to shore up the students' skills since many have not mastered basic math facts like multiplication of fractions and math properties." The school also schedules an intensive writing skills workshop once a week and a regular after-school learning center, and some students complete unfinished work in a school-based summer school. Nathan reports, "Each year we are progressing a bit, becoming better and better. Our inching up on SAT scores is evidence of that, as is the number of students who go on to careers in math and science."

■ At Baltimore's Canton Middle School, teachers make daily recordings of each class's homework assignment. Then, when parents phone the school, they can hear from Mrs. R. who expects her students to turn in their final draft of their persuasive letter arguing for or against the city's building a monument to slavery; from Mr. K., who reports that the next day students will be quizzed on the data in their climatograms; and from Ms. W., who suggests that parents ask their children to summarize the plot of *The Autobiography of Ms. Jane Pittman*. This effort complements after-school tutoring for students who are paired with college students studying for their teacher certification.

■ Willard Junior High School, in Berkeley, California, gives students still developing reading skills the boost they need to succeed in grade-level heterogeneous classes by offering extra (not pull-out) help in "jump start" classes that introduce students to the content of the grade-level curriculum *before* their regular classes tackle a new unit. For example, if the grade-level curriculum calls for reading *Lord of the Flies*, teachers will introduce vulnerable students to the novel's plot, characters, and vocabulary through a viewing and discussion of the movie prior to their reading the book.

■ Tom Browne Middle School in Corpus Christi runs an extended tutorial program for one week beyond the school year for students, many of whom are failing in more than one class, to complete grade-level academic standards. For three hours each morning, the school's own teachers work with students to complete language arts, history, and science assignments left unfinished or unsatisfactory from the spring semester. Some students substitute this time for summer school; others go on to summer school but with the strongest possible foundation for promotion. In 1998, all but a few of the school's students met the district's standards as a result of this opportunity program.

While extra-help strategies vary according to school conditions, district requirements, and available resources, all reflect a basic commitment to student welfare and a commitment to prevent failure before it occurs. But not all middle schools can rely on this strategy alone. In some districts, middle grades schools receive students who may already be two or more years behind their age-appropriate grade, leaving them vulnerable to dropping out with less than a ninth grade education. In response to such students, some middle schools develop additional special programs so that students can receive extra help and catch up with their peers. For example:

■ Faced with some students turning age 17 in the seventh and eighth grades, Aiken County, South Carolina, educators have created a "Seven to Nine" program, which allows students who meet established criteria to jump from seventh to ninth grade. The summer after seventh grade, they go to summer school, then enter ninth grade from that program, where they are assigned a special counselor who provides the personal support for success, including after-school tutoring, reminders to get to school on time, and once-a-week group counseling. Dr. Frank Roberson, Assistant Superintendent for Instructional Services of Aiken County Public Schools, reports that students in the program work harder and are more motivated to graduate in part because they are in the grade they should be in (Grossman, 1998).

■ Understanding that overage students in the middle grades are vulnerable to dropping out far short of their graduation year, some West Palm Beach County, Florida, middle schools are offering students promotion into ninth grade contingent on their participation in a summer program. Then, before entering high school, high school staff meet with students and their parents to sign a contract spelling out attendance and homework expectations as a condition for enrolling as students with"No Limits." Once in ninth grade, students receive close attention in small classes and from counselors who provide study skills support. For many students, the program's offer of a second chance to "do it right" and the opportunity to stay close to their age-cohort provides a significant source of motivation to stay in school (Patrick, 1998).

With the growing number of students retained in grade in the name of standards, the need to develop extra-help responses with personalized support at the individual school level is urgent. Schools must offer extra-help strategies in their appropriate grade level, not as add-ons but within a school culture that reflects school-wide commitment to equal access to knowledge, a "press for achievement," and research-based professional teaching practices (Smith & Shepard, 1989; Oakes, 1989).

Efforts to mandate grade retention and summer school district wide or programs that shuffle failing eighth graders off to a separate transitional school may be well-intentioned, but such programs are likely to fall short of expectations. Simply put, district-designed remedial programs let individual schools off the hook for ensuring that every student succeeds. The knowledge that "there's always the district summer school" may tempt schools to tolerate failure within their own walls, allowing teachers to pass responsibility on to others in separate remedial settings. Likewise, separate transition programs represent less a second-chance than a dead-end placement, the last step before dropping out. In contrast, the examples offered by schools committed to ensuring that all tudents meet standards in the company of their peers illustrate that alternatives to either grade retention or social promotion are within the reach of all schools willing to use resources to design and implement them.

Students require more than talk if they are to take values of effort and risk taking seriously. They also need concrete support and opportunities to learn to make their effort worthwhile. To this end, schools back up the expectation that students will work harder by providing extra help and second chances for turning incomplete work into work that meets standards as a regular feature of school life.

Flexible block scheduling

New structures and practices that support a motivational climate also require changes in schools' schedules so that teachers have the authority to allocate time in ways that meet new expectations for student work. As Charles Jervis of Virginia's Auburn High School notes:

> As a former English, speech, and drama teacher, I can attest to
> the frustrations of not being able to complete a writing assign-

ment (with peer responses and revisions) in a 45-minute lesson and certainly not being able to have much of a play rehearsal!

I believe the key is flexibility in scheduling, whatever form is used. Some shorter periods may be fine, but longer ones are needed as well. The best of all worlds, in my opinion, is when a team has a large block of time and can determine how to structure it on a daily/weekly basis.

Schools that are setting the stage for such learning figure out ways to shift the schedule to fit the expectations of standards-based learning, including both more in-depth curriculum projects and extra help. For example, Paula Hutton, principal of Sullivan Middle School in Lowell, Massachusetts, asserts "Planning for extra help and everything else is harder than you think! I've turned to Lynn Canady for some solutions... and he inspired an idea of my own." As Hutton explains, her schedule accommodates five-teacher teams that include special education or English-as-a-Second-Language teachers, teacher advisories, and student choice:

On *A* day, a student has a core subject: math, science, and writing and a "non-core"(physical education, art, family life, consumer science, tech ed., world language, or music). On B day a student has English/language arts, social studies and an interdisciplinary block. For each marking period, students then take either (1) a challenge, (2) a review, (3) an "I-Search Project" or (4) a T.A.P. (teacher activity period) which is interdisciplinary in nature and connected with a core subject. The student chooses this T.A.P. from a list of selections. In the past these have included selections such as rocketry, city history, Junior Great Books, or geometry. At the end of the day for 25 minutes, each student will also participate in an advisor/advisee period.

From Hutton's perspective, the payoff of this schedule is in the better teacher-student ratios and opportunities for in-depth projects and extended learning. She adds:

The new schedule creates longer blocks of time for instruction (80 minutes instead of 42-47), and it lowers the per-pupil ratio. It allows teachers to see 65 kids per day instead of 130. It's all gains except that if a student is absent, he or she will have to wait one extra day to make contact with those teachers because he will return on an *A* or *B* day. The teachers promise to help them. I have 94% daily attendance, so that should be an acceptable risk.

Schools that set out to ensure that students do work that meets standards and learn for understanding inevitably find that a traditional schedule of 45-minute periods is too tight to allow students to study complex problems, investigate ideas in science labs, and execute projects for a real world audience. Science investigations, cooperative learning, and Socratic discussions followed by reflective writing about literature, for example, all require extended time. When schools take on the commitment of building a culture for standards-based reform, they also take on the commitment of ensuring that school routines support the diversification of curriculum and extra-help opportunities essential to support student engagement in learning.

Challenge, cooperation, and participation in and outside classrooms

Student reports that middle school life is "boring" or "too easy" are signals that a motivational climate must include challenge. At the same time, young adolescent students may find "challenge" difficult to pursue working alone at their seat or at home. In fact, a large body of research indicates that students working together persist longer with more difficult problems than when they are working alone (Cohen, 1986; Johnson & Johnson, 1975; Slavin, 1987). Clearly a motivational climate requires a balance of challenge and cooperation. It also requires redefining competition in inclusive terms to encourage the participation of every student in challenging activities.

Students working together persist longer with more difficult problems than when they are working alone.

In some schools, teachers applying simplistic notions about using competition to motivate students can actually turn students away from effort. Indeed, schools may execute competetive activities in ways that, at best, distort their potential to motivate students to improve on their "personal best" or, at worst, feed interpersonal hostilities and disrupt the school as a community of learners. For example, Pauline Lipman (1998) describes how one school's efforts to motivate its young adolescent students through competition between teams turned ugly and only reinforced negative stereotypes as students from tracked, racially identifiable teams were pitted against one another. In other ways, the emphasis on and recognition of individual success alienated a number of students in the schools Lipman studied, especially African American students who came to identify the academic accomplishments the schools recognized as "a white thing."

In contrast, schools working to build a supportive climate motivate students through challenges that also honor values of cooperation, inclusion, and participation. In Ron Berger's classes, for example, students work together as a class for an entire year to solve a complex mathematics problem from the real world, leaving students proudly reporting at the end of the year, "This was really, really hard, but our class almost solved it." In addition, each year, every student creates an original graphic art piece, in the form of an advertisement for a local business and submits the finished work to the local newspaper for judging and publication. Because Berger routinely expects student to do work that meets standards, every student submits work of high quality. Then, even when they do not win, students can report, "I did lots of drafts. I didn't win, but I really liked what I did."

Some students find challenge in the thrill of competition, putting their skills on the line to determine how they measure up in the larger world. The choice-block at the Devens, Massachusetts, Parker Public Charter School, thus encourages students to pursue personal interests into arenas beyond the school. For example, Parker fields multiple teams in Odyssey of the Mind competitions, regional debate tournaments, and the county math league and MathCounts competitions, all working with choice-block or after-school coaches. Individual students also participate in state chess tournaments, skating competitions, regional orchestras, and visual arts competions, reflecting their diverse callings.

Other students find the right balance of challenge and cooperation in settings where competition is tempered with school-wide goals. For example, in the New Haven, Connecticut, middle grades, the work of school librarians has set off an explosion of reading incentive programs. Within each middle school, librarians create images such as gigantic thermometers to chart the growth in the number of books students throughout the school read during the year. With high goals set by the Library Power Committee in each school, it becomes clear that the more students are reading, the closer the school will come to meeting its own expectations. In addition, at the instigation of West

Hills Middle School librarian Gail Hall, librarians have organized a district-wide reading incentive program, now known as New Haven's annual "Book Bowl." In preparation, students read quality young adult fiction, then answer questions they devise in in-school play-offs. Finally, teams from each school compete in a city-wide tournament. With an emphasis on participation, not on fielding only the smartest, the number of students involved has grown exponentially. One school organized into 15 teams during the first year of participation; in another low-income school, the number participating jumped from 20 to over 100 in one year, and many students were reading whole books for the first time in their school careers. Over all, the "Book Bowl" challenge has meant that more middle grades students in New Haven are reading more good books more often and having fun doing it (Wheelock, 1998b).

Whether in or outside of classrooms, challenging projects are likely to be the ones that stick with students long after the school year has ended. For example, teachers at Campus Middle School in Englewood, Colorado, found that students would describe a perfectly completed spelling test as their "*best*" work because it received an 100% grade from their teacher. However, asked to describe work they found *memorable*, students used words that described effort and engagement: "I never worked so hard, but it was worth it;" "It was really hard but I learned a lot;" and "I spent 12 hours on it, but it was the most fun project I ever did; also I did well on it" (Wasserstein, 1995).

If "challenge" is to motivate all students to do work that meets standards, teachers must ensure that it is woven into the fabric of the school in such a way that it is available to all students. Moreover, when teachers structure challenges to emphasize that students working together will produce the "best" work, whether through addressing real world problems or meeting school-wide goals, students can share the pleasure of challenge, celebrate success, and feel "safe to be smart" knowing that they share both the difficulties and the benefits of hard work in the company of their peers.

If 'challenge' is to motivate all students to do work that meets standards, teachers must ensure that it is woven into the fabric of the school in such a way that it is available to all students.

Counseling and mentoring to match students' aspirations

Establishing a school climate that motivates all students also means connecting with students' individual goals through counseling and mentoring that link students' aspirations to school performance. In particular, these efforts must provide students with information about future opportunities, so that students can make choices that will help them realize their own goals. The necessity for such approaches was made all the more urgent by a recent study that found that information about financial support and course selection are more important than "brains" in determining who goes to college. As reported by the Associated Press (1998), a study for the Department of Education byMathtech, Inc. found that even with high scores on standardized tests, students from low-income families are less likely to attend college than all students from middle- and top-income groups. The study concluded that information in the middle grades about the courses to take and the availability of financial aid boosted students' enrollment in post-secondary education. Reflecting these findings, the Department of Education (1997) advised that the middle-grades years are the time for students to plan for a course of study that will set them up for college.

Middle schools that take this advice seriously focus counseling and mentoring resources on helping all their students develop the plans and resolve that will help them realize their own aspirations for future opportunities. For example, at Crete-Monee Junior High School in Crete, Illinois, classroom-based advisories guide seventh and eighth graders through a structured process for identifying strengths, values, and interests and learning decision-making strategies so that they can make informed choices about their futures. Using a curriculum developed by school counselors called "Pathways to Success: Individualized Educational and Career Plan," students make the connection between their academic programs and possible careers. As a result, by the time they leave eighth grade, students have a clear written plan for the course of study they will follow in high school that matches their personal aspirations and provides them with concrete goals worth working toward.

Classroom-based counseling around developing the knowledge, beliefs, attitudes, and skills that fuel student engagement reaches all students and contributes to a motivational school culture. In some middle schools, students who are deeply discouraged, overage for grade, or need a special hook into school may also need additional mentoring experiences. For example, Baltimore's Canton Middle School principal Craig

Classroom-based counseling around goals of developing the knowledge, beliefs, attitudes, and skills that fuel student engagement reaches all students and contributes to a motivational school culture.

128

Spilman (1996) works in partnership with a downtown hotel to arrange for jobs one day each week for such students. Together the hotel and school condition student employment on students' signing contracts agreeing to improve their attendance and academic performance. After a successful first year, the school extended the program to include an interdisciplinary curriculum linking work and the core curriculum and expanded the number of job sites. The overall results have been improvements in both attendance and discipline.

Although young adolescents' aspirations for future success is well-documented, many students are not convinced that teachers support their strivings. For example, a recent Rhode Island study found that although the state's high school teachers believe that nearly every student can graduate from high school, one quarter of the state's ninth graders do not believe their teachers expect them to graduate; and although high-school teachers believe that more than 80 percent of their students can graduate from a two-year or four-year college, only about 65 percent of the state's ninth graders say that their teachers expect them to go to college (Krieger, 1998a). Counseling and mentoring strategies are concrete means of signaling that teachers are behind their students and willing to help make students' dreams come true. In acknowledging and connecting with students' aspirations, these strategies also help create a school climate that motivates all students to meet standards.

Pulling it all together: The Talent Development Middle School

Success in creating and sustaining a strong school climate that both holds students and motivates them to put forth the effort necessary to "meet standards" depends on a variety of changes in schools' standard operating procedures. Implementing such multi-faceted change benefits from a whole-school change strategy and the guidance of a model grounded in applied research. The Talent Development Middle School model is one that offers such direction and support for schools seeking to create a school climate that nurtures and challenges students at the same time.

The components of the Talent Development model evolve from applied research by the Center for Research on the Education of Students Placed at Risk (CRESPAR), co-directed by staff at Howard University and the Johns Hopkins University. Everything about Talent Development Schools' organization, curriculum, teaching, and student support structures stems from the belief that schools must *develop students' talent*. Talent Development principles argue that schools can do this best when every student has access to an engaging standards-based curriculum in heterogeneous classrooms, and when every student is in classrooms with caring teachers and peers who are "rooting for them to do well, who are encouraging them to give their best in the classroom, and who are doing everything in their power to help them improve their skills and increase their understanding" (Mac Iver & Plank, 1996, p. 1).

As a Talent Development School, Central East Middle School in Philadelphia has set out to prove that every student can succeed in the middle grades by putting into place a set of practices that complement one another and create a school culture that encompasses both caring relationships and challenging learning opportunities. The school fosters positive relationships by organizing students and teachers into teams, with the same group of teachers remaining with their students for three years through the middle grades. Teacher-student advisories mean that every student has an advocate who knows him or her well in the school.

A rich curriculum and innovative instructional approaches, with an emphasis on cooperative learning, provide a huge boost in students' motivation for learning at Cenral East. Students study reading, English, and language arts in a 90-minute block so that teachers can work with fewer students for more extended periods of time. For example, working with a curriculum called *Student Team Literature*, students read award-winning, multicultural young adult fiction, then work in pairs to ask and answer questions, discuss the novel, and master vocabulary from the novel. In mathematics, students all use the Chicago Mathematics textbooks, providing them with an NCTM standards-based course of study, combined with peer assisted cooperative groups. Students' science curriculum draws on recent National Science Foundation-sponsored curriculum projects.

At Central East, teachers receive professional development based on the specific curriculum they will be teaching. In addition to an intensive summer program in the curriculum selected for each subject area, coaching and follow-up workshops help the teachers enact the curriculum during the year. New curricula have been phased in at a pace that sustains momentum but uses resources strategically and does not overwhelm teachers. Thus, language arts teachers have received training in the *Student Team Literature Program*; math teachers received professional development in the Chicago

Mathematics curriculum; and science teachers have had access to professional development in new NSF-supported science curricula materials. Although not all teachers initially bought into staff development for the new curricula, the "low implementers" who have observed benefits are becoming more active users of the new curricula, and observers believe that students will make greater gains as teachers use materials and instructional strategies more widely and adeptly, and as students become more accustomed to the expectations and roles of peer assistance.

Central East has also adopted a variety of ways to extend extra help to students who need a boost to succeed in the heterogeneous standards-based curriculum. For example, the school offers time for reteaching and development of study skills through a homework club where teachers and peer tutors work one-on-one with students. With some students pushed to attend by teachers and others attending on their own, teachers observe students' paying better attention to their work and say more are getting their homework done. Even more effective has been the assignment of some students to an "elective replacement" class in math. This approach provides a double dose of math for students who are significantly behind grade-level expectations and for those who want a boost to compete for a place in college-preparatory high schools. Focused on strengthening procedural knowledge and math skills in daily classes over ten weeks, classes are organized for maximum participation and effect.

Computer-based instruction combined with structured cooperative learning means that students can help one another and develop a commitment to one another's success. In addition, students learn through math games that add diversity to the learning experiences and whole-class instruction that often rehearses students in using math concepts prior to their introduction in the regular math class. As a result of this approach, students at all test-score levels make dramatic gains in procedural knowledge and skills. In addition, teachers are reassured that they can move ahead in a standards-based curriculum grounded in conceptual understanding and reasoning, knowing that their weaker students will be receiving extra help in operational skills in the elective replacement. Johns Hopkins research reports that this intervention is highly cost-effective, costing about one-third as much as extra help offered by contracting out to for-profit vendors like Sylvan Learning Systems (Mac Iver, Balfanz,& Plank, 1998).

Finally, teachers have also implemented an advisory curriculum that guides students in connecting their own aspirations with such personal decisions as high school course selection. In seventh grade, students that follow a curriculum in "Career Exploration and Educational Decision-Making" that begins with students making a "Contract with Myself" to fulfill expectations related to study habits, grades, and effort. Then, over the course of the year, students connect the realities of high school course offerings to their own educational, occupational, and personal interests through a variety of exercises and activities. At various points during the year, students review and renew their personal "contracts" to assess their own status in relation to their goals.

The implementation of Talent Development Schools, like other whole-school change models, is complex, realized by phasing changes into the school over a period of several years. However, data from Central East indicate that the strategy has dramatically elevated the achievement of all students at the school. For example, reading and comprehension scores for students have jumped for students at all score levels, with students with the highest scores thriving in the *Student Team Literature* curriculum (Mac Iver, Plank, & Balfanz, n.d.). These gains, along with those in mathematics, draw from new curriculum and extra academic support, but they also draw from an overall climate that intentionally fosters greater student motivation and engagement based on positive relationships and peer assistance. Outside coaching, focused professional development, and informed leadership all work together to create a supportive context for teachers as well. As Central East demonstrates, developing a motivational climate for learning goes beyond any one change to embrace a set of changes, not as a set of unrelated "add-ons" that characterize "Christmas tree schools" (Bryk, 1993), but to create a coherent culture grounded in research-based strategies for improving student engagement.

Conclusion

Making school a place where students want to be every day and where they pursue "good work" once they get there requires large and small changes in school life. Schools that realize the promise of helping all students produce work of high quality must avoid the many school norms, values, and routines that undermine student motivation. Beliefs that student achievement is limited by "innate ability" along with and the notion that students cannot transcend challenging social circumstances are not compatible with a culture for standards-based reforms. Nor can standards-based reforms take root in school cultures that tolerate tracking and ability grouping, worksheet-based curriculum and instruction, or indifference to students' unique backgrounds and aspirations.

No one aspect of school practice, whether in student-teacher relationships, curriculum and instruction, or support services can create a motivational climate strong enough to ensure that every student will meet standards. Taken together, however, new beliefs, structures, and routines can go a long way to strengthen student motivation for learning and support a culture for standards-based reform. Along with a diversified curriculum, routines that honor challenge, encourage students to ask questions, seek and provide peer assistance, and provide extra support for learning can contribute to a larger school culture where all students feel safe to be smart.

THE THIRD ESSENTIAL BUILDING BLOCK:
A COLLEGIAL COMMUNITY FOR PROFESSIONAL PRACTICE AND ACCOUNTABILITY

Building a culture for standards-based reform means that educators put student work at the forefront of learning, move toward greater instructional coherence, and nurture a more compelling motivational climate. A collegial professional community within each school is essential to this work. Creating such a community goes beyond attending to the professional practice of individual teachers. It also involves enhancing the relationships and interactions of teachers within schools.

As teachers shape their practice to standards, many are working to deepen their knowledge base and expand their repertoire of teaching strategies to meet the expectations of specific curriculum frameworks. However, if teachers remain isolated from one another in schools, lacking opportunities to rethink teaching and learning school wide, even those with extensive knowledge of their subject areas will have difficulty mobilizing all students to learn for understanding. A school culture that can rise to the expectations of standards-based reform must be a culture in which teachers share professional knowledge and skills, exchange ideas and information, and support and cri-

Without a network of professional relationships to nurture teachers' opportunities to learn, standards-based reforms will collapse under their own weight.

tique one another as they implement best practices and press students toward producing better work more of the time. Without a network of professional relationships to nurture teachers' opportunities to learn, standards-based reforms will collapse under their own weight.

"Norms of collegiality"

Developing new relationships within the school community goes against the experience of many teachers who are frequently left on their own to deliver instruction. Indeed, teachers' entrepreneurial spirit and autonomy is often celebrated as key to innovation in schools across the country (Cohen, 1995). But as often as teachers' individualism fosters good practice, it may also breed cynicism in the face of new expectations for standards-based learning. As reformer Michelle Fine (1994) found as she helped teachers develop small learning communities within large urban high schools, the "communitarian damage" that can accumulate over years of neglecting the human connections within schools takes an enormous toll on many teachers' will and skill for taking collective action to improve student achievement. In the absence of a community for professional practice, many teachers will remain incapacitated in the face of new expectations for student learning.

Recent thinking on developing a community for professional practice highlights that professional collegiality is perhaps the most important contributor to teachers' capacity to weather change and take advantage of resources available to advance reform. For example, Berkeley's Judith Warren Little reports that while formal staff development made a contribution to teachers' effectiveness in desegregating schools, even more powerful were the "norms of collegiality" and "norms of continuous improvement" that evolved from educators' relationships in those schools (Sparks, 1993). As she notes:

> In fact, schools that were well organized [around] a robust set of professional relationships were able to take advantage of even what we would all call weak forms of staff development.... They were well-organized to take advantage of the one-shot presentation because they had a capacity to discuss ideas back on their home ground.

Moreover, says Little, "Schools that did not have those norms, in which teachers were isolated and often alienated, were only tangentially and weakly helped by even the best of the formal staff development."

Teacher collegiality is not the same as congeniality or social comfort. Rather collegiality draws on a sense of interdependence among professionals, an awareness that student success depends on sharing responsibility for professional practice, and a realization that one teacher's individual success is limited unless all teachers work together to ensure the success of everyone. Little also emphasizes that a norm of collegiality embraces a respect for teacher initiative and ideas, conversations about student work and teaching, and a shared commitment to student learning goals. It is when teachers exploit collegial relationships to discuss problems of teaching and learning that they can begin to pare down their goals and focus on changing classroom practice to meet those goals.

Making time for conversations about professional practice

Developing a community for professional practice means relearning habits of individual decision making and isolated practice. But teachers cannot nurture professional collegiality without the time to do so. Creating a climate for professional practice, then, first involves scheduling time for teachers to meet together to talk about teaching and learning, review their work in light of research, and engage in conversations about student work.

Good middle school practitioners have long advocated daily common planning time for teacher teams to work together to plan curriculum and solve problems that develop in relation to particular students. Recent research supports schools' experience that common planning time, implemented with other middle school practices, results in improved learning (Felner, Jackson, Kasak, Mulhall, Brand, & Flowers, 1998). In addition, some middle schools are discovering additional approaches that allow for more extended professional conversations. For example:

- Educators at Einstein Middle School in Shoreline, Washington, traded in weekly all-staff meetings and other teacher committees so that they could meet in study groups to examine student work. They also agreed to use funds for professional development, traditionally used for out-of-school workshops, to pay teachers to meet together beyond the contract day (ATLAS Communities, 1997b).

■ Teachers at Philadelphia's Baldy Middle School now devote all the time allocated under their contract for staff development and all annual time that would ordinarily be committed to faculty meetings to whole faculty study groups that meet biweekly before and after school. In addition, some teachers meet together on their own time.

■ Chicago's Hefferan (K-8) School has freed up time for teacher discussions by adopting a weekly schedule that includes four days of intense classroom work with a fifth "Resource Day" for intensive art, music, physical education, and computer lab. With this schedule, teachers meet weekly for a full day of professional learning (Hirsh, 1997).

■ Harbor Middle School, one of several small schools piloting new practices in Boston Public Schools, has formed partnerships with numerous community and youth organizations who offer a variety of enrichment activities one full afternoon each week so that teachers can meet together weekly for a long block of time.

■ In New York City, teachers at New York Prep, a middle school in East Harlem, extend the school day by 25 minutes Mondays through Thursdays, allowing them to release students early on Fridays so that they can enjoy several hours of time together weekly (Steinberg, 1996).

Regular time for teacher conversations goes hand in hand with a more pointed focus on student work. Although standards developed by teachers' own professional associations may outline what students should know and be able to do, teachers in each school must still reach consensus on what "good" student learning looks like, the assignments that will get all students' work closer to that standard, and the ways in which they will make sure that all students get the necessary help to produce that work. Building a culture for standards-based reforms, then, means using time for teacher conversation to develop shared goals, criteria for good work, and tools that communicate those shared standards to students.

Building collegial commitment for change

Professional collegiality also relies on leadership for change. Without a principal committed to developing a collegial community among educators, few schools will be able to sustain a professional climate that can support the ambitious instructional reforms envisioned by new standards. Schools need principals who can access available resources and partnerships to support teachers as they move toward new learning goals. School leaders must also facilitate a variety of approaches to professional development that help teachers connect their own practice to research and school-wide goals and set the tone for the school as a learning community.

Without a principal committed to developing a collegial community among educators, few schools will be able to sustain a professional climate that can support the ambitious instructional reforms envisioned by new standards.

"Inside" leadership nurtures shared commitment to new goals. Finding the time for teachers to meet together is clearly a first step in developing a community for professional practice. It is not sufficient, however. Developing teacher collegiality also means that teacher conversations must ultimately focus on improving teaching and learning within a larger context of shared goals for student learning. In some schools, state or district standards may define these goals. In others, schools themselves may set their own goals in terms of student work quality. In either case, school-based leadership is essential to guide faculty toward new routines that support standards-based reforms. Principals must be willing to persist in asking tough questions, and they must work with teachers to develop school-wide solutions to problems that everyone in the school can "own." In the process of piloting new routines developed school wide, teachers can then begin to rethink their beliefs and practice in the company of other professionals.

For example, Steve Hoelscher, former principal of Southwestern Junior High School in Battle Creek, recalls that in the early years of his school's eight-year reform process, many teachers subscribed to the slogan "All Students Can Learn" without giving it much thought. However, in Hoelscher's view, lip service to this ideal was not enough. As he reports:

> Finally we got everyone together and asked, 'Well, if all kids can learn, how come so-and-so isn't learning?' We'd talk about specific students, and it came down to the fact that kids weren't

learning because they weren't turning in their homework and weren't passing tests. It sounds simple, but it was a place to start.

What Hoelscher calls the "drive toward quality" at Southwestern, a racially mixed school where three-quarters of the students come from low-income families, gathered steam through regular discussions with the faculty as a whole. These discussions at first focused on the gap between professed beliefs and real practices. Under Hoelscher's leadership, growing awareness of this gap created a momentum for change. As Hoelscher explains:

> We asked, "What would we have to do to see that all kids really did learn?" We imagined, "What if we said every kid had to turn in every assignment and pass every test?" We realized we needed to communicate to all kids that we would just not accept substandard work. At first it was a struggle, and we had to discard a whole lot of ideas about which kids would or would not succeed. We couldn't talk any more about problems kids had because they came from single-parent homes. We had to decide that we could make a difference.

Southwestern teachers have learned to make a difference through ongoing professional discussions during "quality time," a biweekly three-hour block of time that the school gains from adding teaching time to other school days. Over the years, these conversations, along with annual summer professional development that involves 80 percent of the faculty, have resulted in significant changes in teaching and learning, with a focus on structured cooperative learning, heterogeneous grouping, extra help for students who may need it, and new grading practices. These new routines coupled with subject area-based professional development have paid off in higher test scores, especially in science and writing, for all student groups. With eight years of steady reform behind them, the percentage of Southwestern students scoring at the "proficient" level in science now stands at five times the rate for the state overall. Differences between White and African American students' test scores have virtually vanished as teachers have backed up their expectation that every student will succeed by multiple changes in classroom practice.

Southwestern's story illustrates the gains middle schools can make when teachers take the time to develop a consensus about school goals and the opportunities to learn new practices to help them reach those goals. Changes in practice or beliefs at Southwestern did not come "naturally." Rather they emerged as school leaders helped teachers try new approaches that were based on learning goals the teachers, as a group, set for their students.

Like other middle schools that begin to create a climate for more professional practice, Southwestern also benefited from a partnership that linked its own "inside" leadership to "outside" partners for change. In Southwestern's case, Steve Hoelscher, once he had pointed his school in a new direction, got a boost from his school's involvement with the Kellogg Foundation's Middle Start Project. Similar partnerships around the country have assisted other school leaders as they adapt to the demands of standards-based reforms. Moreover, schools may join with different partnerships for different purposes during different stages of their reform work. For example, Craig Spilman of Baltimore's Canton Middle School reports that in his school's early years of restructuring, a partnership with his state's middle school reform project yielded many collegial contacts, ideas, and resources for introducing middle school structures to his faculty. In more recent years, as the school has focused more explicitly on improving classroom practice, Spilman has hooked up with Expeditionary Learning as a way to link curriculum and instructional goals to professional development.

"Outside" coaches help teachers negotiate changes in teaching and learning. Besides prodding teachers toward new practice by creating opportunities for professional conversations, some principals in reforming schools also contract for coaching with an outside facilitator as a way of supporting teachers as they move toward standards-based reforms. As educators in one study of a state-wide reform effort noted, "If we are going to be asked to adopt new practices, we need help in doing so," and "We are asked to be a vast support system for our students now more than ever. If we are to be effective, we need a support system ourselves" (New Hampshire Business Roundtable on Education, 1996:29).

Coaches from outside play a variety of roles depending on the needs of the school. In some cases, they can help schools develop new teaming structures and routines. They may also help schools identify assets within the faculty, negotiate internal discords, and connect teachers to professional resources and networks outside their own school. Recognizing the importance of these roles, many school reform projects routinely offer organizational coaching to principals as they engage in a whole school reform process.

Outside coaches working with teachers to adopt new practice can also model relationships of trust for faculty. As Carleen Murphy (1988) notes, teachers must believe that their consultant is going to return to work with them over the long haul, and they must see their consultant as being committed to their success in establishing new practice. Whether through the guidance of an insider or the coaching of an outsider, schools move toward creating a "press for achievement" and higher standards for student work in all classrooms throughout the school when they have stable support over time directed to this purpose.

A collegial culture relies on teachers' learning and working together on common problems of teaching, and one means for developing that peer support is through whole faculty study groups.

Whole faculty study groups help develop a community for professional practice. Ultimately, a collegial culture relies on teachers' learning and working together on common problems of teaching, and one means for developing that peer support is through whole faculty study groups. Faculty- wide discussions about school goals begin with small teacher-based study groups organized to involve every teacher in the school in regular discussions of student work, teaching, and curriculum. This approach has the potential of pointing a whole school faculty toward a common direction for change, setting the stage for further collegial work for standards-based reforms.

For example, at Kentucky's Boyle County Middle School, social studies teacher Jim Spears reports that as a teacher with 24 years of experience, he was just a little too comfortable with the strategies he had developed. Like many teachers, Spears had spent many days in 6-hour professional development workshops designed to expose teachers to innovative teaching approaches. But, as he explains:

> There was no follow-up. You might go back and try something in your classroom, but you never had a chance to experiment with a support system behind you to guide you through or review things. If you didn't immediately succeed, you'd think, 'Well, this may work for some teachers, but it won't work for me, with my kids, in my classroom.'

All this changed after Assistant Superintendent Pam Rogers introduced Boyle County Middle School teachers to Carlene Murphy's approach to "reculturing" schools through whole faculty study groups. Study groups offered a different kind of professional development. Spears elaborates:

> We chose what we wanted to study and met with four, five, or six other teachers who had a common interest. We read research and talked about it. You'd go back to your classroom and try out something. Then you'd come back, share things good and bad. And you follow up like this for an entire year. You can make the changes you know you need to make without fear of the principal or an evaluation.

During the first year, teachers at Boyle County Middle School organized their study groups around elements of the school's own "Transformation Plan," written as required by the Kentucky Education Reform Act. Groups met on alternate Wednesdays for an hour and a half, while non-certified staff supervised students in activities and study halls. Assistant Superintendent Rogers pulled together articles and research relevant to the different topics chosen. One group studied how to schedule the school day to enhance learning. Another examined the new math curriculum. A third evaluated implementation of the school-wide reading program. Two groups studied technology, with one focusing on new uses for technology and the other previewing existing software. Another group studied school-community relations. Spears's group explored strategies for developing higher level thinking skills.

After one year, teachers' study resulted in a variety of changes in teaching and learning. The group studying variations in scheduling recommended the school move away from fixed periods and toward flexible block scheduling. The reading group discovered ways to strengthen the school's approach to reading in the content areas. As Spears's own group looked at specific materials like *History Alive!* (Teachers' Curriculum Institute, 1994) and read articles on diverse learning styles, Spears became more reflective about how well his own teaching matched the varying needs of his students. He recalls:

> As a result of the study group, I started thinking about special needs students. I felt that they were always on the outside looking in. I was looking for ways to break down barriers. So the Language Arts teacher and I wrote a grant to develop curriculum and lessons directed more toward individual learning styles.... I'm teaching differently now. Never in my life had I brought music into my classroom. Native American songs, gospel music from slavery days....

During the second year, Boyle County Middle School teachers continued working in study groups, but this time around they took a different tack. Instead of organizing themselves across disciplines as they had the first year, teachers organized by subject area with the task of aligning the school's curriculum with Kentucky's standards. Without abandoning their "study group mode," teachers examined their curriculum grade by grade, with the intention of connecting curriculum with state standards, then developed assignments and projects that more closely matched those standards. As Spears explains:

> This year we're looking at state standards and at how well what we are teaching matches what the state expects students to learn. We don't waste much time. Now we know what other teachers in prior grades have done or are going to do, and we don't study one topic over and over. We're also starting to face that you can't always spend all your time on your pet subjects.

Spears also notes that study group time may also involve teachers in exchanging ideas, materials, and open-response items they can use in preparing students for state testing. And he reports that, as a result, students assigned to different teacher teams are more likely to have similar opportunities to learn.

Boyle County Middle School's teacher study groups operate on a system of rotating leadership, with a different teacher taking responsibility for facilitating the group from one session to the next. Each group keeps a log, recording minutes of what was discussed and what materials teachers need for further study. On the morning following study group meetings, group leaders for the week meet, bringing copies of the logs for other group leaders. In addition, another copy goes to the assistant superintendent who monitors progress and responds to requests for support. This information loop ensures that the entire process is self-monitoring, with no one lacking information.

From Spears's perspective, whole faculty study groups have shifted the school culture toward stronger professional practice. As he recalls, "We felt the whole school was in a rut. There was a comfort zone for us. Our culture was embedded in traditional ways of teaching." Study groups opened teachers up to new ideas, allowed them to see each other as experts, and fostered new habits of connecting practice with research. As Spears reflects:

There's some peer pressure involved. If we're trying something new, it can be awkward to be the one not to try it. Now there's higher expectations for ourselves as teachers. I'm out of my rut. We think students will improve as a result of our getting better.

As Carlene Murphy (1997) allows, the first hurdle schools face as they begin to implement study groups is finding that one hour each week during which teachers will come together to study teaching and learning. The schools she has worked with have found this time in a variety of ways, ranging from setting aside one hour when all teachers are in study groups to staggering the time blocks allotted for study groups. Sometimes different teachers meet at different hours and days, using existing common planning periods.

Likewise, different schools take different routes toward developing a school wide commitment for change and norms of collegiality. Judith Warren Little notes that the leadership of the principal is essential, as is attention to scheduling time for teacher conversations. Beyond that, says Warren Little, teachers sometimes plant the seeds for a stronger collegial climate by "taking their work public," either through study groups, classroom visitations, or putting student work on the table for group discussion (Sparks, 1993). Although this work feels risky at first, the payoffs are high. For example, describing the support a collegial community offers, one teacher from San Diego's O'Farrell Community School notes:

> There is real teamwork at O'Farrell. We are invited into each other's classrooms and asked to give suggestions about the teaching and learning that we see. And if we have questions or problems, it is always O.K. to ask another teacher to help us out. Sometimes we watch each other to get ideas for curriculum or to learn new strategies. I don't know what I'd do without my educational family(Bachofer & Borton, 1994: 90).

A norm of collegiality, then, develops teachers' sense of efficacy, and when coupled with a school-wide consensus around new goals for learning, forms a solid foundation for further professional development. Drawing from the support of a collegial community, teachers are positioned to take better advantage of opportunities to learn new curriculum and pedagogy. Further, bonded by shared goals, they can make use of a wider variety of tools for understanding student learning and accounting for that learning in terms of professional practice.

Professional development for coherent curriculum and instruction

Standards-based reforms directed toward learning for understanding assume that teachers know their subject matter well and are prepared to work with student groups that are more diverse than ever before in the history of our country. As states move toward systemic reform, then, policy makers exhort educators to align teaching with new curriculum frameworks and assessments. Yet the quality of professional support available to help teachers do this frequently falls short of the need. For example, educational leaders in some states report that much professional development boils down to introducing teachers to content and skills that their students will find on high-stakes state tests. Even among networks of schools reforming to meet design parameters of respected national models, teachers report that training is too general and provides too few concrete ideas for new classroom practices (Smith, Ross, McNelis, Squires, Wasson, Maxwell, Weddle, Nath, Grehan, & Buggy, 1998).

The promise of the standards movement is its focus on learning for understanding in the disciplines. Yet, in the era of standards-based reform, many teachers in all subject areas face a gap between their own knowledge and what they are asked to teach (Darling-Hammond, 1996; Gregg & Leinhardt, 1994). In reality, many teachers themselves have only rarely had the opportunity to learn for understanding or produce work that stands up to criteria for excellence within a discipline. As Paula Evans (1994) of the Coalition of Essential Schools notes:

> Many teachers and principals have not experienced themselves what it means to be pushed intellectually, to exhibit knowledge publicly, to generate knowledge. Adults must experience that firsthand in order to change their thinking about teaching, curriculum, standards, and the role of students. (p. 44)

Not surprisingly then, at the end of the day, after the cafeteria workshop has come to a close, many teachers fall back on the teaching they are most comfortable with, and students' work remains unchanged. In contrast, when schools tie professional development to standards-based curriculum and allow teachers to hone their skills and develop understanding about their disciplines through the very curriculum they will teach to their young adolescent students, teachers and students both benefit. Such professional opportunities to learn increasingly appear to be a critical link between standards-based reform policies and classroom teaching (Ball & Cohen, 1996; Cohen & Ball, 1998). Moreover, this approach seems to result in measurable gains for student achievement. For example, David Cohen and Heather Hill (1998) report that when teachers' learning was rooted in the curriculum students were to study, linked elements of curriculum, instruction, and assessment, and extended over a period of time, professional opportunities to learn contributed notably to improved student achievment in mathematics

Professional development linked to specific new school-wide curriculum also offers a useful tool in building school cultures centered on student work. Teachers who have shared opportunities for enacting a standards-based curriculum are more likely to design assignments that generate real student work and share an understanding for what constitutes excellent work. Preparing to use a specified curriculum provides teachers with common experiences and a language for talking about student work. In particular, teachers develop shared expectations when training and curriculum offer concrete examples of the range of student work possible, explain the reasoning behind the examples of student work, and demonstrate different ways teachers can respond to students' questions about the content (Ball & Cohen, 1996). Such preparation offers teachers valuable opportunities to think deeply about the questions intellectual tensions that inform both their content areas and students' developing understanding.

When teachers from the same school prepare together to teach new curriculum school wide, they also increase the likelihood that as they implement the curriculum, they will communicate a consistent set of expectations for what it means to be a student in that curriculum. For example, teachers receiving students who have used *Junior Great Books* in earlier grades notice that students benefit from the consistency of expectations for student learning across the school and report that the school's culture for learning gains strength from that consistency. As one teacher in a school using *Junior Great Books* school wide observed, "It all depends on the teachers beforehand. If they've followed the approach, the students are more aggressive with the program." Over time, these common expectations strengthen the school's culture for learning.

In-class coaching strengthens school-wide instructional coherence.
Extended summer institutes for teacher teams represent a beginning step for introducing teachers to standards-based curriculum. Follow-up coaching for

teachers implementing that curriculum also raises the chances that teachers will actually enact that curriculum with consistency across the school and fidelity to the intentions of the curriculum. This strategy takes professional development out of the "hot house" and into real classrooms with real students. It ensures that teachers have opportunities to observe multiple demonstrations of new strategies, practice these strategies themselves in a supportive context, and receive feedback about their practice. These learning opportunities are essential if professional development is to stick (Joyce & Showers, 1988; Murphy, 1988).

Classroom coaching is complex and labor intensive, but it provides a powerful boost to instruction as teachers shift from teaching a coverage curriculum to teaching for the in-depth understanding implied by the standards of the professional associations. Such teaching often calls for changes in the ways teachers relate to students, involving, for example, more Socratic questioning as opposed to questioning for *the* right answer, better listening skills, or the direct teaching of group roles and skills. It may also require greater awareness of the range of solutions that one problem, whether in mathematics, science, or social studies, might generate.

Some curriculum developers offer classroom coaching as part of the professional development attached to the curriculum. Following summer workshops to prepare teachers as discussion leaders, the *Junior Great Books Program* offers schools intensive coaching to help teachers begin and sustain regular "shared inquiry" discussions about literature with diverse students (Wheelock, 1998a). Over the school year, coaches offer demonstration lessons and provide immediate feedback based on observed discussions. Like personal trainers, coaches shape their assistance to teachers' individual styles, skills, and confidence levels. Responding to immediate and long-term concerns, coaches help teachers move from novice to expert levels of competence. Observing teachers in action, coaches can attend to how students react to the discussion, assess students' readiness for pursuing more ambiguous questions, and reflect their observations back to teachers. As one coach explains:

> I have to analyze each situation, then figure out what one piece
> I can reinforce, and what one bit of advice I can give them that
> might help them try something new. If I can just plant a small
> suggestion, I can see progress.

Even the most skilled teachers gain from in-class coaching about their work on *Junior Great Books*. Coaches help those who are already leading good discussions become even better as they co-lead shared inquiry conversations with teachers, modeling ways of pushing students deeper into the text and providing teachers with a chance to try new techniques. This kind of support helps teachers sustain their commitment to new curriculum in the face of initial challenges. As one teacher reports,"Without follow-up, I might have been discouraged... If I'd been left isolated without visitations, I don't know if I would have continued.... You need a support."

Outside curriculum coaching does not substitute for a principal who is an instructional leader. However, coaching can give principals extra leverage as they nudge their teachers toward a school-wide commitment to teaching for understanding. As one principal in a school using *Junior Great Books* school wide reflects, "[Our coach's] visits make us refocus. If it's in the top of your mind that [she] is coming, you make sure you're working through the stories with your students." Moreover, coaches play a role that principals cannot fill. Because coaches do not evaluate teachers, teachers can try out new approaches and learn from mistakes without fear of high stakes appraisals. As another principal points out, "It's really good for teachers to have someone from the outside giving them feedback. It's not so stressful. It's friendlier when it's not tied to a rating."

Outside curriculum coaching does not substitute for a principal who is an instructional leader.

By reducing teachers' isolation, classroom coaching to help teachers enact a particular curriculum can be a key strategy for developing a norm of collegiality among teachers. For example, in one Chicago school using *Junior Great Books* school wide, teachers are now relying less on their outside coach and turning to each other for ideas and support. To encourage classroom visitations and peer consultations, the principal assures teachers that she will arrange for substitutes to cover classes for this purpose.

When tied to particular curriculum adopted school wide, coaching acts as a post-training booster shot to reinforce teachers' move toward teaching for understanding, and it can prevent teachers from falling back into comfortable but less effective ways. Coaching that is non-evaluative, classroom-based, and individualized helps teachers feel their way toward greater competence as they practice these new skills in a safe context. As all teachers begin to use those skills, they contribute to greater instructional coherence across the school.

Teachers' opportunities to learn based on standards-based curriculum and follow-up coaching illustrate two routes to developing a professional culture which fosters teachers' commitment to learning for understanding. These professional development approaches offer teachers a set of common experiences that encourage greater instructional coherence while helping teachers deepen their own knowledge of the content areas. In addition, they reinforce a larger culture for standards-based reforms by zeroing teachers' attention in on their classroom practice, and the ways in which students are at work in the classroom.

Linking professional conversations, student work, and standards

Individual teachers who seek to know more about how well their own students are meeting standards often look for evidence of how well students actually grasp a subject as they grade tests, homework, and assignments. But improving student work across an entire school requires teachers to come out of their classrooms, share, compare, debate, and discuss the work among themselves. Such conversations can help teachers consider connections between students' work, the assignments they give students, and their expectations for learning. Looking at student work provides a window on students' grasp of content and understanding of how to use that content.

Improving student work across an entire school requires teachers to come out of their classrooms, share, compare, debate, and discuss the work among themselves.

Just bringing teachers together on a regular basis, of course, does not guarantee collaborative discussions to promote high quality work. In fact, in many middle schools, teacher teams are already meeting regularly, but the discussion is frequently on administrative matters or "why Johnny didn't bring his books today" rather than on student work and teaching. As professional development consultant Carlene Murphy points out: "It's very scary for teachers to open up and share problems. They want to stay on safer ground, to focus on something like materials rather than on what they are actually doing in the classroom."

Discussions about student work that also reveal information about classroom practice can be especially uncomfortable when they unearth evidence of low expectations, thoughtless teaching, or learning activities that are "fun" but unconnected to larger learning goals or curriculum standards. But such discussions are critical to building a culture for standards-based reform. Making these discussions meaningful means that educators must set aside time specifically for this purpose. Moreover, teachers must get the support they need to move forward to look honestly at their practice in looking, and for many schools, outside facilitators provide such support.

Developing shared standards from real student work. Bringing teachers together to talk about student work is a critical part of building a culture for standards-based reform in every school. For teachers who may have had few opportunities to work collaboratively over many years, such conversations can be difficult. However, over time, teacher discussions about student work can lead to standards that all teachers develop, agree on, share, and support, and these standards can begin to reshape the culture of the school.

To this end, some teachers are beginning to use their time together to look at the work their students do as a way of reflecting on their own practice. Different teachers in different schools are taking on this effort in different ways. Some look at the work students do in response to a single assignment that is common among many teachers. In other cases. one teacher at a time may take the lead by bringing student work to a group of colleagues for discussion. Still others may meet to discuss what a "standard" suggested by the state or profession actually "looks like" in practice in their own school and develop a common understanding for what teachers will expect from students. For example, imagine this scene:

Some teachers are beginning to use their time together to look at the work their students do as a way of reflecting on their own practice.

In this middle school, science teachers have never talked about the kind of assignments they give, the work their students do, or their criteria for awarding grades. The district has recently adopted "standards," and now all eighth graders must "meet the standard" for "communicating science ideas." But what in the world does this look like? Among those who understand that a culture of high standards is critically linked to high quality student work, this is the question teachers ask first. As Grant Wiggins of the Center for Learning, Assessment, and School Structures (CLASS) notes, "Once we decide what it is we want students to know, we quickly have to ask 'What will it look like when they know it?' and 'What do we want to see students doing to demonstrate that they have learned what we want them to learn?"

Figuring this out means looking at the work that students are already producing. So teachers gather together, with a coach who serves as outside facilitator, to look at their best examples of work that their middle grades students from all classes including special education, bilingual, advanced, or regular have produced. The best examples are diverse: weather maps students have copied from the newspaper and mounted on poster board; graphs students have created that describe the frequency of bird sightings in their area; a page of dictionary-perfect definitions of scientific terms; science fiction stories that incorporate notions of gravity and motion; letters written to scientists; a box of bugs discovered behind the school and mounted on pins; a field guide to the neighborhood surrounding the school; a lab report describing results of a water quality analysis.

This is the first time teachers have ever seen examples of what students are doing in classes other than their own. Each teacher has some unexpressed thoughts about the work samples others have brought. To the regular seventh grade teacher, it looks as if the sixth grade work does not reflect the understanding of science concepts that will be expected in his class. The advanced teacher is a little alarmed that the "regular" work is not much different from that of her students. The bilingual teacher feels a little smug that her students' work is more detailed and carefully executed than that of the other teachers. The eighth grade teacher suddenly feels a little defensive that the work he brings is hardly more polished than that of the earlier grades.

Together, the teachers pool the work each has contributed. Then, each teacher studies one piece of work at a time and on a "post-it" note stuck to the back, marks it as demonstrating an *exemplary, proficient, developing,* or *beginning* understanding of "communicating science ideas." After each teacher has considered and rated all pieces of student work, the group collects them in four piles representing the different assessment categories, but this means resolving differences in judgment and more hard work as teachers explore the sometimes widely divergent perspectives each other brings to the table. "Why does one teacher rate one piece of work as *proficient*, while another sees it as *developing*?" "Can the same piece of work be considered *exemplary* in some ways and judged to have reached only the point of *developing* in other ways?" "Which aspects of a particular piece of work are seen as valued outcomes; which are not?" In the process, teachers debate in what way sixth-grade work might reasonably be different from eighth-grade work and what the standards for overall science work should look like.

From this conversation, the teachers must determine the characteristics of student work that "really count," the aspects of work they wish to emphasize, the dimensions of learning that they value, all reflected in how students are communicating science ideas. And based on the work they have before them at that time, they must glean the characteristics of student work at each performance level. This means answering tough questions: "What do you have to know and be able to do to communicate science ideas?" "What distinguishes one piece of work from others?" "Why does that piece of work show only *beginning* understanding overall?" "What are the qualities of *proficient* work?"

In the process of doing all this, teachers begin to talk about the kinds of assignments and opportunities to learn that result in *beginning* or *exemplary* work. They learn that the opportunities to read and discuss ideas in young adult science fiction that occur in one class may never be allowed in another; that opportunities for field trips afforded one class may not be considered for another. Such conversations can also reveal biases: about students who teachers believe cannot be trusted with lab equipment; about students who become anxious when they are asked to pose questions as well as answer them. They can reveal that student work is often only so good as the assignment, that some teachers emphasize quick recall while others allow for work to be rewritten. They can unveil the expectations of the different grade level teachers who become aware that the assignments they have habitually given in eighth grade are little more than repetitions of the sixth grade assignments.

With more work and discussion, teachers can develop rubrics that represent teachers' consensus on what constitutes work that meets standards for communicating science ideas. Teachers can share this rubric with students and parents to help them understand the quality of work expected. Teachers can also take the examples of work at each level of competency and display them to students and parents to guide their understanding for "what the teacher wants."[4]

Outside coaches help teachers look at student work. In schools that are building a culture for standards-based reform by putting student work and a coherent instructional program at the center of learning, the next logical step is to develop routines that allow teachers together to look at student

[4]This example draws on observations at the 1995 Winter Summit of the Performance Assessment Collaboratives in Education (PACE), Forth Worth, Texas. The author is grateful to Dennie Palmer Wolfe and her staff for permission to attend this meeting.

work and use that work to formulate standards as defined in rubrics and selection of exemplars for use beyond a few classrooms. To this end, some schools are finding that outside coaches can be helpful in working with teacher teams or departments. Coaches can help teachers weave together new expectations for students, the assignments they give students, and the way they assess the quality of work they receive from students. Such coaching requires sustained contact, and coaches often meet with teacher teams on a weekly basis to facilitate a process in which different teachers describe an assignment and present a packet of student work for review and discussion.

Schools that have devoted extensive teacher time to looking at student work also begin to develop new norms for what "the best" work looks like. In the process, teachers begin to revise assignments and learning goals to reflect higher expectations for the work of every student. Others may also rethink their own teaching. For example, one coach working with teachers to review student work noted:

> A teacher in one district realized when the group looked at the work from his class that he needed to teach the whole concept again. The work showed that the students hadn't learned what he thought he was teaching.

In some cases, as teachers begin to examine their students' work in a systematic way, they may identify a need for changes that go beyond the classroom to generate more support for both teachers and students. For example, one coach notes that better assignments require scheduling changes and reports, "We are now trying to figure out how to ratchet-up the conversation of what is curriculum, and how it can be constructed in a very different way than in isolated, daily 45-minute bits."

The process of looking at student work to develop standards for that work does not magically produce better teaching and learning. For example, as one coach explains:

> [In one school] there have been some very good conversations with teachers, most of whom have never done this kind of thing before.... And, although there are some very nice examples of individual teachers trying things out – for example, a 30-year veteran social studies teacher trying out a graphic organizer prior to students' writing a report for the first time in his

career – it is also distressing how little of what we discuss about teaching during our meetings is really tried in classrooms.

In fact, documenting the impact of the process of reviewing student work to improve assignments, researchers from the Philadelphia Education Fund found that as implemented in their district, the process of looking at students work and developing common scoring guides did elevate teacher expectations for assignments and helped teachers attend more closely to the *work* students produced rather than student personalities. However, the process was most likely to affect practice when teachers had solid content knowledge and a wide repertoire of teaching techniques, and when teachers had sustained support, expert facilitators, and regular opportunities to meet with colleagues to discuss the quality of student learning (Coe & Useem, 1996).

Taken together, these findings indicate that when schools have already put into place new curriculum and instruction that generates student work products, and when teachers have had professional development to support that curriculum, the process of looking at that student work can develop a stronger sense of professional collegiality and further refine teachers shared expectations for the work all students do. Over time, as teachers make the common examination of student work a regular part of their own work week, they can begin to develop the habit of continuously challenging one another to rethink practice. Then standards for exemplary work become "living" tools for helping teachers and students strive for ongoing improvement.

Looking at student work to strengthen subject area teaching. In some schools, teachers are now using a process of examining student work to help them improve teaching and learning in specific subject areas. These efforts are helping develop greater coherence for subject area teaching across the whole school. Further, teachers are finding these discussions help them understand better what constitutes quality learning for understanding in the disciplines.

For example, five years ago, the principal of Hoover Middle School in Long Beach, California, presented his history teachers with a challenge: Why not apply for a California Demonstration Grant to strengthen their department? Although they knew it would mean a lot of time, teachers agreed, and the school received $25,000 a year for the next three years to buy primary source materials, other new teaching tools, and most important, their own professional development. After three years of working with historians and polishing their practice, these teachers wanted to learn more about how their own learning linked up with their students' learning. History teacher Mary Massich recalls:

> We felt there was a critical piece missing. We felt the need to sit back and reflect on our own teaching and look at how the staff development was actually showing up in our lessons. Was it trickling down to the kids? (Focused Reporting Project, 1997b).

With a fourth-year grant, the group expanded to include specialist teachers in special education and English language development and began to look systematically at student work to see if students were learning what teachers wanted them to learn. Massich reports:

> I had been teaching American History in 8th grade for eight years, and I have a real passion for it, but I was beginning to feel content-weary.... Then we started this process of analyzing student work, and I realized that I needed to make some big changes in my teaching. My weariness vanished.

Now, as the Hoover teachers pursue this process, they focus primarily on examining specific assignments and student work, with reference to standards and assessments proposed by their professional association or district. For example, at one meeting, teacher Massich asked her colleagues to help her think through a proposed U.S.history assessment that called on students to "identify the Bill of Rights and its relevance to everyday life." Massich wanted some new ideas for making this content more meaningful to students. So after fellow teachers read the assignment and scoring rubric, they rated the quality of their own assignments in the context of their department's expectations for students' understanding of history. Then with the help of their UCLA coach Linda Whitney, the group discussed the quality and purpose of the assignment. By the end of the discussion, Massich had plenty of ideas to refine her work. Over the subsequent hour, the group proceeded with a similar process. This time, they reviewed sixth graders' work brought by another teacher, and using their own rubric, they identified critical gaps in the work and the kinds of teaching strategies that might address those gaps.

When the teachers first met to talk among themselves about their practice, discussions like these were "comfortable," revolving around such "safe" questions as "What was your objective?" Over time, they became tougher as teachers asked each other what student work indicated teachers were doing to help every student meet the district's standards. Such questions shifted the group's focus to what students need to learn. As special education team member Yvette Gow notes, lessons that had been teacher-centered and based on "what the teacher wants to teach or is most comfortable teaching" began to change. Now, she says:

> By working with the history department group, I've really come to ask, "What is it my students need most? And how am I going to deliver that?" If I weren't with this group, I would not be at the level of lesson preparation and execution I am now.

Hoover teachers note that it is controversy and critical feedback that ultimately generate improvements in teaching. Recognizing that you have to "put your ego on hold," they also believe that the give and take of criticism in a climate of trust is part of growing. They note that an outside coach and guidelines for structured discussion can help keep discussion focused away from personalities and on the work. The bottom line, they say, is that the process results in teaching that more closely matches what students need to learn. As Massich explains:

It is controversy and critical feedback that ultimately generate improvements in teaching.

> Maybe we think we've developed a good lesson, but the review of student work tells us that it's just not helping enough kids meet standards. So we have to change, to experiment, to try something else. Often we'll get ideas about how to do that from others in our group, or from our coach, or from our outside research. But we accept, up front, that developing alternative teaching strategies are part and parcel of this work.

The process is ultimately a professional development experience, and different teachers draw different lessons from participating. For example, new teachers find support as they try new strategies. Veteran teachers begin to realize the importance of content knowledge to high-quality teaching. The presence of specialists ensures that all teachers will give as much attention to the work of students with disabilities or those whose first language is not English as they do to that of general education students. Regardless of experience, all agree that, as sixth grade teacher Janet Leis, reports, "Two, and three, and four heads are better than one.... Together we can come up with something really awesome, but by ourselves we just don't get the same product."

Others who have observed the process agree. Hoover principal Gary Graves has given clear support to the history team to encourage them to continue their study of student work. Moreover, he has encouraged the school's English teachers to follow suit. Grants of $5,000 for each subject area team to use to design their own professional development activities further connect the history teachers' efforts to those of others in the school. The team's coach, historian Linda Whitney, hopes that eventually the process will extend to other middle schools but is also well-aware of the challenges teachers face when they "risk their ego" in conversations about their work. She notes that teachers have to understand that the discussions are about students' learning, not teachers' imperfections, and she emphasizes that looking at student work is about continuous improvement. "These aren't mistakes we're looking at. They're examples of a teacher's work that's going through the process of getting better and better," she explains.

Hoover's teachers emphasize that their effort demands time and energy. They typically spend two hours a week discussing their lessons and student work, supported with a stipend derived from a state department of education grant. As a result of reflecting on their practice, they find they are working both harder and "smarter" and their students are producing better work. Moreover, the work of the Hoover history teachers has triggered discussions among other Long Beach teachers about how to make student work the focal point of their team meetings. Teachers have presented their work to their colleagues at an all-day conference for all middle school teachers sponsored by the district. In

Just as the relationships they have developed among themselves sustain them, the connections they are making with others across the district are building a broader community for professional practice, founded on conversations about teaching, learning, and student work.

this way, just as the relationships they have developed among themselves sustain them, the connections they are making with others across the district are building a broader community for professional practice, founded on conversations about teaching, learning, and student work.

Using school-wide teacher study groups to look at student work. While teachers in some schools are working team by team to look at student work, other schools are using study groups school wide to involve every single teacher in the process of critiquing student work to improve teaching. In Philadelphia and several other districts, some middle schools have joined forces with the ATLAS school reform project to do just that. The ATLAS Communities (1996a,

1996b) have made school-wide study groups a front-and-center strategy for focusing teacher discussions on student work and developing a shared commitment to quality. The key question study groups raise in their meetings together as they look at student work is a simple one: "Is this work good enough?"

To keep conversation focused on teaching and learning, ATLAS study groups borrow from the Coalition of Essential Schools' "Tuning Protocol," a process involving a carefully structured five-step discussion lasting about 25 minutes. First, one teacher offers a selected piece of student work for discussion and describes the assignment, without providing any further information about the student's background or academic record. Second, group members take five minutes to gather information about the work by describing and making observations about the evidence of learning in the work. Third, the group uses the evidence in the work to infer what the student was thinking and why, what the student does and does not understand, what the student was most interested in, and how the student interpreted the assignment. Fourth, the group discusses implications for teaching and assessment in the classroom, identifying what other kinds of assignments and assessments could lead to more desirable qualities in the work. Fifth, the group reflects on the process using such questions as "What did you learn about how this student thinks and learns?," "What new perspectives did colleagues provide and how can you use those perspectives?," and "What would you like to try in your classroom as a result of looking at this student's work?" As groups following this protocol meet over and over, every teacher benefits from professional exchange about work drawn from his or her own classrooms.

As groups following this protocol meet over and over, every teacher benefits from professional exchange about work drawn from his or her own classrooms.

While this protocol is common to all study groups engaged in the ATLAS project, the approach is not a "one size fits all" model of prescribed staff development. Instead, teachers can adapt the approach to the special themes of each school. For example, study groups at Philadelphia's Baldy Middle School look at student work and discuss teaching strategies in part through the lens of their school-wide theme of multicultural learning. Moreover, to reinforce this theme, groups are cross-disciplinary and include teachers responsible for both students in general education and those learning English as a second language. The mix keeps teacher expectations high for all groups, and keeps teachers from developing a dual set of standards within the school.

As Principal Richard Shohen notes, "It's important for the regular teachers to see the kind of work the ESL kids do. These are bright kids. Just because their English still needs work doesn't mean they can't do the work."

Over time, Principal Richard Shohen expects study groups will also close in on the district's standards for learning, noting:

> Standards-based reforms are not something that can be mandated. It's something people have to buy into. The way we make change is by having the teachers come together and have them talk to one another, bring samples of student work from all disciplines. Study groups have them talking about standards and student work.

Study groups at Baldy Middle School have just begun to rekindle some excitement for teaching and learning in a veteran staff. For example, Shohen reports that more teachers are beginning to try out research-based strategies like cooperative learning. He also notes that teachers are beginning to think of themselves as lifelong learners. For example, stimulated by their study group conversations, one group has planned their own summer study in Japan with support from the World Affairs Council, a first-time event.

Teachers are beginning to think of themselves as lifelong learners.

The ATLAS Project is only one of a number of school reform networks insisting that teachers' working together to examine and discuss student work is an essential element in the effort to strengthen teaching and learning. Others involved in similar efforts include the Coalition of Essential Schools, Harvard University's Project Zero, the National Center for Restructuring Education, Schools, and Teaching (NCREST) at Columbia Teachers College, Performance Assessment Collaboratives in Education (PACE), Expeditionary Learning, the Center for Learning, Assessment, and School Structures (CLASS), the Appalachian Education Laboratory, and the Education Trust. Schools involved in these and other networks see multiple benefits from looking at student work in a routine and collegial way. Through this process, teachers can explore questions like:

■ *What is our shared understanding of what 'excellent student work' looks like and how do we communicate these standards to every one of our students?*

■ *How close does the work our students do come to the standards of excellence we set for ourselves and the standards of excellence that others have set?*

■ *How do our assignments contribute to helping students produce excellent work? How well do they match standards of the professional associations?*

■ *What does student work tell us about any gaps between our own district's learning goals and standards developed by the professional associations?*

■ *How can we improve our teaching to help our students do better work?*

Teacher groups formed to look at student work contribute to a school culture for high standards by moving everyone in the school toward a common understanding of what quality in teaching and learning looks like. The student work teachers bring for discussion sheds light on the quality of assignments teachers offer students, and it can reveal how different learning opportunities and expectations vary from classroom to classroom within schools. As teachers become more familiar with the process, discussions begin to include disagreement among teachers. As these discussions about student work unearth controversy and reveal differences in perspectives among adults in a school, they become "counter-cultural," potentially capable of shaking up entrenched ways of looking at students and what they can learn and do (Jervis & McDonald, 1996).

When student work is on display for others to see, teachers themselves are pushed to think about the relationship of that work to their teaching and curriculum. Looking at student work forces teachers and whole schools to set priorities for learning, clarify what students have to do and why, identify points of connection between subjects, make interdisciplinary approaches real rather than fabricated, and tailor coaching to individual students (Darling-Hammond, Ancess & Falk, 1995). Looking at student work pushes teachers to take the question "What is good enough?" out of the private discourse between teacher and student and make it a stimulus for professional discussion.

Professional accountability and standards of practice

One hallmark of the standards movement is faith in bureaucratic approaches to accountability. Such approaches typically involve states and districts in the gathering of outcome data about schools and reporting these data to the public. As a sign that such managerial approaches have captured the hearts of policy makers, the *New York Times* (Steinberg, 1998) reports that 35 states now issue school report cards, and 20 warn schools deemed to be in "academic distress" that they are subject to takeover. Yet, while such policies are meant to shame schools into better performance, the extent to which they work to this effect is not clear. For example, of 24 Alabama schools put on the "academic alert" list in 1996, only two subsequently improved enough to be taken off the list, and nine (38 per cent) performed at the same level or worse. In New York City, a record 15 of the state's list of 100 struggling schools in 1997 showed enough improvement to be removed from the list, but only after the state coupled the threat of closing these schools with extra resources for their improvement.

Data on the outcomes of schooling disaggregated by community, school, grade, and race are essential for monitoring the effects of policy. As public institutions responsible for educating all children, schools do have an obligation to account for their practice. However, only professional approaches to accountability can encourage genuine reflection about professional practice at the school and district level. By requiring teachers to explain and account for their practice in terms of professional standards, professional accountability connects teaching and learning to student work and so helps build a culture for standards-based reform.

Standards of professional practice. A culture of standards-based reform is also a culture based on '"standards of professional practice" – the beliefs, norms, and practices recognized by the teaching profession as contributing to the well-being and achievement of students. As Linda Darling-Hammond (1992;1993) notes, standards of practice reflect a professional "duty of care," the obligation teachers have to apply knowledge and practice in wise and responsible ways to benefit student learning and avoid student harm. Standards of practice direct attention to the quality of decisions teachers make about teaching and learning.

A school culture that embraces standards of professional practice depends on teachers who do more than march toward outcome goals set by policy-makers, leaving teachers to decide on the means for reaching those goals. Rather, as Douglas Mitchell (1989) explains, true accountability for professional practice means that educators must also be involved in determining the kinds of outcomes that are desirable and select the appropriate interventions for achieving those results. As Mitchell notes:

> In authentic professional settings (law, medicine, architecture, accounting, etc.) we do not measure performance by outcomes. Thus, for example, we expect criminals to be found guilty, despite outstanding defense. Accountability means accepting responsibility for pursuing the results on the basis of work strategies that have known effects.

A professional community, then, works to set up processes that allow teachers to account for the kinds of things they do in their classroom to other professionals and to the wider community. Professional norms expect that teachers will document not simply the outcomes of school practices but also those indicators that describe the context of schooling, and in particular, those aspects of schooling that enable student achievement, including access to knowledge and conditions for professional practice (Oakes, 1989).

Fostering professional accountability. If bureaucratically oriented and outcomes-driven accountability measures do not improve teaching and learning or help create a school culture of high standards, what sorts of professional accountability offer greater promise for doing so? Schools that are building a culture for standards-based reform develop greater professional accountability through collegial reviews of school quality and student surveys. Some schools are further deepening professional practice and accountability by developing means for viewing instructional reforms through the eyes of their students, the ultimate consumers of schooling.

Schools that are building a culture for standards-based reform develop greater professional accountability through collegial reviews of school quality and student surveys.

School quality reviews. Just as other professions "account for" their practice by opening their work up to the scrutiny of their peers, educators too are beginning to devise ways to explain their work to their colleagues. School quality reviews are one way of doing this. These extended reviews ask schools to make their work "public" so that teachers within schools reflect on their practice with a wider group of colleagues. School quality reviews go beyond the bureaucratic modes of outcomes-based accountability to gather information about teaching and learning in individual schools in ways that can guide improvement.

As Mark Barth and Elaine Frankonis (1996) of the New York State Education Department explain, the School Quality Review (SQR) process in New York sets out to establish a school culture that values reflection on professional practice. A key part of the SQR process is a school-wide self-review that triggers reflection on three questions: (1) What do we know about our school now? (2) What do citizens want and educators expect our children to know and be able to do? and (3) How can the school meet and exceed those standards? Individual schools answer these questions in different ways, ranging from intensive staff discussions to curriculum mapping.

In addition, the state has trained hundreds of "critical friends" who participate in teams of 7 to 12 external reviewers, at least half of whom are practicing teachers. These teams visit schools that request an external review for a period of a week, collecting evidence for teaching and learning through class observations, student shadowing, and interviewing students and adults in the school. Reviewers also review student work through the lens of state curriculum frameworks. Finally, the team meets as a whole to consolidate all findings into a "collective perspective" honed through rigorous discourse. The team's final report avoids recommendations or judgment; rather it provides an outside perspective on how close a school is coming to meeting its own goals. In addition, it offers evidence of good practice along with questions designed to trigger further reflection, inquiry, and discussion at the school.

Over time, New York has seen a number of effects of SQR. Schools participating in SQR begin to incorporate norms of reflection into regular school routines and relationships. In local communities, many schools have made the final reports available to the public and have benefited from greater public recognition for their work. In addition, educators report they have developed a clearer picture of their own improvement process and reforms as they put various reform activities temporarily on hold while they reconsider the value of each. Others note that the SQR process paves the way for peer evaluation practices as a substitute for administrative reviews. Still others credit the process with enhanced school capacity to work on common goals related to teaching and learning. As a result, some schools have expanded opportunities for students to learn more rigorous content as the SQR process revealed the limitations of multiple track and non-Regents courses.

Establishing the SQR process is not all smooth sailing. Both schools and the state have encountered hurdles in contract rules and tight budgets that inhibit teacher participation. Moreover, many of the state's least effective schools have such a high degrees of instability and inexperience in their administrative and teaching staff that they have limited capacity for supporting a sustained, reflective process. Because both external and internal reviews are labor-intensive, schools must reschedule time for all teachers to participate.

However, the process clearly nurtures stronger norms of collegiality. Ultimately, as Barth and Frankonis point out, the major constituency of the process is the teaching faculty. By demanding teachers to be more public, SQR also invites the public to know the teaching profession better.

Although New York State has devolved responsibility for directing the SQR process to the state's intermediary professional development centers, state education department staff are encouraged about the prospects for continuing the process. As Mark Barth reports:

> Over the last four to five year the tools to do self-reflection have gotten better. Our unit at SED has been working with Joe McDonald of the Coalition of Essential Schools in conducting Reviews of Learning Experiences – it takes review of student work much further by allowing observers/reviewers to see the whole learning context. A review format allows for critical friends to query and praise.

As teachers themselves become accustomed to using these tools, they can develop more reflective, and therefore more effective, responses to their students' work. Whether they participate as either inside or outside reveiwers, teachers participating in SQRs have to "account for" their practice in terms of standards of practice and student work. Over time, schools can sustain the climate of collegiality that develops through guided and monitored self-reviews after the initial SQR is carried out.

Using student surveys and drawings to reflect on classroom practice. As part of a larger commitment to developing greater professional accountability, some school leaders are going beyond an examination of data provided by their administrators to emphasize data gathered from students about their own classroom experiences. These educators agree that outcomes are important, but they also understand that the daily life of students in schools is equally important to learning. From their perspective, students' views can provide key information for helping teachers reflect on the impact of their practice. As Walt Haney of the Center for the Study of Testing, Evaluation, and Education Policy (CSTEEP) at Boston College explains:

> Focusing only on outcome data, without simultaneously gathering data on the nature of students' school experiences provides very little leverage for improvement. In our work with school reform efforts, we have tried to encourage schools to gather data on processes as well as outcomes for the simple reason that without evidence on processes, evaluation efforts are reduced to "black-box" inquiries with little potential to explain outcomes, be they good or not good.

Gathering information from students can take different forms. For example, for several years in a row, San Diego City middle schools, in partnership with CSTEEP, have surveyed students to help them reflect on their progress in developing standards-based reforms. The first part of the questionnaire gathers student responses on questions of particular interest to district and school educators, including questions drawn from the National Assessment of Educational Progress that allow for national comparisons. The second part elicits student responses to such questions as "When your teachers read your essays and papers, how do they decide when your work is excellent (A) or very good (B)?" and "What are the most important things you have learned at your school this year?" Over several years, San Diego has been able to use responses to these questions to chart changes in students' perceptions of standards-based reform, and to describe students' learning experiences in each school. The patterns of responses help both individual schools and the district as a whole understand the context for improving or declining test scores and suggest the kinds of strategies teachers might expand or eliminate from their practice.

In addition to written questions, some schools are adding to the data they collect by soliciting student drawings that portray teachers at work in their classroom. For example, to stimulate teachers' thinking about their practice, San Diego and Corpus Christi middle schools along with middle schools participating in the national CO-NECT (Cooperative Networked Education Community for Tomorrow) Project, have prompted student drawings of instruction in their classrooms, then have allotted teachers professional time to reflect on those drawings.[5] In small groups, teachers peruse the drawings, then discuss the patterns they see and the reasons they think those patterns might occur. Finally they discuss how they might change their practice in response to student views of their classrooms.

The process of reflection that results from teachers' review of drawings is sometimes painful but always interesting, and teachers can be surprised that what students portray may fall short of their own faculty goals. For example, at the Scott Middle School in Hammond, Indiana, principal Frank Lentvorsky explains that teachers had set a school-wide goal to use more group work in class. However, as Lentvorsky explained, when they reviewed the drawings, "Teachers were taken aback to see the traditional guru at the blackboard. We realized that we revert back to traditional modes of teaching more than we thought we did." With teachers more focused on their own goals, subsequent surveys have documented changes, and now student drawings depict teachers working as goup facilitators, desks arranged in circles, and increased use of computers (Tovey, 1996).

Using multiple indicators to assess and account for professional practice. Student surveys are probably most useful as part of a larger process for professional accountability that also includes a review of school-based outcomes data, in-school examination of student work, and school quality reviews from visiting colleagues. However, because drawings are gathered as part of an internal review process and are never made public, they offer a unique tool for professional reflection. Like information from student surveys, student drawings can suggest how teachers as a whole faculty might adjust classroom practice. Moreover, as teachers make classroom changes, drawings can document those changes and help teachers account for the patterns revealed in more traditional outcomes-oriented data.

Establishing a climate for professional accountability depends on teachers' gathering data from multiple sources, then using those data to improve student achievement. Sources of data that provoke conversation about student learning might include standardized tests that assess reading, writing,

---

[5]Research on the use of student drawings to foster teacher reflection is continuing at the Center for the Study of Testing, Evaluation, and Education Policy at Boston College. Matching student drawings with videotaped classroom conditions, Cengiz Gulek has found the prompt that elicits drawings that most closely resemble actual classroom practices reads, "Think about the kinds of things you have done in your classroom today. Draw a picture of what a video camera would have seen."

Establishing a climate for professional accountability depends on teachers' gathering data from multiple sources, then using those data to improve student achievement.

and basic math, disaggregated to report on the progress of different student groups and reported for a three-year period; student portfolios with work that illustrates the progress individual students have made over time; data gathered through observations and interviews conducted by colleagues and constituents who, while outsiders to the school, understand the school's workings in relation to its community; and public events at which school staff report on the school's progress and answer questions from parents, students, and citizens.

While many states gather information from testing programs, then feed test results back to schools, few support schools in using other sources of evidence to consider school progress. In short, bureaucratic methods for accountability remain dominant at the state level, leaving schools and districts to shape their own strategies for developing deeper commitment to professional accountability. Despite this lack of support, some schools are taking the risk of "accounting for their work" by going public with that work. In fact, student work-centered routines – exit presentations and exhibitions, student-led conferences, and assignments that engage students in producing real work for real audiences – themselves set the stage for that process. In this sense, an emphasis on professional accountability reinforces a focus on student work, and brings the process of developing a culture for standards-based reform full circle.

Conclusion

Building a school culture for standards-based reform in the middle grades requires shifting the focus of the whole school toward student work, with student work intimately tied to the school's curriculum and instructional program. Making this shift depends to a great extent on teachers' adopting a variety of practices that strengthen students' motivation to work harder to demonstrate in-depth learning in that curriculum. But however effective they are as individual practitioners, teachers cannot effect these changes on their own. They need a supportive professional community grounded in norms of collegiality and a commitment to accounting for and improving professional practice.

The importance of creating norms of collegiality as prerequisites for schools' effective use of resources for reform has clear implications for the future of professional development. As Dennis Sparks, Executive Director of the National Staff Development Council asserts:

> New forms of professional development will more often have teachers working with colleagues in identifying and solving their own problems through various collaborative processes both within their schools and with those at other sites.

Building a culture for standards-based reform, then, involves multiple changes in professional practice. Teachers' developing new knowledge is important, as is coaching for skills. But the success of these approaches ultimately hangs on the ways in which schools nurture more professional relationships among teachers both within and across subject areas and throughout the entire school. In the absence of the fruitful professional relationships and interactions that are the foundation for a collegial community, teachers are unlikely to forge new practices essential for learning for understanding. Creating schools in which all students are producing work that "meets standards" – the essence of standards-based reform – benefits from effective leadership; making reforms "stick" requires all teachers working in interdependent ways toward shared goals in a culture that values professional practice and reflection. ◨

In the absence of the fruitful professional relationships and interactions that are the foundation for a collegial community, teachers are unlikely to forge new practices essential for learning for understanding.

IV. What Districts and States Can Do To Promote a Culture of High Standards in Every School

Developing a culture for standards-based reform is much more difficult than adopting lists of content goals and selecting new curriculum and assessments to match those goals. The work of shifting cultural norms toward learning for understanding is intensely social, involving diverse personalities with varying kinds of commitments to change. It is also highly personal, for it requires changing deeply held beliefs about learning that often support comfortable but dysfunctional practices. Given these challenges, it is not surprising that the need for developing such new school cultures to match the aspirations for more meaningful achievement for more students goes largely unacknowledged in policy circles.

Realizing a vision of all schools organized for standards-based reform requires district and state leaders to support educators in a variety of new ways. But once districts and states have worked through the process of writing new learning goals and curriculum frameworks, selected new assessments, and trained teachers on the standards, what exactly is their role? In many states and districts, policy makers have determined that their next step is to set up system for "accountability," one that involves monitoring test scores, feeding outcomes data back to the schools, and using the process to push schools toward modifying their instructional program to produce better results. However, little evidence exists that these approaches translate into better teaching and learning (Stake, 1998). In fact, given the explosion of testing across the country and the ensuing "testing culture" that is developing in many schools, these policies may actually undermine schools' attempts to develop a culture for standards-based reforms, one based on teaching for understanding and improving student work, and on the complementary relationships and routines that motivate students and teachers to work hard at meaningful tasks.

To date, in most districts and states, strategies for improving teaching and learning to match the vision of the standards movment have largely fallen short of their desired effect. For one thing, as researchers James Spillane and Charles Thompson (1997) learned when they studied nine districts in Michigan, local capacity for understanding and leading reform varies dramatically from district to district. At the same time, when Spillane and Thompson began to probe the districts' strategies for realizing "ambitious instructional reform," they found that local district offices in "high capacity" districts took distinct steps to foster reform through leveraging "human capital," (teachers linked to networks so as to promote norms of trust and collaboration) "social capital" (resources outside the schools supporting new norms), and financial resources for reform.

These findings imply that just as states should work with districts to change their cultures, districts must work with schools to build capacity for developing a culture for standards-based reforms in every school. What specifically can district and state leaders do? Current "standards policy" offers little assistance. However, the experiences of standards-oriented reformers to date suggest a variety of new directions.

Send clear messages

As districts and states are currently organized, both are vulnerable to a variety of forces that results in their sending mixed messages to schools. Whether seen in terms of what Judith Warren Little calls "goal overload" (Sparks, 1993) or what Linda Darling-Hammond (1997) calls "policy collision," districts and states often charge school-based educators with conflicting mandates. However, when district leadership sets out to clarify the purpose of schooling in terms of teaching for understanding and improved student work, and backs that message up with real support and resources, schools can develop the kinds of cultures that support deeper student learning.

When district leadership sets out to clarify the purpose of schooling in terms of teaching for understanding and improved student work, and backs that message up with real support and resources, schools can develop the kinds of cultures that support deeper student learning.

For example, in District 2 in New York City, the message that every aspect of school operations should result in better instruction, trumpeted consistently over ten years, has made significant contributions to the development of a powerful culture for standards-based reform that touches almost every school district wide (Elmore, 1997). This message has come from the top through the superintendent and his staff. To underscore this message, the district first mobilized all its resources to address the top-ranked goal of literacy development. But support did not end there. In addition, the district infused every level of operations with opportunities for professional development, involving teachers in planning for curriculum and instruction, assessment, leadership and teacher development, and school reorganization to serve the goal of improved literacy. Every district staff meeting, monthly principals' meeting, school site visits, and performance review also focused on literacy learning.

The focus on literacy was just the beginning. The district's initial foray into focused professional development established a culture of high expectations for staff, risk taking and reflection. The initiative also consolidated and strengthened the instructional leadership in every school. As a result, there was no question as to the purpose of schooling, and "goal overload"diminished among principals and faculty. Over the years, the district took on reform of other content areas and grade levels with the same intense focus. Having mobilized the entire district for improved literacy learning, the shift to content areas, again emphasized in every area of school operations, was relatively easy.

In District 2, the sending of a clear message about the priority of instructional improvement over any other aspect of school reform was not a management tool designed to standardize practice across schools. Rather, it set the stage for creating a district-wide culture based on higher expectations for better work from both teachers and students, persistent effort, continuous improvement, and professional collegiality. In addition, by communicating that instruction counted for more than anything else in the districts' work, district and school staff were able to move schools away from a "project"mindset and establish an expectation that every single employee in the system would be continuously involved in learning, planning, piloting, and reflecting on instructional improvement.

Promote cross-program collaboration around curriculum innovation

The lack of coherence around purposeful reform in many schools should not be surprising given schools' need to respond to different sets of laws and regulation that themselves may have little overlap. District and state operations are often equally fragmented, with different departments and programs operating independently of one another, sharing neither goals nor resources. Given the emphasis of the standards movement on the disciplines, some content areas departments may move full-speed ahead toward standards-based reform, leaving those responsible for "special populations" outside of both planning for curriculum and instructional reforms and their implementation. If standards-based reform is to benefit every single student, including those whose first language is not English and those with disabilities, greater coordination for a shared purpose is necessary at state, district, and school levels.

If standards-based reform is to benefit every single student, including those whose first language is not English and those with disabilities, greater coordination for a shared purpose is necessary at state, district, and school levels.

District offices play a key role in ensuring that content-focused reforms will benefit all students. For example, in working to promote inquiry-based science for all students through eighth grade in urban districts, the Center for Urban Science Education Reform (CUSER) at the Education Development Center, Inc. realized that many districts were planning reforms in science curriculum and instruction in the absence of any consultation with staff responsible for special programs. Moreover, they realized that professional development for new curriculum often excluded staff who would be working directly with students most in need of the enriched opportunities to learn offered by new curriculum. To address this lack of coordination, CUSER staff pulled together central office teams consisting of science curriculum leaders along with staff responsible for special programs, including special education, Title I, and bilingual or ESL education, for a weekend retreat of conversation and planning. This was the first time many participants had worked together for a common curricular purpose. As a result, science reformers within the district office now include special program staff in district level planning, and they are promoting similar kinds of cross-program implementaion in every school. Further, some districts like South Bend, Indiana, and Spring Branch, Texas, have started involving bilingual and special education para-professionals along with professional staff in professional development around new science curriculum.

Nurture principals as instructional leaders

Of all the things district leadership can do to support school cultures for standards-based reform, identifying, recruiting, and developing principals as instructional leaders is perhaps the most important. Districts must match skilled educators to schools that fit their strengths and nurture principals' knowledge and skills so that they can, in turn, work with teachers to build a culture focused on teaching and learning for understanding. For example, as part of New York City's District 2's thrust toward instructional effectiveness through professional development, principals who are instructional leaders are now in place in nearly every school.

How is *instructional leadership* defined in practice? As Richard Elmore and Deana Burney (1997) found in their study of that district's approach to systemic change, instructional leadership begins with beliefs about learning that set the stage for common expectations for student and professional performance. In District 2, principals exert instructional leadership and strengthen norms of collegiality in their own schools by expanding teachers' participation in networks, study groups, and district meetings. Principals also initiate visits to other schools to observe specific teaching strategies, and they travel with their teachers on those visitations. With teachers, they also attend district meetings designed to raise awareness of instructional improvement in particular subject areas. In their own schools, they conduct demonstration lessons in classrooms. District 2 principals see these activities not as add-on professional development activities, but part of their regular responsibilities as principals.

District 2 has nurtured principals as instructional leaders in a variety of ways. For example, principals participate in regular monthly meetings, held in principals' own buildings, that focus on matters of instruction. Some principals also meet regularly with smaller support groups of four or five peers. New principals are assigned as "buddies" to more experienced administrators, and they spend up to two days a month in their buddy's school for their first two years on the job. When principals encounter particular difficulties, district staff encourage them to consult with other principals experienced in solutions to specific problems (Elmore, 1997).

Building school cultures for standards-based reform clearly requires principals who are prepared to act as educators with the knowledge and skills for leading teachers in adopting ambitious instructional reforms. The district's responsibility is to assign such professionals to every school in the district.

Stabilize professional staff in each school

Habits of trust and professional collaboration require a stable professional community, including continuity of principals. However, in some schools, especially in urban districts, this stability is hard to come by. Not only does high staff turnover limit the development of a collegial community; it also affects students' opportunities to learn and meet standards. For example, Dick Corbett and Bruce Wilson (1997b) found that the number of Philadelphia seventh graders who had multiple or long-term substitutes was "sizable." Such holes in the teaching staff represented a major "crack in the classroom floor," undermining consistency in expectations and instruction, time spent on learning, and meaningful adult-student relationships that might foster motivation. Moreover, when students had long-term substitutes for teachers assigned to two or more core subjects (science and math, for example), they felt the negative effects in 50 percent of their core classes. These circumstances make it virtually impossible to build a culture for standards-based reform and learning for understanding.

District offices must take proactive steps to identify those schools that suffer most from staff turnover and take steps to address the circumstances contributing to persistent teacher vacancies. Remedies are likely to vary according to circumstances, but assigning principals who are strong instructional leaders to the most needy schools and allowing them as much latitude as possible to hire their own staff is a first step. In districts like Baltimore, principals and district staff have been able to work with such organizations as Teach for America to fill gaps. Central office staff can also train principals in more rigorous teacher evaluation procedures that can result in encouraging uncommitted teachers to find work outside education and can develop a set of incentives and recognition mechanisms to encourage experienced teachers to teach in high turnover schools.

Help schools reschedule to make time for professional learning within schools

Whether schools are focused on providing extra help to students so that all can meet standards or strengthening professional collegiality, teachers in schools need more time to develop new routines and beliefs for standards-based reforms. However, as a RAND report(Purnell & Hill, 1992) noted, creating blocks of time within the traditional structure of the school day and year remains "one of the major hurdles to accomplishing change" (p. 40). District office staff can consult with schools to assess use of time and provide technical assistance in maximizing use of time for purposes of standards-based reforms. Technical assistance must identify ways in which schools can supplement existing staff with more adults – additional teachers, community volunteers, staff from school-university partnerships – so that groups of teachers can use time within the school day to plan new curriculum, examine student work, and engage in professional development to implement new teaching strategies. Some districts have helped principals identify various self-study tools they can use with teachers as a stimulus for assessing teachers' use of time.

Support teacher networks and study groups

District staff can also take proactive steps to sponsor teacher networks around new curriculum in the subject areas and around instruction for authentic pedagogy. In fact, in some districts, teachers have already organized themselves into study groups to provide peer support for new instruction like Socratic seminars and peer learning in subject areas. For example, some 14 percent of Philadelphia's teachers are affiliated with networks of science resource leaders, math resource leaders, and the Philadelphia Writing Project (Useem, Culbertson, & Buchanan, 1997).

But without district support, teacher networks can atrophy. Networks need not only funding; they also need support for setting up meetings, recruiting new members, and cultivating leadership. Districts stand to gain from such support as they use teacher networks to identify teacher leaders and teachers who may ultimately become principals.

Whether at the district or state level, administrators can also work collaboratively with teacher networks to test new policies related to standards reforms. Teacher study groups, for example, can provide planners with important information about the effects of policies, and connect standards-based reforms at the policy level to the realities of schools and classrooms. For example, during the process of developing an early set of curriculum frameworks, the Massachusetts Department of Education explicitly encouraged statewide teacher study groups to help policy makers understand the impact of new frameworks on teaching and learning. First the department allocated federal and state funding to promote school- and district-based study groups for the purpose of generating real world comments on the state's draft content standards. Then, across the state, districts themselves organized study groups where teachers reviewed draft standards, posed research questions around the state's content-focused curriculum frameworks, and field-tested recommended units designed to answer their questions. Through this process, teachers developed an understanding of new expectations for student learning and, at the same time, helped standards writers at the state level fine-tune the frameworks documents.

Support processes for school-based reflection on school performance and student work

Districts and states can play a key role in supporting schools to be accountable for their practice by de-emphasizing bureaucratic models of accountability and focusing on what schools are doing inside schools to help students produce work that meets standards. Policy-level staff, for example, can provide technical assistance for gathering data on schools' instructional programs, using student surveys, and identifying means of making the work of all students more public. Districts themselves can also routinely gather data on "context indicators" that reflect aspects of schools' cultures. These might include teachers' beliefs about learning, assignments, use of rubrics and exemplars, and evidence of learning applied outside of school. Data gathering on students' opportunities to learn content that opens doors to understanding in the disciplines, along with data on the number and percentage of students leaving eighth grade and enrolling in a college-preparatory high school program, is especially critical.

Districts and states can play a key role in supporting schools to be accountable for their practice by de-emphasizing bureaucratic models of accountability and focusing on what schools are doing inside schools to help students produce work that meets standards.

Developing professional accountability also means that districts should assist schools in analyzing trends in school-based data and link schools to resources so they can act on those data to improve student work, teaching, and learning. Districts should train school teams to use such tools as the Los Angeles-based Achievement Council's guide for examining school data, *Setting Our Sights* by Ruth Johnson (1996). This handbook provides a wealth of tools for assessing the steps individual schools can take to use data to realize a high achievement culture. Tools include student, parent, and teacher surveys, a guide for identifying high-performing counseling practices that support high achievement, and an assessment of the status of institutional supports for an academic culture.

Convene teachers system wide to develop rubrics and identify exemplars

Districts and states can also take steps to foster a shared definition of what constitutes high quality student work by bringing teachers together across schools and districts to examine student work. This strategy can serve the purpose of developing shared expectations for student work while communicating that student work is as important as test scores. At the district level, teachers may come together to describe how student work derived from a common complex task fits different levels of performance. For example, in separate summer institutes, Long Beach, California, and San Diego City Schools have both pulled teachers from all grades together to score student work. In San Diego, some 400 teachers have worked to score some 32,000 Literacy Assessment Portfolios from Grades 3, 4, and 8. As a result, more teachers have a better idea of the concrete expectations for student work, and the district as a whole is better informed about student progress toward meeting newly-adopted language arts standards.

State departments of education can lead similar work on a state-wide level. For example, the Minnesota Department of Children, Families, and Learning is investing in a multi-year effort to develop a common understanding of what constitutes good work in every district in the state. Beginning in the summer of 1997, the state convened teachers from all over the state to discuss the quality of student work in the context of the state's standards initiative.

Beth Aune, the project's coordinator and Minnesota's Director of Post-Secondary Relations, explains how state policy is focused on infusing higher expectations for better quality work through improving professional practice and shaping collegial discussions about student work. State-facilitated discussions have helped teachers formally look at student work as a way of discussing learning assignments that link to the complex reasoning processes called for in the state's standards. Aune reports:

> We had a process that involved teachers in looking at a wide range of the student work they brought with them to our summer meeting. We knew that over time we wanted to develop rubrics, and we wanted to create a better understanding of what good evidence that students have met the standards looks like. It was a tough couple of days because we were tying our discussions to standards. Some teachers would bring a project and

say, "Look how good this is!" and we would have to say, "Yes, but it's irrelevant."

During their time together, teachers looking at student work identified several pieces that were so outstanding they could be considered exemplars. For some teachers, these will be key to rethinking expectations. "They've never seen a model," Aune explains. She adds:

> Some teachers became aware that they were not expecting enough from their students. In one evaluation, a teacher wrote, "I didn't realize kids this age could do this kind of work. I'm going to raise my expectations."

Over several years, Minnesota will replicate this process in regions around the state, with the goal of deepening all Minnesota teachers' understanding of what constitutes quality work. Aune notes that the summer process generated a few exemplars along with a set of four-point guidelines for scoring work, and that eventually more exemplars and rubrics will be available to describe expectations for work on each of the state's 24 "learning profiles." She also notes that principals and district leaders are beginning to appreciate the value of the process for their own schools. In fact, Wayzata, Minnesota, Public Schools Director of Assessment and Evaluation Roger Anderson echos her assessment, reporting that gathering teachers together to develop exemplars and rubrics is a "terrific staff development tool and way to get a department on the same page." For Minnesota educators, then, the state's support for professional discussions leading to agreement of what constitutes quality work offers a policy context that reinforces what individual teachers and schools are doing to develop a culture of high standards. At the same time it provides a vehicle for extending this culture beyond individual classrooms and schools to redefine professional practice across the state.

Gathering teachers together to develop exemplars and rubrics is a 'terrific staff development tool and way to get a department on the same page.'

Identify resources to match the goals of standards-based reform

Districts and states can also leverage education budgets to support steps that will result in stronger school cultures for standards-based reform. For example, districts and states should ensure that schools where large numbers of students need extra help receive both the funding and technical assistance necessary for building extra help opportunities directly into the school day. Budgeting should be strategic, that is it should be calculated to apply funds to those strategies most likely to bring about desired results. For example, in New York City's District 2, former Superintendent Alvarado made professional development visible in the district budget to communicate the priority the district was placing on instructional reform (Elmore, 1997). In addition, to reinforce this focused strategy, district staff drew funding from multiple sources, including local tax revenue, Title I, special education, and state categorical programs like magnet schools.

Resources go beyond funding, however. Districts and states can foster networks of schools and link both individual schools and network to national school reform organizations. Districts must also be more pro-active in identifying specific curriculum materials and outside resources that can support the goals of learning for understanding. As districts identify high-quality standards-based curriculum, they should also put in place a process for professional development and follow-up coaching to support teachers who begin to use that curriculum. Further, they should identify a process for making those schools using that curriculum demonstration sites so that other teachers can learn about innovative curriculum.

In addition, districts should identify materials suitable for all student groups, including those students whose first language is not English. In fact, the absence of content-rich materials is especially pronounced for students in bilingual and ESL classes. Even schools with high numbers of students whose first language is not English find it is difficult to identify materials that incorporate the high content contemplated by the standards and curriculum frameworks (Lara, 1995). Coordinated support for these schools is essential both to ensure high-quality materials and to save schools duplication of effort as they undertake such a search on their own.

The need for concrete resources in terms of books and facilities improvement cannot be overestimated as a way of mobilizing teacher commitment to reform. For example, many schools have space for libraries, but they do not have full-or part-time librarians assigned to work with teachers; and 30 percent of high poverty schools in particular, do not meet staffing levels recommended by The American Association of School Librarians (AASL) (National Center for Education Statistics, 1995). This deficiency leaves many teachers without in-school support for developing resource-based curriculum units.

When schools do meet AASL standards, librarians can serve multiple roles as instructional leaders for developing integrated curriculum units and introducing teachers to standards-based instruction with positive results (DeWitt Wallace-Reader's Digest Fund, 1998).

Develop public support of learning for understanding

As schools begin to implement standards-based reforms to benefit all students, events around the country provide ample evidence in support of the observation of researchers working on the massive Study of Schooling of the mid-1980s:

> Reformers who emphasize quality, and who mean by it higher expectations for all, will be tolerated only to the point where they can find a willing audience; beyond that point they will be resisted. The idea that serious mastery is possible and necessary for most Americans is simply not widely shared. (Powell, Farrar, & Cohen, 1985, p. 6)

Rhetoric to the contrary, many Americans still may not believe that 'all children can learn at high levels.'

Rhetoric to the contrary, many Americans still may not believe that "all children can learn at high levels." For example, in Kentucky, a statewide poll has revealed that most citizens do not believe that all students can learn for deeper levels of understanding (Roberts & Kay, Inc., 1993).

Districts and states play a key role in developing the wider public support for higher standards so that schools can take the necessary steps to develop stronger cultures for learning for understanding. Districts, for example, can promote opportunities for the public to see student work through the grades. They can also provide opportunties for school boards, parents, and the public to experience the kinds of teaching that produce exemplary student work as a way to generate support for new classroom practices.

In specific content areas, districts and states can also partner with professional organizations to sponsor large-scale community events to increase public awareness of the implications learning for understanding. For example, the Delaware Council of Teachers of Mathematics and the Delaware Mathematics Coalition Board routinely co-sponsor a Saturday Math Fair at a shopping mall to demonstrate new approaches to the mathematical learning envisioned by NCTM standards. In this public event, teachers from ten schools demonstrate new methods of teaching mathematics using manipulatives, calculators, and computers. Parents, students, and the public can view exemplary student projects and work on standards-based mathematical puzzles and games themselves. The group distributes pamphlets describing various initiatives in math education, and business and universities highlight the application of mathematics in real-world settings(NCTM News Bulletin, 1995, p. 3). While this biennial fair serves as a means of communicating to a citizen audience the meaning of higher achievement in mathematics, it also suggests an approach that could be used to take work from all learning domains into the community and develop support for teaching and learning grounded in student work.

Districts can also provide support so that schools themselves can reach out to their communities and explain their work in public settings. For example, in Vermont, every school in every town in every part of the state holds a School Report Day to talk about student achievement and school performance. Districts can also provide funding for schools expressly for the purpose of introducing parents to student work and new teaching strategies. For example, schools in South Deerfield, Massachusetts hold regular Family Math nights as an way for parents to view student work, thus making NCTM standards come alive for the community.

Charting new territory

Almost a decade into the standards movement, there is little evidence that relying on top-down efforts to reform schools through high stakes testing and new assessments

There is little evidence that relying on top-down efforts to reform schools through high stakes testing and new assessments has produced much change in teaching and learning.

has produced much change in teaching and learning. In contrast, some emerging evidence from districts like District 2 in New York City suggests that when districts focus more explicitly on instructional reform, they can create a momentum for change that is compatible with the need to build a culture for standards-based reform in every single school. If districts and states want to make a difference to schools, they are well-advised to choose the path of supporting instructional reform and nurturing a system-wide commitment to professional practice.

If districts and states want to make a difference to schools, they are well-advised to choose the path of supporting instructional reform and nurturing a system-wide commitment to professional practice.

In choosing to throw their weight behind ambitious instructional reform, districts assume responsibility for taking on demanding new roles. Rather than keeping schools at a distance, they must engage closely with schools, interacting with teachers and principals at the school site. They must move away from acting bureaucratically as regulators and "aligners" of curriculum, instruction, and assessment in an abstract way. Instead, they must act more proactively to create norms of continuous improvement and collegiality, to cultivate and nurture relationships so that professionals can use their own expertise and that of their peers for better teaching and learning. They must also act directly to serve as instructional coaches within specific curriculum areas. In short, just as each school needs instructional leaders, district and state-level educators must also assume roles of consultants and coaches informed about instructional matters. This path, rather than the path to more standardized curriculum and testing, has many challenges, but it is likely to result in more lasting and systemic reforms in teaching and learning. ◻

V.   Conclusion

*The best kind of learning is learning all together, in little
groups or big groups; it's a really good way to teach kids.
Learn with each other, not just alone. Kids who don't learn
this way are really missing out. I think it's a privilege for us to
be able to have this kind of education. People who just learn
the traditional way, just by themselves, who don't get help, it's
like, totally un-nineties. It's also scary.*
— Julia Devanthery Lewis, sixth grader,
John M. Tobin School, Cambridge, Massachusetts
(quoted in Coles, 1998, p. 15).

T he standards movement was born with good intentions. Seen in its
best light, it offers the impetus for educators to infuse opportunities
for all students to learn for understanding into every aspect of school life. At
its worst, it reinforces practices that our best educators know to be ineffective
routes to real learning. Standardized testing and curriculum, grade retention,
ability grouping, and tracking are all reemerging in the guise of "standards-
based reform," especially in those districts enrolling large numbers of our
most vulnerable students. To the extent that these practices become proxies
for "standards," the vision of all students learning for understanding will
remain unrealized.

The cost of mistaking old practices for new standards is high. First, because these practices institutionalize narrowly defined and unequal achievement, they are counterproductive to the goals of improved learning for all
students. Moreover, these practices, heralded as standards, take a toll in less
measurable ways. Taken together, they ensure that schools will remain places
where few adolescents dare to excel and where many will feel that *being
smart* is fraught with danger. For young adolescents, danger lies in being
separated from friends and social circles; it lies in being forced to choose
between individual success and group loyalties; it lies in being asked to do
work that undermines one's sense of dignity. To avoid these dangers, stu-

dents may "tune out," pretend indifference to learning, or defer from asking questions that invite too much attention from teachers. At the same time, they may hide mistakes that could suggest incompetence. To avoid labels that reflect on their ability, they may dodge difficult assignments or situations that require hard work, all to circumvent the danger of being judged on the "smartness" continuum. In settings marked by sorting and labeling practices, *being smart* is to be different, and few adolescents feel safe to be different.

In contrast, a school culture for standards-based reform allows every student to feel *safe to be smart*. Such a culture puts the focus on student work and communicates explicit expectations for the work required from every single student. It draws strength from relationships of trust and beliefs about learning that allow students to risk working hard, making mistakes, and persisting. It is grounded in assignments that every student can find engaging, and its credibility rests on routines that build the support students need to succeed into the regular school day. It communicates that every student will learn by asking for help and by helping others do good work, so that it is not only *safe* but exciting to *be smart*.

This report does not offer a fool-proof process for creating school cultures for standards-based reform. It does describe an assortment of practices that can shape such a culture. Every day, educators around the country are venturing to discover different ways to help more students to do better work more of the time. No one single report could describe all these efforts with any sense of finality. It remains to educators working together in their own schools to find the right mix of practices that will turn their schools into places where students demonstrate an understanding of challenging problems in the disciplines through carefully and thoughtfully executed work. In these schools all students are acquiring and using the skills and knowledge they need for citizenship, work, and lifelong learning in a democracy.

This report, then, is a *work in progress* delineating a number of approaches some middle grades educators are taking to build school cultures for standards-based learning. Yes, the standards of the professional associations offer helpful clues to thinking about what "all students should know and be able to do." But in the absence of school cultures organized around a compelling vision of the work young adolescents can do, routines that communicate the value of effort and perseverance, and human relationships that sustain students through difficult times, all the curriculum objectives in the world will not result in learning that lasts beyond the final exam or that opens doors to future educational opportunity.

In the end, the standards movement rises and falls on the meaning teachers and their students make of it in individual schools. The challenge for practitioners and policy makers alike is to mobilize the commitment of those in every school to develop school cultures that celebrate work worth doing well and work well done. If the standards movement can energize our commitment for that task, young adolescents in the country's middle schools may yet benefit. ◼

REFERENCES

Academy for Educational Development. (1995, December). *Expeditionary Learning Outward Bound Project: Final report.* Unpublished paper.

Adler, M. (1982). *The Paideia proposal: An educational manifesto.* New York: Macmillan.

Aguilar, M. (1997, November 28). Homework help at middle school, *Daily Hampshire Gazette.*

Alexander, K.L., & Entwisle, D.R. (1996). Educational tracking during the early years: First grade placements and middle school constraints. In A.C. Kerckhoff (Ed.), *Generating social stratification: Toward a new research agenda* (pp. 75-105). Boulder, CO: Westview Press.

Allington, R.L. (1994). The schools we have. The schools we need. *Reading Teacher, 48* (1), 14-29.

Anderman, E.M., & Maehr, M.L. (1994). Motivation and schooling in the middle grades. *Review of Educational Research, 64* (2), 287-309.

Appalachia Educational Laboratory. (1996). Five years of reform in rural Kentucky: Notes from the field. *Education Reform in Rural Kentucky, 5* (1), Charlestown, WV: Author.

Ascher, C., Ikeda, K., & Fruchter, N. (1998). *Schools on notice: A policy study of New York State's 1996-97 schools under registration review process. Final report to the New York State Education Department.* NY: Institute for Education and Social Policy, New York University.

Asimov, N. (1998, January 6). Reform - no sure cure: S.F. primary school struggles despite radical overhaul, *San Francisco Chronicle*, p. A13.

Associated Press. (1998, August 11). Family money top factor in college attendance: Income, preparation beat scores in study. *Washington Post*, p. A08.

Association for Supervision and Curriculum Development, (1997). *Presentation digest: Designing authentic tasks and scoring rubrics*. Alexandria, VA: Author.

ATLAS Communities. (1996a). *Guide for study groups*. New American Schools Development Corporation.

ATLAS Communities. (1996b). *Learning from student work*. New American Schools Development Corporation.

ATLAS Communities. (1997a). *ATLAS in practice*, An interview with Ted Sizer, *Spring,* 8-11.

ATLAS Communities. (1997b). Principals' institute (Unpublished proceedings). April.

Atwell, N. (1998). *In the middle: New understandings about writing, reading, and learning*. Portsmouth, NH: Heinemann-Boynton/Cook.

Bachofer, K.V., & Borton, W.M. (1994, December). *Restructuring: The dream lives on. The continuing evolution of O'Farrell Community School: Center for Advanced Academic Studies*. San Diego: San Diego City Schools, Planning, Assessment, and Accountability Division.

Ball, D.L., & Cohen, D.K. (1996). Reform by the book: What is - or might be - the role of curriculum materials in teacher learning and instructional reform? *Educational Researcher, 25* (9), 6-8, 14.

Barry, C. (1995). Putting standards in their own words. *Voices from the Middle* (Journal of the National Council of Teachers of English), *2* (1), 38-41.

Barth, M.J., & Frankonis, E. (1996). *The necessity of reflection: Public inquiry and accountability through school quality review.* Unpublished paper. Albany, NY: New York State Education Department.

Berger, R. (1996a). *A culture of quality: A reflection on practice.* Providence, RI: Annenberg Institute for School Reform.

Berger, R. (1996b). Water: A whole school expedition. In D. Udall and A. Mednick (Eds.), *Journeys Through Our Classrooms* (pp. 115-125). Dubuque, IA: Kendall/Hunt.

Blum, R.W., & Rinehart, P.M. (1977). *Reducing the risk: Connections that make a difference in the lives of youth.* Minneapolis, MN: University of Minnesota Printing Services.

Braddock, J.H. (1990). Tracking in the middle grades: National patterns of grouping for instruction. *Phi Delta Kappan, 71* (6).

Brady, L. (1996). 'The world is mine. Soon. I hope.' The struggle to raise standards. In D. Udall and A. Mednick (Eds.), *Journeys through our classrooms* (pp. 1-15). Dubuque, IA: Kendall/Hunt.

Bryk, A.S., Easton, J.Q., Kerbow, D., Rollow, S.G., & Sebring, P.A. (1993, July). *A view from the elementary schools: The state of reform in Chicago.* Chicago: Consortium on School Research.

Budde, A., & Johnson, S. (1998). Investigations. In M. Campbell, M. Liebowitz, A. Mednick, & L. Rugen, (Eds.), *Guide for planning a learning expedition* (pp. 129-147). Dubuque, IA: Kendall/Hunt.

Burke, D.L. (1996). Multi-year teacher/student relationships are a long-overdue arrangement. *Phi Delta Kappan, 77* (5), 360-361.

Campbell, M., Liebowitz, M., Mednick, A., & Rugen, L. (1998). *Guide for planning a learning expedition.* Dubuque, IA: Kendall/Hunt.

Carnegie Council on Adolescent Development. (1989). *Turning points: Preparing American youth for the 21st century.* New York: Carnegie Corporation.

Cheney, L. (1997a, August 11). Creative math, or just fuzzy math? *New York Times.*

Cheney, L. (1997b, September 29). A failing grade for Clinton's national standards. *Wall Street Journal.*

Clinchy, B.M. (1997). The standardization of the student. In E. Clinchy (Ed.), *Transforming public education: A new course for America's future.* New York: Teachers College Press.

Coe, C., & Useem, B. (1996, September). *Bringing standards into the classroom: A report on the summer work of Partnerships for Standards-Based Professional Development.* Unpublished paper. Philadelphia Education Fund.

Cohen, D.K. (1995). What is the system in systemic reform? *Educational Researcher, 24* (9), 11-17, 31.

Cohen, D.K., & Ball, D. (1998, July). Instruction, capacity, and improvement. Photocopied paper. Ann Arbor, MI: University of Michigan.

Cohen, D.K., & Hill, H. (1997, August). Instructional policy and classroom performance: The mathematics reform in California. Photocopied paper. Ann Arbor, MI: University of Michigan.

Cohen, E. (1986). *Designing groupwork: Strategies for heterogeneous classrooms.* New York: Teachers College Press.

Coles, R. (1998, September 27). In school. *Boston Globe Magazine*, pp. 14-17, 21.

Connected Mathematics Project. (n.d.). Problem-centered teachering: The focus of CMP teaching and learning. Available: http://www.math.msu.edu/cmp/ProbTch.html#Analysis.

Corbett, H.D., & Wilson, B.L. (1997a). *Cracks in the classroom floor: The seventh grade year in five Philadelphia middle schools.* Philadelphia: Philadelphia Education Fund.

Corbett, D., & Wilson, B. (1997b). *Urban students' perspective on middle school: The sixth grade year in five Philadelphia middle schools.* Philadelphia: Philadelphia Education Fund.

Corbett, D., Wilson, B, & Williams, B. (1997). *Assumptions, actions, and performance: First year report to OERI and the participating school districts.* Providence, RI: Northeast and Islands Regional Educational Laboratory at Brown University.

Cotton, K. (1996). School size, school climate, and student performance. *Close-up Number 20.* Portland, OR: Northwest Regional Educational Laboratory.

Cziko, C. (1996). Brother, can you spare a dime? Designing a learning expedition on the Great Depression. In D. Udall & A. Mednick (Eds.), *Journeys through our classrooms* (pp. 77-88). Dubuque, IA: Kendall/Hunt.

Daniels, H. (1994). *Literature circles: Voice and choice in the student-centered classroom*, York, ME: Stenhouse.

Darling-Hammond, L. (1997). *The right to learn: A blueprint for creating schools that work.* San Francisco: Jossey-Bass.

Darling-Hammond, L. (1992-1993, Winter). Standards of practice and delivery for learner-centered schools. *Stanford Law and Policy Review,* 37-52.

Darling-Hammond, L. (1996). *What matters most: Teaching for America's future. Report of the National Commission on Teaching and America's Future.* New York: Columbia University, Teachers College Press.

Darling-Hammond, L. (1996). The quiet revolution: Rethinking teacher development. *Educational Leadership, 53* (6), 4-10.

Darling-Hammond, L, Einbender, L., Frelow, F., & Ley-King, J. (1993). *Authentic assessment in practice: A collection of portfolios, performance tasks, exhibitions.* New York: National Center for Restructuring Education, Schools, and Teaching, Teachers College, Columbia University.

Darling-Hammond, L., & Falk, B. (1997). Using standards and assessments to support student learning. *Phi Delta Kappan, 79* (3), 190-199.

Dean, M. (1997, October 2). Critics say Hornbeck's report card needs improvement. *Philadelphia Daily News.*

deLone, R. (1979). *Small futures: Children, inequality, and the limits of liberal reform.* New York: Harcourt Brace Jovanovich.

Delpit. L. (1995). *Other people's children: Cultural conflict in the classroom.* New York: New Press.

Dentzer, E., &Wheelock, A. (1990). *Locked in/locked out: Tracking and placement practices in Boston Public Schools.* Boston: Massachusetts Advocacy Center.

DeWitt-Wallace Reader's Digest Fund. (1998). *Library power: Strategies for enriching teaching and learning in America's public schools.* New York: Author.

Diegmueller, K. (1996, August 7). By AFT's standards, only 15 states deserve passing grade. *Education Week.*

Dow, P.B. (1991). *Schoolhouse politics: Lessons from the Sputnik era*. Cambridge, MA: Harvard University Press.

Dweck, C., Kamins, M., & Mueller, C. (1997, April). *Praise, criticism, and motivational vulnerability*. Symposium paper delivered at the biennial meetings of the Society for Research in Child Development, Washington, DC.

Education Development Center. (1997, June 5-6). National forum to accelerate middle-grades school reform. Proceedings of Meeting.

Elmore, R.F., with Burney, D. (1997, August). *Investing in teacher learning: Staff development and instructional improvement in Community School District #2, New York City*. New York: National Commission on Teaching and America's Future, Teachers College, Columbia University (with the Consortium for Policy Research in Education, University of Pennsylvania).

Elmore, R.F., & Burney, D. (1997, October). *School variation and systemic instructional improvement in Community School District #2, New York City*. Unpublished paper.

Evans, P. (1994, October 19). Getting beyond chewing gum and book covers. *Education Week*, 44.

Farkus, S., & Johnson, J. (1997). *Kids these days: What Americans really think about the next generation*. New York: Public Agenda.

Farrell, E. (1990). *Hanging in and dropping out: Voices of at risk high school students*. New York: Teachers College Press.

Feldman, S. (1997). Passing on failure. *American Educator. 21* (3), 4-10.

Felner, R.D., Jackson, A.W., Kasak, D., Mulhall, P., Brand, S., & Flowers, N. (1997). The impact of school reform for the middle years, *Phi Delta Kappan, 78* (7), 528-532, 541-550.

Fine, M. (Ed.) (1994). *Chartering urban school reform: Reflections on public high schools in the midst of change*. New York: Teachers College Press.

Fine, M. (1991). *Framing dropouts: Notes on the politics of an urban high school*. Albany, NY: SUNY Press.

Fine, M. (1986). Why urban adolescents drop into and out of public high school. *Teachers College Record, 87* (3).

Flanders, J.R. (1987). How much of the content in mathematics textbooks is new? *Arithmetic Teacher, September.*

Focused Reporting Project. (1995). How will Chattanooga know when students are achieving more? *School reform in Chattanooga, 1* (2). New York: Edna McConnell Clark Foundation.

Focused Reporting Project. (1997a). What students say about rubrics. *Changing schools in Long Beach, 1* (2). New York: Edna McConnell Clark Foundation.

Focused Reporting Project (1997b). History teachers dig deep into their students' work and their own teaching. *Changing schools in Long Beach, 2* (1). New York: Edna McConnell Clark Foundation.

Fordham, S., & Ogbu, J. (1986). Black students' school success: Coping with the 'burden of acting white.' *Urban Review, 18* (3).

Fullan, M. (1991). *The new meaning of educational change.* New York: Teachers College Press.

Gardner, H. (1993). *Frames of mind: The theory of multiple intelligences* (Tenth Anniversary Edition). New York: Basic Books.

George, P.S., & Alexander, W. (1993). *The exemplary middle school.* New York: Harcourt Brace Jovanovich College Publishers.

Ginsberg, R., & Berry, B. (1991). Experiencing school reform: The view from South Carolina. *Phi Delta Kappan, 71* (7).

Glovin, D., & Casey, M. (1998, July 7). Schools have kids cram for state tests. *Bergin (NJ) Record,* p. A1.

Goals 2000: Educate America Act. (1994, March 31). Public Law 103-227.

Gonzalez, D. (1997, June 28). Going ahead, grounded in reality. *New York Times,* p. A1.

Goodlad, J.I. (1984). *A place called school.* New York: McGraw-Hill.

Gregg, M., & Leinhardt, G. (1994). Mapping out geography: An example of epistemology and education. *Review of Educational Research 16* (2), pp. 311-361.

Grossman, W. (1998, March 3). Program helps teens get back on track. *USA Today*, p. A1.

Haberman, M. (1991). The pedagogy of poverty versus good teaching. *Phi Delta Kappan, 72* (4), 290-294.

Haberman, M. (1997). Unemployment training: The ideology of nonwork learned in urban schools. *Phi Delta Kappan, 78* (7), 499-503.

Hackman, D.G. (1997). Student-led conferences at the middle level. *ERIC Digest No. ED 407 171.*

Hammond, R., & Howard, J.P. (1986). Doing what's expected of you: The roots and rise of the dropout culture. *Metropolitan Education* (2).

Harp, L. (1997, July 23). High-stakes tests make security a big issue. *Lexington Herald Leader.*

Hart, J. (1997, November 16). Teaching from the heart: Educator shares her passionate philosophy of reaching out to students. *Boston Sunday Globe*, Learning Section, pp. L5, L6.

Henderson, V., & Dweck, C. (1900). Motivation and achievement. In S. S. Feldman & G. R. Elliott (Eds.). *At the threshold: The developing adolescent.* Cambridge, MA: Harvard University Press.

Henry, T. (1998, July 14). Schools pay a price for raising standards. *USA Today*, p. A01.

Herman, J.L., Aschbacher, P.R., & Winters, L. (1992). *A practical guide to alternative assessment.* Alexandria, VA: Association for Supervision and Curriculum Development.

Hibbard, M. (1996). *A teacher's guide to performance-based learning and assessment.* Arlington, VA: Association for Supervision and Curriculum Development.

Hilliard, A. (n.d.).Cultural pluralism in education. In Dickinson, D. (Ed.), *Creating the future: Perspectives on educational change.* Seattle, WA: New Horizons for Learning.

Hirsh, S. (1997, October 3). Investing the time to learn. *NSDC Results* (Newsletter of the National Staff Development Council).

Holland, H. (1997). The Brown vs. the Department of Education. *Louisville Magazine, October*, 38-48, 74-79.

Hoover, M.N., Zawojewski, J.S., & Ridgway, J. (1997, March). *Effects of the connected mathematics project on student attainment*. Paper presented at the annual meeting of the American Educational Research Association, Chicago, IL. Also available at http://www.math.msu/cmp.

Hopfenberg, W.S., Levin, H.M., & Chase, C. (1993). *The accelerated schools resource guide*. San Francisco: Jossey-Bass.

Hower, W., & Kurtz, M (1998, July 24). Summer school a testing time. *Durham News and Observer*, p. 01.

Ilka, D. (1997, December 2). State salutes 9 innovative schools in Oakland and Macomb. *Detroit News.*

Indelicato, A. (March 1998). Teachers questionnaire on standards implementation in the classroom. Summary included in the *Minneapolis Public School Quarterly Report to the Edna McConnell Clark Foundation,* (December 1, 1997-April 14, 1998).

Institute for Education in Transformation. (1992). *Voices from the inside: A report on schooling from inside the classroom*, Claremont, CA: Claremont Graduate School.

Jackson, A. (1997). The math wars: California battles it out over mathematics education reform. *Part I, Notices of the American Mathematical Society, 44* (6), 695-702.

Jervis, K., & McDonald, J. (1996). Standards: The philosophical monster in the classroom. *Phi Delta Kappan, 77* (8), 563-569.

Johnson, D. (1997, June 1). Chicago schools are setting a standard. *New York Times*, p. 6.

Johnson, R. (1996). *Setting our sights*. Los Angeles: The Achievement Council.

Johnson, D.W., & Johnson, R.T. (1975). *Learning together and alone*. Englewood Cliffs, NJ: Prentice-Hall.

Jones, K., & Whitford, B.L. (1997). Kentucky's conflicting reform principles: High stakes school accountability and student performance assessment. *Phi Delta Kappan, December*, 276-287.

Jones, R., & Mezzacappa, D. (1998, January 13). Testing slighted students' abilities. *Philadelphia Inquirer*

Jones, S.L. (1997, September 27). Ranking of schools rankles many. *San Diego Tribune*, B1:7; 2:5.

Joyce, B.R., & Showers, B. (1988). *Student achievement through staff development*. New York: Longman.

Katz, N.L. (1998, July 6). Summer term trips students. *New York Daily News*, A3.

Kellaghan, T., Madaus, G.F., & Raczek, A. (1996). *The use of external examinations to improve student motivation*. Washington, DC: American Educational Research Association.

Klonsky, M. (n.d.). *Small schools: The numbers tell a story*. Chicago: Small Schools Workshop, University of Illinois-Chicago.

Kohl, H. (1992) I won't learn from you! Thoughts on the role of assent in learning. *Rethinking Schools, 7* (1), 16-17, 19.

Koretz, D. (1988). Arriving in Lake Wobegon: Are standardized tests exaggerating achievement and distorting instruction?. *American Educator, 12* (2), 8-15, 46-52.

Koretz, D.M., Barron, S., Mitchel, K.J., & Stecher, B.M. (1996). *Perceived effects of the Kentucky Instructional Results Information System (KIRIS)*. Santa Monica, CA: RAND.

Kozol, J. (1991). *Savage inequalities*. New York: Basic Books.

Krieger, E. (1998a, August 18). Teachers rate their schools, students. *Providence Journal*, p. 01.

Krieger, E. (1998b, August 19). Most parents satisfied with their children's schools. *Providence Journal*, p. 01

Kreitzer, A., & Madaus, G.F. (1995). The test-driven curricululm. In D. Tanner & J.W. Keefe (Eds.), *Curriculum issues and the new century* (pp.23-28). Reston, VA: National Association of Secondary School Principals.

Kurtz, M. (1997, August 29). Retention rate rises sharply for Durham eighth-graders. *Durham News and Observer*.

Ladson-Billings, G. (1994). *Dream-keepers: Successful teachers of African American students*. San Francisco: Jossey-Bass.

Lara, J. (1995). *Second-language learners and middle school reform: A case study of a school in transition*. Washington, DC: Council of Chief State School Officers.

Levin, H.M. (1998). Educational performance standards and the economy. *Educational Researcher, 27* (4), 4-10.

Lipman, P. (1998). *Race, class, and power in school restructuring*. Albany, NY: State University of New York Press.

Lipsitz, J. (1984). *Successful schools for young adolescents*. New Brunswick, NJ: Transaction Books.

Lounsbury, J., & Clark, D. (1990). *Inside grade eight: From apathy to excitement*. Reston, VA: National Association of Secondary School Principals.

Mac Iver, D.J. (1990). Meeting the needs of young adolescents: Advisory groups, interdisciplinary teaching teams, and school transition programs. *Phi Delta Kappan, February*, 457-464.

Mac Iver, D.J., & Plank, S.B. (1996, September). *The talent development middle school. Creating a motivational climate conducive to talent development in the middle schools: Implementation and effects of student team reading. Report No. 4*. Baltimore/Washington, DC: Johns Hopkins University and Howard University, Center for Research on the Education of Students Placed at Risk.

Mac Iver, D.J., & Reuman, D.A. (1993/1994). Giving their best: Grading and recognition practices that motivate students to work hard. *American Educator 17* (4), 24-31.

Mac Iver, D.J., Ruby, A., Balfanz, R., Plank, S., & Prioleau, A. D. (1998). *Looping: Helping middle school teachers to be caring and caring*. Working paper submitted to Division K (Teaching and Teacher Education): Section on Teaching and learning in the contexts of teachers' work.

Mac Iver, D.J., Balfanz, R., & Plank, S.B. (1998). An 'elective replacement' approach to providing extra help in math: The talent development middle schools' Computer- and Team-Assisted Mathematics Acceleration (CATAMA) Program. Manuscript submitted for publication.

Mac Iver, D.J., Plank, S.B., & Balfanz, R. (n.d.). *Working together to become proficient readers: Early impact of the talent development middle school's Student Team Literature Program*. Unpublished paper. Baltimore: Center for Research on the Education of Students Placed at Risk, Johns Hopkins University.

Madaus, G.F. & Kellaghan, T. (1993). The British experience with 'authentic' testing. *Phi Delta Kappan, 74* (6): 458-469.

Manzo, K.K. (1997, June 11). With vote set, Mass. Board still at odds over history standards. *Education Week*, p. 1.

Markley, M. (1998, March 23). HISD doesn't shine on national test. *Houston Chronicle*, p. A1.

Marzano, R.J., Pickering, D., & McTighe, J. (1993). *Assessing student outcomes: Performance assessment using the dimensions of learning model*. Alexandria, VA: Association for Supervision and Curriculum Development.

Mathews, J. (1997a, May 21). A math teacher's lessons in division. *Washington Post*, p. D1.

Mathews, J. (1997b, September 24). In Virginia schools, A new focus on facts: Some teachers fear state tests will mean a return to rote learning. *Washington Post*, p. A1.

Mayer, D.P. (1998). Do new teaching standards undermine performance on old tests? *Educational Evaluation and Policy Analysis, 20* (2), 53-73.

McDonald, J. (1996). Foreword to Berger, R. *A Culture of Quality: A Reflection on Practice*. Providence, RI: Annenberg Institute for School Reform.

McEwin, C.K., Dickinson, T.S., & Jenkins, D.M (1996). *America's middle schools: Practices and progress — A 25 year perspective*. Columbus, OH: National Middle School Association.

McGill-Franzen, A., & Allington, R. (1993). Flunk 'em or get them classified. *Educational Researcher, V* (4), 20.

McNamara, E. (1998, July 4). The daily test of teaching. *Boston Globe*, p. B1.

McNeil, L.M. (1988). *Contradictions of control: School structure and school knowledge*. New York: Routledge and Kegan Paul.

McQuillen, P.J. (1998). *Educational opportunity in an urban American high school: A cultural analysis.* Albany, NY: State University of New York Press.

Mehrens, W.A. (1998, July 13). Consequences of assessment: What is the evidence? *Education Policy Analysis Archives, 6* (13). Available: http://epaa.asu.edu/epaa/v6n13.html.

Meier, D. (1995). How our schools could be. *Phi Delta Kappan, 76* (5): 369-373.

Mezzacappa, D. (1997, October 9). Hornbeck allies become opponents. *Philadelphia Inquirer.*

Mid-continent Regional Education Laboratory. (1984-85). *Noteworthy, Winter.* Author.

Midgley, C., & Urdan, T. (1995). Predictors of middle school students' use of self-handicapping strategies. *Journal of Early Adolescence, 15* (4), 389-411.

Mitchell, D.E. (1989). Measuring up: Standards for evaluating school reform. In T.J. Sergiovanni, & J.H. Moore, (Eds.), *Schooling for tomorrow: Directing reforms to issues that count.* Needham, MA: Allyn and Bacon.

Mosley, S. (1995, September 18). Writing down secrets. *The New Yorker,* 52-61.

Muncey, D., & McQuillen, P. (1993). Preliminary findings from a five year study of the Coalition of Essential Schools. *Phi Delta Kappan, 74,* 486-489.

Murphy, C. (1997). Finding time for faculties to study together. *Journal of Staff Development, 18* (3), 29-32.

Murphy, C. (1998). *Whole faculty study groups: A powerful way to change schools and enhance learning.* Thousand Oaks, CA: Corwin Press.

National Council of Teachers of Mathematics. (1989). *Curriculum and evaluation standards for school mathematics.* Reston, VA: Author.

National Science Foundation. (1996). *National Science Foundation review of instructional materials for middle school science.* Paper available from National Science Foundation, Division of Elementary, Secondary, and Informal Science Education.

Neufeld, B. (1996, August 30). Standards-based reform: Baseline data report for Jefferson County Public Schools. Interim evaluation report submitted to the Edna McConnell Clark Foundation. Cambridge, MA: *Education Matters*.

New Hampshire Business Roundtable on Education. (1996). *Gathering of lessons learned: New Hampshire school improvement program*. Concord, NH: Business and Industry Association of New Hampshire.

Newmann, F.M., Marks, H.M., & Gamoran, A. (1995, Spring). Authentic pedagogy: Standards that boost student performance. *Issues in restructuring schools*. Madison, WI: Center on Organization and Restructuring Schools.

Newmann, F.M., & Wehlage, G.G. (1995). *Successful school restructuring: A report to the public and educators by the Center on Organization and Restructuring of Schools*, Madison, WI: Board of Regents of the University of Wisconsin System.

Nieto, S. (1992). *Affirming diversity: The sociopolitical context of multicultural education*. White Plains, NY: Longman.

Noble, A.J., & Smith, M.L. (1994). Old and new beliefs about measurement-driven reform: 'Build it and they will come.' *Educational Policy 8* (2), 111-136.

Noddings, N. (1992). *The challenge to care in schools*. New York: Teachers College Press.

Northwest Regional Education Laboratory. (1994). *Improving science and mathematics education - A toolkit for professional developers*. Portland, OR: Author.

O'Leary, M. (n.d.). The quality school grading policy. Available: http://www.pnh.mv.net/ipusers/oleary/reform.html#essay2.

Oakes, J. (1985). *Keeping track: How schools structure inequality*. New Haven: Yale University Press.

Oakes, J. (1989). What educational indicators? The case for assessing the school context. *Educational Evaluation and Policy Analysis, 11* (2), 181-189.

Oakes, J. (1990). *Multiplying inequalities: The effects of race, social class, and tracking on opportunities to learn mathematics and science.* Santa Monica: RAND Corporation.

Oakes. J., & Wells, A.S. (1996). *Beyond the technicalities of school reform: Policy lessons from detracking schools.* Los Angeles: UCLA Graduate School of Education and Information Studies.

Patrick, K. (1998, July 18). Class bridges learning gap to high school. *South Florida Sun Sentinel*, p. 01.

Perlman, C. (1994). *The CPS performance assessment idea book.* Chicago: Chicago Public Schools.

Pham, Alex. (1994, November 9). California math rush: When Houghton Mifflin texts won OK, reformers cried foul. *Boston Globe*, p. 55.

Pipher, M. (1996). *The shelter of each other: Rebuilding our families.* New York: G.P. Putnam.

Popham, W. J. (1997a). The standards movement and the emperor's new clothes. *NASSP Bulletin, 81* (590), 21-25.

Popham, W. J. (1997b). What's wrong - and what's right - with rubrics. *Educational Leadership, 55* (1):72-75.

Powell, A., Farrar E., & Cohen, D. (1985). *The shopping mall high school: Winners and losers in the educational marketplace.* Boston: Houghton Mifflin.

Purnell, S., & Hill, P. (1992). *Time for reform.* Santa Monica, CA: RAND.

Pyle, A. (1997). In the loop: Better discipline, relationships cited as benefits of keeping students and teachers together over time. *Middle Ground, 1* (1),15.

Raudenbush, S.W., Rowan, B., & Cheong, Y.F. (1993). Higher order instructional goals in secondary schools: Class, teacher, and school influences. *American Educational Research Journal, 30*, 523-553.

Ray, S. L. (1996) Risking to learn: Let's teach students that mistakes are not synonymous with failure. *Middle Ground, Spring*, 6-7.

Resnick, M.D., Bearman, P.S., Blum, R.W., Bauman, K.E., Harris, K.M., Jones, J., Tabor, J., Beuhring, T., Sieving, R., Shew, M., Ireland, M., Bearinger, L.H., & Udry, J.R. (1997, September 10). Protecting adolescents from harm: Findings from the National Longitudinal Study on Adolescent Health. *Journal of the American Medical Association, 278*, 823-832.

Richards, M. (1987). A teacher's action research study: The 'bums' of 8H. *Peabody Journal of Education, 64* (2), 65-79.

Roberts and Kay, Inc. (1993, September). *Kentuckians' expectations of children's learning: The significance for reform*. A public report prepared for The Pritchard Committee for Academic Excellence and the Partnership for Kentucky School Reform.

Rothman, R. (1995). *Measuring up: Standards, assessment, and school reform*. San Francisco: Jossey-Bass.

Russell, M., & Haney, W. (1997). Testing writing on computers: An experiment comparing student performance on tests conducted via computer and via paper-and-pencil. *Education Policy Analysis Archives, 5*(3). Available: http://olam.ed.asu.edu/epaa/v5n3.html.

San Diego City Schools. (n.d.). *Looking at ourselves: The middle level studies itself*. San Diego: San Diego City Schools, Planning, Assessment, Accountability, and Development Division.

Sapon-Shevin, M. (1994). Cooperative learning and middle schools: What would it take to really do it right? *Theory Into Practice, 33* (3), 183-188.

Sarason, S. (1982). *The culture of school and the problem of change*. (2nd ed.) Boston: Allyn & Bacon.

Sarason, S.B. (1996). *Revisiting the culture of school and the problem of change*. New York: Teachers College Press.

Secretary of Labor's Commission on Achieving Necessary Skills. (1991) *What work requires of schools: A SCANS Report for America 2000*, Washington, DC: U.S. Department of Labor.

Schaps, E. (1994). Kind kids and challenging curriculum: We *can* have both. *What's a teacher to do? New curriculum for new standards*, Pittsburgh, PA: New Standards Project.

Shepard, L.A. (1991). Will national tests improve student learning? *Phi Delta Kappan, 73* (3), 232-238.

Sizer, T.R. (1984). *Horace's compromise: The dilemma of the American high school.* Boston: Houghton Mifflin.

Sizer, T.R. (1992) *Horace's school: Redesigning the American high school.* Boston: Houghton Mifflin.

Sizer, T.R. (1996). *Horace's hope: What works for the American high school.* Boston: Houghton Mifflin.

Slavin, R.E. (1987). Cooperative learning: Where behavioral and humanistic approaches to classroom motivation meet. *Elementary School Journal, 88* (1).

Smith, J.B. (1996). Does an extra year make any difference? The impact of early access to algebra on long-term gain in mathematics attainment. *Educational Evaluation and Policy Analysis, 18* (2), 141-153.

Smith, L., Ross, S., McNelis, M., Squires, M., Wasson, R., Maxwell, S., Weddle, K., Nath, L., Grehan, A., & Buggy, T. (1998, April). *The Memphis Restructuring Initiative: Analysis of activities and outcomes that impact implementation success.* Paper presented at the American Educational Research Association Annual Meeting, San Diego, California.

Smith, M.L., & Rotenberg, C. (1991). Unintended consequences of external testing in elementary schools. *Educational Measurement: Issues and Practice, Winter.*

Smith, M.L., & Shepard, L., (Eds.) (1989). *Flunking grades: Research and policies on retention.* New York: Falmer Press.

Smith, M.L. (1997, March 26). *The consequences of measurement-driven reform in Arizona: A case of integrated methods.* Paper presented at the Annual meeting of the American Education Research Association, Session 24.17, Chicago, Illinois.

Smith, M. L. (1997). *Reforming schools by reforming assessment: Consequences of the Arizona Student Assessment Program (ASAP). Equity and teacher capacity building.* [CSE Technical Report 425]. University of California, Los Angeles: National Center for Research on Evaluation Standards and Student Testing.

Sparks, D. (1993). *Professional development in school reform.* Interview with Judith Warren Little. Audiotape. Oxford: OH: National Staff Development Council.

Spillane, J.P., & Thompson, C.L. (1997). Reconstructing conceptions of local capacity: The local education agency's capacity for ambitious instructional reform. *Educational Evaluation and Policy Analysis 19* (2):185-203.

Spilman, C.E. (1995/1996). Transforming an urban school. *Educational Leadership, 53* (4), 34-39.

Spurlock, H.L., Munford, R.L., & Madhere, S. (1995, July). *Effects of gender, race, and grade retention on the developmental progression of self-efficacy perceptions.* Paper presented at the American Psychological Society Conference, New York.

Stake, R. (1988). Some comments on assessment in U.S. education. *Education Policy Analysis Archives, 6* (14): Available: http://epaa.asu.edu/epaa/v6n14.html.

Stecklow, S. (1997, September 2). Kentucky's teachers get bonuses, but some are caught cheating. *Wall Street Journal,* pp. A1, A5.

Steele, C.M. (1997) A threat in the air: How stereotypes shape intellectual identity and performance. *American Psychologist, 52* (6), 613-629.

Steinberg, J. (1997, November 27). California goes to war over math instruction. *New York Times.*

Steinberg, J. (1996, November 8). Study finds secret of successful schools. *New York Times.*

Steinberg, J. (1998, January 7). Underachieving schools are shamed into improvement. *New York Times.*

Steinberg, L., Brown, B., & Dornbusch, S. (1997). *Beyond the classroom: Why school reform has failed and what parents need to do.* New York: Simon and Schuster.

Stevenson, C. (1997). Portfolios and self knowledge. *VAMLE Focus, 3* (7) (Newsletter of the Vermont Association for Middle Level Education).

Strauss, V. and Mathews, J. (1998, July 9). DC summer school still scrambling for supplies, teachers. *Washington Post,* p. D01.

Strauss, V. (1998, July 23). 4,500 too many take summer classes. *Washington Post*, p. D08.

Swirko, C. (1997, August 17). Performance, attendance standards hit middle-schoolers. *Gainesville Sun*.

Teachers Curriculum Institute. (1994). *History alive! Engaging all learners in diverse classrooms.* Reading: MA: Addison-Wesley.

Texas Education Agency. (1996). *Comprehensive biennial report on Texas public schools: A report to the 75th Texas Legislature.* Austin, TX: Author.

The idea box. (1995, April 3). *NCTM News Bulletin*.

Tomlinson, C.A., Moore, T.R., & Callahan, C.M. (1998). How well are we addressing academic diversity in middle school?. *Middle School Journal 29* (3), 5-9.

Tovey, R. (1996). Getting kids into the picture: Student drawings help teachers see themselves more clearly. *Harvard Education Letter, XII* (6), 5-6.

U.S. Department of Education. (1997, October 20). *Mathematics equals opportunity.* White Paper prepared for U.S. Secretary of Education Richard W. Riley, 20 October.

Useem, E., Culbertson, J., & Buchanan, J. (1997, October). *The contributions of teacher networks to Philadelphia's school reform.* Philadelphia Education Fund.

Viadero, D. (1996, May 8). Math texts are multiplying. *Education Week*, 33-34.

Vobejda, B. (1997, September 10). Love conquers what ails teens, study finds. *Washington Post*, p. A1.

Wasserstein, P. (1995). What middle schoolers say about their schoolwork. *Educational Leadership, September*, 41-43.

Wehalge G., & Rutter, R. (1986). Dropping out: How much do schools contribute to the problem? *Teachers College Record, 87* (3).

Weitzman, M. (1985). Demographic and educational characteristics of inner city middle school problem absence students. *American Journal of Orthopsychiatry, 55 (3)*.

Wheelock, A. (1992). *Crossing the tracks: How 'untracking' can save America's schools.* New York: New Press.

Wheelock, A. (1994). Chattanooga's Paideia Schools: A single track for all—and it's working. *Journal of Negro Education, 63* (1), 77-92.

Wheelock, A. (1995, November). *Standards-based reform: What does it mean for the middle grades?* Paper prepared for the Edna McConnell Clark Foundation, Program for Student Achievement.

Wheelock, A. (1998a). *The Junior Great Books Program: Reading for understanding in high-poverty urban elementary schools.* Case study prepared for the Junior Great Books Program, Great Books Foundation, Chicago, Illinois.

Wheelock, A. (1998b). *National library power evaluation, case studies summary report.* A Report Prepared for New Haven Public Education Fund, Inc., New Haven, Connecticut. Based on case studies by Nancy Curran, Ken Doane, and Anne Wheelock. Madison, WI: School of Library and Information Studies, University of Wisconsin-Madison.

Wheelock, A., & Dorman, G. (1988). *Before it's too late: Dropout prevention in the middle grades.* Boston: Massachusetts Advocacy Center and Chapel Hill, NC: Center for Early Adolescence.

Wiggins, G. (1993). *Assessing student performance: Exploring the purpose and limits of testing,* San Francisco: Jossey-Bass.

Wilgoren, D. (1998, February 2). Exercises in frustration at P.R. Harris: Lack of supplies, student skills, teacher training spell little progress. *Washington Post*, p. A01.

Williamson, D. (1998, August 5). Teachers give ABC project poor marks, say it does not help. *Carolina News Services.* Available: http://www.unc.edu/news/newsserv/research/jonesgal.htm

Woodhams, F. (1998, February 25). U.S. high schoolers trail counterparts. *USA Today*, p. A1.

Yonazawa, S., Wells, A., & Serna, I. (1996, April). *Choosing tracks: 'Freedom of choice' in detracking schools.* Paper presented at the Annual Meeting of the American Educational Research Association, New York

National Middle School Association

National Middle School Association was established in 1973 to serve as a voice for professionals and others interested in the education of young adolescents. The association has grown rapidly and now enrolls members in all fifty states, the Canadian provinces, and forty-two other nations. In addition, fifty-six state, regional, and provincial middle school associations are official affiliates of NMSA.

NMSA is the only association dedicated exclusively to the education, development, and growth of young adolescents. Membership is open to all. While middle level teachers and administrators make up the bulk of the membership, central office personnel, college and university faculty, state department officials, other professionals, parents, and lay citizens are members and active in supporting our single mission – improving the educational experiences of 10-15 year olds. This open and diverse membership is a particular strength of NMSA.

The association provides a variety of services, conferences, and materials in fulfilling its mission. The association publishes *Middle School Journal*, the movement's premier professional journal; *Research in Middle Level Education Quarterly*; *Middle Ground, the Magazine of Middle Level Education; Target*, the association's newsletter; and *Family Connection*, a newsletter for families. In addition, the association publishes more than sixty books and monographs on all aspects of middle level education. The association's highly acclaimed annual conference, which has drawn approximately 10,000 registrants in recent years, is held in the fall.

For information about NMSA and its many services contact headquarters at 2600 Corporate Exchange Drive, Suite 370, Columbus, Ohio 43231, TELEPHONE: 800-528-NMSA; FAX: 614-895-4750; WWW. NMSA.ORG.